GETTING TO REPARATIONS

ALSO BY DOROTHY A. BROWN

The Whiteness of Wealth

GETTING TO REPARATIONS

How Building a Different America
Requires a Reckoning with Our Past

DOROTHY A. BROWN

CROWN
NEW YORK

CROWN
An imprint of the Crown Publishing Group
A division of Penguin Random House LLC
1745 Broadway
New York, NY 10019
crownpublishing.com
penguinrandomhouse.com

Library of Congress Cataloging-in-Publication Data is available upon request.

Hardcover ISBN 978-0-593-59361-5
Ebook ISBN 978-0-593-59362-2

Editor: Madhulika Sikka
Assistant editor: Fariza Hawke
Production editor: Liana Faughnan
Text designer: Andrea Lau
Production: Christopher Andrus
Copy editor: Janet Biehl
Proofreaders: Kevin Clift, Robin Slutzky, Miriam Taveras, and Andrea Peabbles
Publicist: Stacey Stein
Marketer: Chantelle Walker

Manufactured in the United States of America

1st Printing

First Edition

The authorized representative in the EU for product safety and compliance is
Penguin Random House Ireland, Morrison Chambers, 32 Nassau Street,
Dublin D02 YH68, Ireland, https://eu-contact.penguin.ie.

For Uncle Billy . . . because of his fearlessness.

CONTENTS

GETTING TO REPARATIONS

INTRODUCTION

The past is never dead. It's not even past.

—WILLIAM FAULKNER, *REQUIEM FOR A NUN*

On the night of January 12, 1865, twenty black ministers were summoned to a meeting in Savannah, Georgia—a meeting that could have changed the trajectory of our country. It was a singular opportunity to right a grievous wrong. Even the setting met the moment.

The convening occurred at the Green-Meldrim House, with 7,300 square feet and fifteen-foot ceilings, majestic columns, and Italian Carrara marble fireplaces that were surely burning that night. The house served as General William Tecumseh Sherman's wartime headquarters. The meeting was the brainchild of Secretary of War Edwin M. Stanton, and the agenda was to discuss "matters relating to the freedmen of the State of Georgia."[1] For the first time in American history, the US government would be asking the formerly enslaved what they wanted for their futures now that they were free.[2]

Among the delegation of twenty black men, primarily from

Georgia and South Carolina, was great diversity. Nine had remained in bondage until the Union Army entered their states, three had bought their freedom outright, three had been emancipated by will following their enslavers' deaths, and five were born free. They ranged in age from twenty-six to seventy-two, with varying degrees of experience and service in the church, some commanding local congregations as large as eighteen hundred people and managing church property worth as much as $20,000. Garrison Frazier, though he was no longer in charge of any congregation as his health was failing, was chosen by his peers to lead the group and "express their common sentiments." As the scholar Charles Elmore describes him, Frazier, an eloquent and imposing man, was "well over 6 feet tall."[3] Only eight years before, Frazier had secured freedom for himself and his wife with a payment of $1,000 in gold and silver.[4]

Sherman and Stanton put their questions to Frazier and the other clergymen. They asked them to state their understanding of slavery along with their definition of freedom.

"Slavery is receiving by irresistible power the work of another man, and not by his consent," Frazier replied. Freedom, he continued, would have the effect of "taking us from under the yoke of bondage and placing us where we could reap the fruit of our own labor, and take care of ourselves, and assist the Government in maintaining our freedom."

The very next question the officials asked Frazier, logically, was just how newly freed men would take care of themselves.

Frazier replied: "The way we can best take care of ourselves is to have land, and turn in and till it by our labor—that is, by the labor of the women, and children, and old men—and we can soon maintain ourselves and have something to spare." (Black women, by reference to our ability to work, made our only appearance here.) Black people, according to Frazier, wanted the opportunity to work and build wealth for themselves, instead of continuing to do so for their former enslavers, as they had been doing for well over two hundred years. "We want to be placed on land until we are able to buy it and make it our own," he concluded.

When they asked Frazier whether freedmen preferred to live among whites or in separate black colonies, he said: "I would prefer to live by ourselves, for there is a prejudice against us in the South that will take years to get over; but I do not know that I can answer for my brethren." Each minister had a chance to answer for himself. They all agreed with "brother Frazier" except for James Lynch, a twenty-six-year-old minister from Baltimore, Maryland, where he had been born free. In contrast to Frazier and the others, he felt that black and white "should not be separated but live together."

The next question may have stung Frazier and the other black men: "Do you think that there is intelligence enough among the slaves of the South to maintain themselves under the Government of the United States, and the equal protection of its laws, and maintain good and peaceable relations among yourselves and with your neighbors?" Frazier's reply was brief and to the point: "I think there is sufficient intelligence among us to do so."

General Sherman listened closely to what Reverend Frazier and the other men had to say and deliberated on his next move. The truth was, he had a problem that desperately needed solving. As his troops marched through the South to the coast, liberating the enslaved as they went, a growing number of dispossessed black people trailed behind his army. Sherman didn't have the resources or the time to feed and shelter the country's newly freed population—he still had a war to win.[5]

On January 16, 1865, four days following his meeting with the black clergymen, General Sherman, with the approval of President Abraham Lincoln, issued Special Field Order No. 15, reallocating 400,000 acres of confiscated property for land grants to freed black men and women. The territory outlined for redistribution included Georgia's Sea Islands and a swath of coastline from Charleston, South Carolina, down to the St. John's River in Florida.[6] The field order was a direct response to what he heard from the black ministers.

"By the laws of war, and the orders of the President of the United States, the negro is free and must be dealt with as such," Sherman's order proclaimed.[7] Each family would be granted forty acres of "tillable ground" where "they might locate their families and work out for themselves a living and respectability."[8] The field order also provided that "no white person whatever, unless military officers and soldiers detailed for duty, will be permitted to reside; and the sole and exclusive management of affairs will be left to the freed people themselves, subject only to the United States military authority and the acts of Congress." The ministers' wish for land and self-determination was seemingly fulfilled.

Sherman later added that the army could loan mules to assist the formerly enslaved, and word of the "forty acres and a mule" promised to them spread quickly. Many came forward to claim the land being offered, including Baptist minister Ulysses Houston, forty-one years old and one of the twenty clergymen who had met with General Sherman. Houston led efforts to resettle one thousand black Americans on Skidaway Island in Georgia and became the first "black governor" of their self-governing community.[9]

Field Order No. 15 had been intended merely as a stopgap

measure until the Civil War ended. Whether General Sherman even had the legal authority to issue such a sweeping and transformative redistribution of Southern land outside the context of a war remained an open question. After all, the land set aside was only enough to resettle ten thousand families.

On March 3, 1865, Congress established the Freedmen's Bureau in the War Department, in order to administer the field order and assign legal title to the forty-acre plots. On April 15, 1865, less than a week after the Confederate Army surrendered at Appomattox, John Wilkes Booth assassinated President Lincoln. In his place, Vice President Andrew Johnson assumed the presidency. By the fall of 1865, President Johnson had reversed Sherman's order and returned the land to the former enslavers. And so died the promise of that January 12 meeting, along with black self-determination and wealth building.

The unfulfilled potential of Field Order No. 15 has haunted this country and black Americans ever since Andrew Johnson reversed course in 1865. It was a missed opportunity that has cost us more than we will ever be able to calculate or recover. Had it been allowed to stand and extended throughout the South to provide for the 4 million newly freed black Americans, we could have become a *different* America.

That America would be one where the subsequent ratification of the Thirteenth Amendment on December 6, 1865, which made 4 million black Americans legally free, meant the end of chattel slavery and the death of white supremacy. In that America, it would have been commonplace for black Americans to thrive—and resulted in a better future for all Americans. That is because white supremacy has the potential to hurt everyone—including white people—as you will discover in these pages. A nation structured to ensure the success of the formerly enslaved would have been designed for all Americans' success. Instead, we created a country that did everything it could to keep the freedmen in bondage—through violence if necessary, while harming others along the way.

Surprising even myself, I have concluded that today all roads to our redemption lead to black reparations. Surprising, because for a long time I believed, as do many people in America, that reparations for black Americans were unrealistic and impractical, a fantasy housed only in our dreams. Then one day something happened that put me irrevocably on the path to believing that reparations can and must become a reality in my lifetime.

It began several years ago at my summer home on Martha's Vineyard, where my then-colleague Carol Anderson, currently the Robert W. Woodruff Professor of African American Studies at Emory University, was visiting me. It was late morning, and I was working on my second cup of coffee. We were sitting in the dining room as she told me about one of her classes. Carol casually mentioned that the United States had paid reparations for the lynching of Italians in New Orleans.

"Wait a minute," I said. "Are you telling me that the United States paid reparations for white people who were lynched, but not for any black people who were lynched?"

"That's right," Carol replied.

I'm sure I threw out an F-bomb in response. While the discussion moved on, I never did. That untold story is one of the building blocks of *Getting to Reparations*.

Get ready to put aside everything you thought you knew about the case for reparations. I'm not going to make the argument you're expecting me to make. The stories I'm going to tell you shocked me—a scholar who studies race in America for a living. What I discovered was that compensating for the types of loss experienced by black people in America is as American as apple pie. That's when I became a believer.

Getting to Reparations tells the story of how the federal government has historically paid cash compensation: to white enslavers, for the "harm" of ending slavery in the District of Columbia; to Italy, on behalf of Italian immigrants lynched by private white citizens in Louisiana; to Tribal Nations, for the land we stole from them; and to Japanese Americans, for their mass incarceration when our government made their racial identity a crime during World War II. But it has never made any payments to black Americans for comparable losses. The central question raised by these examples is, if the federal government paid compensation to others for the end of slavery, for failure to be protected from lynching, for economic exploitation, and for mass incarceration, then why not to black Americans who experienced each one?

These four instances of federal cash compensation are more than just data points. When we connect the dots, they establish something called "precedent." For a lawyer and law professor like me, precedent is the holy grail of legal arguments because it means that since we have done something in the past, we can do it again today. The answer was there all along, staring us right in the face. If cash payments to Tribal Nations, Japanese Americans, former white enslavers, and even the country of Italy—everybody but black Americans—were possible, totaling a whopping $2.5 billion, then that is a well-established *precedent* for the federal government to make long-overdue restitution to black Americans for the harm inflicted after slavery was supposedly ended under the

Thirteenth Amendment. The government failed to protect black Americans from being re-enslaved through convict leasing and sharecropping, threats of racial violence and lynching, sundown towns, eminent domain, Jim Crow policies that were designed for black economic exploitation, and mass incarceration under the guise of a war on drugs. The fact that the United States has stubbornly refused to compensate black Americans for centuries of continuous harm is not a justification for doing nothing today.

While the payments to Italy and Japanese Americans have previously been described as reparations, the other two instances were not. I define *reparations,* however, as compensation for governmental harm inflicted directly, or indirectly due to their failure to prevent others from inflicting injury. That definition also includes the payments to white enslavers for the "harm" of ending slavery and Tribal Nation members for stolen land. And if we could pay white enslavers for ending slavery, we can certainly pay black people for what the government did to them directly and indirectly *after* chattel slavery ended.

Governmental harm is of a higher magnitude than harm at the hands of private parties. It creates a devastating loss because our government is supposed to provide protection and not leave us vulnerable or exploit us. Such a unique experience of harm should influence the remedies we consider. Reparations, which is an extraordinary remedy, should be available for the types of harm that black Americans have suffered, particularly given how other groups have received payments from the government.

Cash payments are often the first thing that usually comes to mind when reparations are mentioned. It was the form of payment in each of the four case studies. But reparations can mean so much more. When I speak about reparations, I am talking about more than money paid to individual black people, because what we have with the black community is not just one type of harm, like those experienced in the case studies. We have a group of people, black people, who have been harmed in all those ways—through slavery, through lynching, through economic exploitation, and through mass incarceration—and so much more. The list continues with being denied the right to full citizenship, including the right to vote, travel, and enjoy other fundamental rights guaranteed by the Constitution. An entire race of people— the black community—has experienced harm. And that harm also requires community-based reparations.

The reparations I am talking about must include fundamental changes to our present systems for economic opportunity and prosperity that currently exclude black Americans (and so many others). Getting to reparations means moving beyond not only the idea of reparations as cash payments but also what reparations can buy you on the other side.

In the process of unearthing America's hidden history, I uncovered a piece of my own. I have always known that I descended from enslaved people. My father's family is from Georgia, and my mother's is from South Carolina. Most black people from those states are descended from enslaved people. But only recently was part of my great-uncle Billy's story revealed to me.

William Blakely James (Uncle Billy) was born on January 10, 1903, in Sumter, South Carolina. He was my maternal grandfather's baby brother and the only lawyer in my family tree.[10] His father, my great-grandfather, was likely born enslaved. Uncle Billy's story offers a glimpse into the promise and perils of black life a single generation after slavery.

I remembered Uncle Billy as a kind man. When I was about nine years old, he told my mother that if I didn't become a lawyer, I would miss my calling. Why? Because I had an answer for everything.

As I started writing this book, I wondered about my family history and talked to my mother about it. She reminded me of Uncle Billy. What I learned from her filled me with pride. This kind man was also a badass who was run out of South Carolina by the Ku Klux Klan for the "crime" of being too uppity.[11] Uncle Billy was a fierce warrior for black people. As one of his friends would later describe him, "he was not afraid, which is very unusual for the times."[12]

I needed to know more about his story, so I got the help of the intrepid librarians at Georgetown Law. Between 1947 and 1954, Uncle Billy worked in private practice in Sumter. He and his wife, Aunt Lucille, whom he married in 1929, owned a home, and I imagine they had a nice middle-class life. Then one day he made the fateful decision to run for a seat on the Sumter City Council. Not long after he lost, a cross was burned on his lawn. Aunt Lucille left town immediately. After he lost the election, Uncle Billy remained for almost two more years to wind down his practice.

My mother always thought he had been run out of town because he took civil rights cases, but that's not what the research revealed. He was run out of town because he *ran* for city council. He wanted to wield power over his white neighbors, and that was a bridge too far. As a result, he was forced to close his practice and flee north.

Uncle Billy and Aunt Lucille sold their home in January 1955 for $2,514.23. They had purchased the property in March 1950 for $650.[13] Was that a fair price, given that he had to sell? Stripping property from black people was often at the root of racial violence, as you will discover in this book. But leaving money on the table when they sold their home in a hurry was better than the alternative. At least my great-aunt and great-uncle lived to tell their story. They started over in Washington, DC, where they both had family, and around 1960 Uncle Billy was able to begin a new life as a government lawyer working for the Federal Trade Commission. Subsequently, in 1966, he became head of the DC Consumer Protection Office, where he remained until retirement around 1971.

In 1975 he left Washington and went back into private practice in Sumter, South Carolina. Uncle Billy and Aunt Lucille's daughter had recently died, and they decided to go back. There, Uncle Billy started making good trouble again. He integrated a neighborhood and befriended one of his white neighbors, who later told a story about Uncle Billy's return to Sumter. One of the first things he did was visit the courthouse. When he didn't see any black employees working there, other than janitors, he threatened to sue. What happened next? They hired more black workers who were not janitors.[14]

Uncle Billy also initiated a campaign to reform at-large elections for the Sumter County Council. At that time, county council elections were county-wide, meaning that the black vote was diluted when combined with the white vote from the entire county. As a result, a black candidate had virtually no chance of getting elected. But in a single-member district, where black voters might comprise a majority, a black candidate had a good chance of getting elected. Uncle Billy served as the "legal engineer" of an eight-year battle that resulted in single-member districts for Sumter County Council.[15]

And once again, white people in South Carolina tried to run him out of town. But this time the outcome was different, as he later told my mother. "By jingles, you're not going to do it to me this time, because I have a gun just like you have a gun, and I'm not afraid," Uncle Billy declared. He continued to practice law in Sumter until the end of his life. He died of natural causes in 1989 at the age of eighty-six.

—————

Getting to Reparations sets out an argument for reparations and the path to getting them for black Americans in the twenty-first century. This book is written for skeptics, of which I counted myself one until very recently. Your objections were my objections. But what you will see unfold in these pages is a story that many people don't want you to know. Florida, Georgia, Mississippi, and Utah (among others) are already making it illegal to teach this history to your children if it might make them feel guilt or shame.[16]

Although chattel slavery ended legally in December 1865, when Georgia became the twenty-seventh state to ratify the Thirteenth Amendment, the institutionalized racism of slavery refused to die with it. (Mississippi was the last state to ratify the Thirteenth Amendment, on March 16, 1995, nearly 130 years later, but it did not notify the US archivist, which did not make the ratification official until 2013.)[17] In different forms, black labor exploitation, black wealth stripping, and white wealth building continued, legally in many instances, throughout most of the twentieth century. As Reverend Frazier said, "The prejudice against us in the South . . . will take years to get over." Unfortunately, he underestimated the sticking power of racism, a viral contagion that knows no geographical or temporal boundaries and that follows black people wherever they go.

The failed effort to provide land to newly freed families was followed by 150-plus years of exploiting black labor and building white wealth, via different means. You could work for your former enslavers under onerous "sharecropping" agreements that made them rich and kept you poor. If you refused, your unemployment would make you guilty of the crime of "vagrancy" and allow you to be locked up and "leased" to individuals, small businesses, and large companies like U.S. Steel to work for no pay. Blackness was criminalized.

At times, those mechanisms did not prevent blacks from achieving self-sufficiency, and through some miracle, black people still managed to own things and benefit from their own labor. But when that happened, private white actors used racial violence to strip property away from blacks and award it to white Americans who neither tilled nor toiled. States employed racially discriminatory legal actions like eminent domain to do the same, while sundown towns—places where black Americans could work but had to be gone by sundown or put their very lives at risk—made sure black people were forbidden from living there, much less building wealth there. These are just a few of the headwinds that black Americans have faced *after* chattel slavery ended.

This book details how the federal and state governments, courts, and private individuals worked in concert to re-enslave black people or get as close to it as possible. It discloses the sanctioned white theft of black wealth. And at its heart, it tells a hidden side of American history, a story of the discrimination inflicted on black people wherever they went. And despite this dark chapter in our history, I believe there is a path ahead that leads to a brighter future. But we will get there only if we, as a nation, choose to face some difficult truths.

Getting to Reparations proceeds in three parts. Part I presents the four instances when the United States paid cash compensation to nonblack people for harms similar to those experienced by black people. These include reparation payments to enslavers in Washington, DC, Italian lynching victims, Tribal Nations for land theft and economic exploitation, and Japanese Americans for their mass incarceration. Our history of compensating other groups demonstrates that the complexities of such a massive undertaking can be worked out.

Part II catalogs the harms experienced by black people after chattel slavery ended. It describes the many ways in which slavery-like conditions were maintained, both legally and by force, to thwart black wealth building and progress. From the labor exploitation of sharecropping, convict leasing, and sundown towns, to lynching that resulted in black property being transferred to white lynchers, to the economic exploitation of Jim Crow's "separate but equal" system of racial subordination, to the use of eminent domain, and finally to the so-called War on Drugs and the school-to-prison pipeline, black Americans have long been thwarted in creating economic security and building intergenerational wealth. It also documents the twenty-first-century harms that impact all of us because of our refusal to address the past.

Part III is where I outline the practical steps to getting reparations for black Americans. Based on the results of focus group testing that I commissioned, I demonstrate that the right kind of messaging can change the hearts and minds of those initially opposed to reparations. I lay out the case for creating a commission, by executive order from the president, to collect evidence and testimonies, publicize its findings through a series of televised hearings, and finally issue recommendations, building public support along the way. Compensation should include not only cash payments to individuals but also funding for systemic reforms. I explain why these payments would be legal, how we will calculate the cost, how we will pay for them, and how they are the inevitable next step in righting the wrongs done to black Americans.

Ultimately, the case for compensating black Americans for the harms they experienced *after* chattel slavery ended is also a case for American democracy. America has unfinished business regarding its black citizens. In order for *all* Americans to reach their full potential, the United States must add black Americans to the list of those compensated for extraordinary losses experienced at the hands of the government—and of individual white Americans. Until we recognize and make amends for the persistent and residual harms of slavery and its aftermath, which are still very much with us in the present day, we as a country will forever be stuck in a downward spiral of division, despair, and recrimination. If black people are ever going to get out "from under the yoke of bondage" and experience the freedom Reverend Frazier spoke of, we must compensate them and transform those systems that continue to exploit them.

Perhaps most important, *Getting to Reparations* shows us what life *could* be like on the other side. It defines both the moral and practical case for making our country whole—and for finally enabling black Americans to walk the road to true freedom, where we will "reap the fruit of our own labor, and take care of ourselves." If black Americans can walk free, it becomes easier for everyone to walk free.

And like my great-uncle Billy, I'm not afraid.

PART I

OUR HIDDEN HISTORY

Truth is powerful and it prevails.

—SOJOURNER TRUTH

White Enslavers' Payday

The road to emancipation started, in the early 1860s, with an "experiment" in the District of Columbia. Would white enslavers be more supportive of ending slavery if they knew they would receive cash compensation for each enslaved person the law set free?

That idea resulted in the District of Columbia Compensated Emancipation Act, which became law in April 1862 and ended slavery in the District of Columbia. It required cash payments to white enslavers for each enslaved person legally freed. The federal government allocated $1 million for the effort. The final Treasury report referred to these payments as "claimed compensation."[1]

One of those enslavers was Margaret Catherine Adlum, who was born on May 29, 1810, in Maryland. Her father, Major John Adlum, served as a corporal in the Revolutionary War and came from a prominent family that aided him in building his fortune as a land surveyor. Her mother, also named Margaret C. Adlum, was Major Adlum's first cousin and likewise came from a prosperous farming family. The Adlum family wealth came from landowning, surveying work, and human trafficking. The Adlums were enslavers.

Around 1837, Margaret married Cornelius Barber. The following year the newlyweds purchased a seventy-three-acre estate for $3,000 ($96,000 today) in the lush green hills overlooking Georgetown in Washington, DC, and turned it into a working farm they called Northview. In the years that followed, Margaret gave birth to six children. By 1850, with a growing family and a farm to take care of, the Barbers enslaved eleven people to lighten their load, eight of whom Margaret inherited from her parents.

As recorded in the 1850 US Census, "Female, Black, 60 y.o., Born in 1790," "Male, Black, 25 y.o., Born in 1825," and "Female, Black, 25 y.o., Born in 1825" were some of the enslaved people who lived and worked at Northview. They weren't even given the basic dignity of having their names recorded, consistent with standard practice. Collectively, they spent their entire lives serving Margaret, her parents, or other enslavers. They built up the Barbers' wealth while being stripped of their own. Many had been bought to serve for life and could only dream of becoming free. They tended to their tasks, inside the house and out in the fields, day in and day out. They were never paid wages for their labor, and if they had ever invented anything, they would have been deprived of their intellectual property rights.[2]

The enslaved people at Northview were silent observers who watched as the Barbers experienced seasons of joy and sorrow, all the while growing wealthier at their expense. They witnessed the tragedy that struck in 1849, when Margaret's five youngest children died of dysentery, leaving the oldest son, John Adlum Barber, the sole survivor. The couple buried their sadness by throwing themselves headlong into the construction of a new family home.

Over the next four years, an extravagant mansion, designed by renowned local architects, was erected on the highest point of the property. The house boasted two ballrooms, "countless bed and drawing rooms, crystal chandeliers, and enormous mirrors."[3] The candlelit drawing rooms in the big house were in sharp contrast to the slave quarters on the far side of the property, way out past the stables and the corn crib.

In 1853 catastrophe struck the Barber household yet again when Cornelius died at age fifty, one month after making his will. Widowed at the age of forty-four, Margaret and her surviving son, John, now fifteen, were left to manage the farm on their own. As a tribute, Margaret commissioned prominent artist Thomas Sully, famous for his paintings of former presidents including George Washington in *The Passage of the Delaware,* to paint portraits of her and her late husband. Cornelius's painting cost her $100 (just under $4,000 today).

While it was customary for husbands to leave their property in a trust for their widow, based on the assumption that a woman would be unable to manage the property, Cornelius left all his property to Margaret outright. Running the estate was a tall order. As Mary Mitchell notes in her book *Divided Town,* "A woman of less character would have sold her farm and moved into town."[4] By 1860, the farm had grown to include the mansion and carriage house, twenty-nine enslaved people (including many that she inherited upon the death of her husband),[5] slave quarters, hay sheds, and hen houses.

For the enslaved people at Northview, little changed other than the type of work they were tasked with. When there was not enough work on the farm to keep them all busy, Margaret rented them out to other merchants and families in the area. She shrewdly hired out ten of the men to slaughterhouses and tanneries and seven of the women to other households as cooks and house servants. This left just over half of the enslaved at home to work the farm and make it as self-sustaining as possible. By renting out the others, she earned an annual income of roughly $1,500 a year (a little over $47,000 today).[6] While it is true that some enslavers allowed enslaved workers to keep a small share of the income they earned when hired out, enslavers still kept the lion's share, further exploiting black Americans.

Cornelius had been right to place his trust in Margaret's business acumen. According to the 1860 Census, there were

3,185 enslaved people in the District of Columbia; twenty-nine belonged to Margaret, and two years later that number grew to thirty-four, making her the second largest enslaver in the district.

The outbreak of the Civil War in the spring of 1861, however, likely jeopardized Margaret's balance sheet, as the value of enslaved people plummeted. But there was the other side of the ledger to consider, namely how the enslaved now thought about the future. The promise of emancipation was no longer limited to daydreams: It now seemed not only possible but probable. "All the slaves in the South think they will be freed soon, even those in this neighborhood," Lieutenant Benjamin F. Fisher of the US Signal Corps at Georgetown declared that fall.[7]

After the Civil War began, Margaret's life and those of her enslaved people took a dramatic turn. Five of her men, four of whom she hired out—Mortimer Briscoe, Townley Yates, Rezin Yates, Andrew Yates, and William Cyrass—wasted no time in liberating themselves. More upheaval was soon to follow.

With the start of the war and the secession of eleven Southern states, there emerged for the first time a realistic chance of ending slavery in the District of Columbia. A draft bill was introduced in the nation's capital in late 1861. The legislation's most vocal supporters—Henry Wilson, Charles Sumner, and William Fessenden—all had abolitionist backgrounds and supported emancipation because they believed it was morally right. Other proponents argued that emancipation would boost Union morale and powerfully highlight what the war was truly about while also delivering a blow to Southern morale. Once slavery ended in the district, they argued, it was only a matter of time before it was ended throughout the rest of the country. Since the Compensated Emancipation Act required enslavers who requested compensation to take an oath of loyalty, the bill would effectively codify a loyal population in the District of Columbia to help defend against any Southern incursions from neighboring Virginia, which was a slave state and part of the Confederacy. Finally, those in favor of abolition saw the symbolic importance of banishing slavery in the nation's capital.

Meanwhile, opponents of the bill argued that emancipation would encourage more resistance from the South and embolden the Confederacy to fight harder against the Union. A minority insisted that Congress did not have the power to end slavery in the District of Columbia. Many white Americans expressed fear that the bill would attract large numbers of runaways hoping to secure their freedom. What's more, detractors believed that the enslaved were unfit for freedom because they were unable to take care of themselves and that they would most likely become dependent on their former enslavers. Emancipation, critics predicted, would lead to a race war. Free blacks would be able to compete with white workers for jobs, thereby harming white livelihoods.

The bill was not popular with residents in the District of Columbia. They were especially troubled by the effort to "deprive them of their property without a fair equivalent," since they viewed the $300 average compensation as woefully inadequate. (Postwar valuations of enslaved persons were low given the uncertainty of slavery, whereas prewar values for adults "without blemish" were much higher.) Many also believed they would be forced to take care of the newly freed, whom they viewed as incapable of caring for themselves. The inhumanity of slavery was built on the white supremacist view that black Americans were inferior beings. Whippings were necessary because they were lazy. Slavery was in fact good for all involved. The enslaved didn't have to worry about providing for themselves and would not be tempted by "idleness." Ending slavery, opponents argued, would actually harm enslaved people.

On March 21, 1862, the *Washington Evening Star* ran an editorial titled "Twenty Reasons Why the Bill to Emancipate the Slaves in the District of Columbia Should Not Pass." The piece gave voice to a long list of concerns and grievances and was signed anonymously by "Justitia." The editors were likely afraid of being accused of disloyalty, which could result in their imprisonment.[8] Anonymity was less risky. Reasons one through three claimed that no one had asked for emancipation, not "the owners, who are the principal parties," not "the general people of the District," and not "the Slaves themselves, if unincited thereto by the originators of the measure." Point nine argued that "numerous widows, and orphans, and aged and helpless persons of both sexes who have been left dependent on the wages of servants, would in a great measure be deprived of the means of subsistence." According to reason number sixteen, any effort to emancipate enslaved people should lead to their removal; if they remained in the country, they would only prove to be "a perpetual burden and annoyance to the whites."

The most damning argument of all was the assertion that emancipation would lead to black equality: "The same power that can liberate our negroes against our will, can and perhaps will confer upon them equality in civil and political privileges with the whites, so, for instance, that negroes may vote for municipal or other officers; may hold such offices themselves; and sit as jurors, magistrates and judges in our courts."[9] All of the editorial's arguments against emancipation were focused on how it would negatively affect enslavers and white Americans but not on how it would affect the enslaved. When the editorial considered the enslaved at all, it was merely as projection, because no one had bothered to ask them what they thought.

Residents of the District of Columbia, however, had no representatives in Congress to advocate for their position. In the end, the majority of Congress, made up of 106 Republicans, 42 Democrats, and 28 Unionists,[10] ignored their complaints and passed the bill. Many of those most opposed to the bill— pro-slavery congressmembers from states that had seceded to join the Confederacy—were no longer around to vote in opposition. However, members from the loyal slave states of Delaware, Maryland, Kentucky, and Missouri remained in Congress and did vote against the bill. As a result, the vote was not even close: 29 to 14 in the Senate and 92 to 38 in the House.

President Lincoln signed the DC Compensated Emancipation Act on April 16, 1862, freeing all enslaved people residing there. The act included a financial provision that set aside $1 million ($30 million today) for compensation—to be paid to the enslavers, not to the enslaved—in exchange for their loyalty to the Union, among other things.[11] The bill also provided additional money to assist the newly freed black Americans to leave the country.[12] Ultimately, the Compensated Emancipation Act freed roughly 3,100 people and cost the federal government $993,406.35, just shy of the allocated $1 million.[13] But the bill's passage marked only the beginning of the hurdles to come.

Figuring out how much enslavers should be paid was no easy task. To determine the valuation of each enslaved person, the commissioners needed to consult someone knowledgeable in the slave trade. They hired Bernard M. Campbell, a Baltimore slave dealer, one of the very men who was put out of business by the legislation. Complicating matters was the fact that the Civil War had caused values to fluctuate widely. Plus, many enslavers like Margaret hired out their slaves, but calculating their value based on rental income would have taken too long to verify and slowed down the process. Dealing with complexity was a critical part of the process and required establishing rules on how to split compensation if two parties petitioned claims on the same enslaved person. The commission devised and implemented detailed protocols that would enable a resolution in a timely manner. The perfect was not allowed to become the enemy of the speedy implementation of the act.

In other words, the government's goal was to compensate the enslavers quickly. The country was at war and fighting for its future existence; time was of the essence. The commission used prewar values from 1859 and 1860 as a baseline when sales were frequent, then reduced valuations so as to not exceed the $1 million maximum allowed by law.

Congress requested detailed documentation from those seeking compensation. Initially, petitioners were asked to submit their claims to the commission clerk within ninety days of the act's passage, before July 15, but the deadline was later extended to August 15. Each petition, which cost enslavers fifty cents to file, consisted of a four-page form with an accounting of each enslaved person, including "the names, ages, and personal description of such persons, the manner in which said petitioners acquired such claim, and any facts touching the value thereof." Wills had to be consulted, deeds were pulled out of storage, and conversations were initiated with older relatives to ascertain the required details. In addition, the act required petitioners to declare their "allegiance to the Government of the United States, and [to swear] that he has not borne arms against the United States during the present rebellion, nor in any way given aid or comfort thereto." Two people had to be willing to attest to the petitioner's loyalty to the Union. This process was not an easy one to navigate, but enslavers were incentivized to jump through all the hoops in order to wring every last penny they thought was due to them from the government.

By the time the DC Compensated Emancipation Act was passed, Margaret Barber was a fifty-two-year-old widow living with her twenty-four-year-old son, John, and thirty-four enslaved people on the seventy-three-acre farm at Northview.[14] Her property holdings included $75,000 in real estate, $25,000 in enslaved people, and 258 ounces of silver. Her wealth, like that of her parents before her, largely came from owning land and enslaving people. Ever the skilled businesswoman, Margaret filed her petition quickly on May 22, 1862, little more than a month after the act was written into law.

Margaret Barber's petition was one of the most precise— "Where other owners measured their people in inches, she did so in quarter-inches."[15] She described those she enslaved, ranging in age from four months to sixty-five years, in detached detail and included information such as their name, sex, color, and height along with their "work" experience. She even included a request for $100 for Samuel Yates, age twenty-four, described as a "dark mulatto" at 5 feet 2½ inches tall, a "house servant" who was "deformed, having a curved spine."[16] The government awarded her no money for Samuel.

She valued "Dennis Carroll, aged seven, light mulatto," at $300. She was awarded $219. Peter Jenkins, sixty-five, was described as black, 5 feet 8½ inches tall, and a "number one farm hand." She valued him at $250. She received $65.70. What's more, her petition provides unequivocal proof of the physical toll of chattel slavery. John Thomas, age forty-one, "had three fingers on his left hand injured by a corn sheller and has lost two joints of his little finger, one joint of his first finger, and his second finger is stiff. But he can drive the carriage and work as well as before." She valued John at $1,200 and was awarded $350.40. That he could work as well as before, even with a mangled hand, provided little incentive for enslavers like Margaret to create safe working conditions. She recorded Susan Carroll as female, age thirty-six, "dark mulatto," height 4 feet 11⅞ inches, value $400, and noted "at home. Seamstress and house servt." She was awarded $87.60. Mortimer Brisco, thirty-nine, black, 5 feet 10 inches tall, was a good farmhand who "had one of his toes frost-bitten but is otherwise sound." She valued him at $1,000 and received $394.20. "Daniel Toyer is male and aged four months" was all she wrote of the baby listed. She valued him at $25 and received $21.90. Margaret was tenacious in her desire to get as much wealth out of this system as possible.

MARGARET BARBER'S PETITION[17]

No.	Name	Sex	Age	Color	Height	Value	Particular Description
1.	Peter Jenkins	male	65	black	5' 8½"	$250	Number one farmhand and hires for $70 a year.
2.	Mary Jenkins	female	58	black	5' 2"	$200	Number one cook and her wages are $72 a year.
3.	Ellen Jenkins	female	60	black	5' 7"	$250	A good cook and her wages are $82 a year.
4.	Susan Carroll	female	36	dark mulatto	4' 11⅞"	$400	To serve until she is 44 years old. A seamstress and house servant. She is delicate and cannot bear outdoor work and exposure.
5.	Dennis Carroll	male	7	light mulatto	3' 10"	$300	
6.	Ann Maria Carroll	female	3	light mulatto		$150	

No.	Name	Sex	Age	Color	Height	Value	Particular Description
7.	William Carroll	male	2	light mulatto		$100	
8.	Richard Williams	male	25	dark mulatto	5' 10$\frac{1}{2}$"	$1,500	Shoemaker, carpenter, and a first-rate farmhand. At home.
9.	Chapman Toyer	male	45	black	6—'	$1,000	A good farmhand and his wages are $100 a year.
10.	Sarah Toyer	female	51	black	5' 1"	$600	Good laundress and her wages are $72 a year.
11.	Mary Young	female	59	black	5—'	$400	Good cook and her wages are $60 a year.
12.	Kitty Silas	female	37	light mulatto	5' 2$\frac{1}{2}$"	$1,200	A number one cook and laundress. She is at home. She is rather deaf.
13.	Gilbert Silas	male	8	light mulatto	4' 2$\frac{1}{2}$"	$300	At home.
14.	William Silas	male	5	light mulatto	3' 10"	$300	At home.
15.	Philip Silas	male	8 mos.			$25	At home.
16.	Samuel Yates	male	24	dark mulatto	5' 2$\frac{1}{2}$"	$100	House servant. He is deformed, having a curved spine.
17.	Judah Yates	female	31	dark mulatto	5' 3$\frac{1}{2}$"	$600	She is a house servant at wages of $72.
18.	John Thomas	male	41	black	5' 8$\frac{3}{4}$"	$1,200	Coachman at wages of $120.
19.	Henry Toyer	male	25	dark mulatto	5' 10$\frac{1}{2}$"	$1400	Farmhand at $120 wages.
20.	Joseph Toyer	male	24	black	5' 8$\frac{1}{2}$"	$1,400	Farmhand at $120 wages.
21.	Louisa Toyer	female	23	black	5' 7"	$1,200	Good cook at wages of $72. She was sickly about nine months ago but is healthy now.
22.	Daniel Toyer	male	4 mos.			$25	
23.	Eliza Toyer	female	18	dark mulatto	5' 1"	$1,000	Good house servant. Wages.

No.	Name	Sex	Age	Color	Height	Value	Particular Description
24.	Jane Yates	female	36	dark mulatto	5' 1¹/₄"	$1,200	Good house servant. Wages.
25.	Mary Brown	female	20	light mulatto	5' 7¹/₈"	$800	A house servant and is at home. She is delicate and cannot bear outdoor work and exposure.
26.	Betty Brisco	female	16	dark mulatto	5' 2"	$1,000	House servant.
27.	Milly Brisco	female	11	dark mulatto	4' 6"	$400	House servant.
28.	Margaret Brisco	female	2	black		$100	
29.	John Chapman	male	34	black	5' 9¹/₂"	$1,200	First-rate farmhand and his wages are $120 a year.
30.	Mortimer Brisco	male	39	black	5' 10"	$1,000	Good farmhand and his wages are $120.
31.	Townley Yates	male	24	dark mulatto	5' 10"	$1,400	Good farmhand and his wages are $120.
32.	Rezin Yates	male	33	dark mulatto	5' 9"	$1,200	Good hostler and farmhand at $120 in wages.
33.	Andrew Yates	male	20	dark mulatto	5' 8³/₄"	$1,200	Good currier.
34.	William Cyrass	male	14	dark mulatto			

[Table 1]

After submitting her petition, Margaret received a summons to appear in person before the commissioners to have her property evaluated and her loyalty to the Union proven. This meant she had to bring her formerly enslaved people along with her for examination. As the petitioner, she was also responsible for locating any of the formerly enslaved who had left after the act was signed into law. In order to be compensated for them, she would have to bring them before the commission at City Hall, where "under gaslight chandeliers, in one or another of the courtrooms as it happened to be vacant, sat the tribunal and a slave dealer from Baltimore."[18] If the formerly enslaved could not be found, then the petitioner had to bring a witness who could attest to their characteristics.

Of Margaret's thirty-four enslaved people, she was able to bring in twenty-nine who still resided on her property. She made efforts to track down the five who had set off on their own at the start of the war. Every time one of them was found, they had to be brought into the district and submitted as "evidence." This kept her two attorneys and eight witnesses quite busy; each had to make at least one visit apiece, sometimes multiple trips.

Margaret Barber was resilient if she was anything. As the second-largest enslaver to file a petition in the district, she received one of the largest payments. In total, she requested compensation of $22,550 (about $650,000 today), and the US Treasury paid her $9,351.30 ($235,000 today).[19] She used the cash to purchase government gold bonds.[20]

TREASURY REPORT EXCERPT[21]

Number of Claim	Name of Petitioner or Claimant	Name	Value ($)	Total	To Whom Paid
366	Margaret C. Barber	Peter Jenkins	65.70		
		Mary Jenkins	87.60		
		Ellen Jenkins	65.70		
		Susan Carroll	87.60		
		Dennis Carroll	219.00		
		Ann Maria Carroll	65.70		
		William Carroll	43.80		
		William Cyrass	372.30		
		Richard Williams	591.30		

Number of Claim	Name of Petitioner or Claimant	Name	Value ($)	Total	To Whom Paid
		Chapman Toyer	131.40		
		Sarah Toyer	109.50		
		Mary Young	131.40		
		Kitty Silas	350.40		
		Gilbert Silas	175.20		
		William Silas	87.60		
		Philip Silas	43.80		
		Samuel Yates	No value		
		Judah Yates	262.80		
		John Thomas	350.40		
		Henry Toyer	613.20		
		Joseph Toyer	613.20		
		Louisa Toyer	438.00		
		Daniel Toyer	21.90		
		Eliza Toyer	438.00		
		Jane Yates	284.70		
		Mary Brown	394.20		
		Betty Brisco	503.70		
		Milly Brisco	306.60		
		Margaret Brisco	43.80		
		John Chapman	481.80		
		Mortimer Brisco	394.20		
		Townley Yates	525.60		
		Rezin Yates	481.80		
		Andrew Yates	569.40		
				$9,351.30	M. C. Barber

[Table 2]

In total, the commissioners reviewed 966 petitions, of which 909 were easy to approve because ownership was clear, as was the petitioners' loyalty to the Union. The 909 included eight black people who were seeking compensation generally for their family members whom they previously purchased with the likely intent to set them free.[22] The commissioners' overall goal was to interpret the act liberally: If the enslaved worker resided in the district and warranted freedom, then the enslaver would generally be compensated. But "they considered 111 slaves too young, too aged, or too infirm to merit compensation, so their freedom was uncompensated."[23] They rejected a handful of petitions either because the enslaved workers ran away more than two years earlier, the enslavers were considered disloyal, or the title to those enslaved were in doubt.[24]

Of all the claims, only fifty-seven merited further deliberation. These included cases with petitioners who had signed the Virginia ordinance of secession in May 1861 or who admitted to having sons or husbands who had joined the Confederate Army. Several were formerly enslaved black Americans who had purchased their freedom before 1861 and were still in the process of raising the money to free their wives and children; they sought compensation for the money they previously paid. Their claims were denied.

Ultimately, "bending over backwards to be fair," according to the records of the Columbia Historical Society, "the commissioners at length decided that an overt act of disloyalty or the bearing of arms against the Union, would be the definitive test."[25] They intended to compensate as many enslavers as possible. As long as the enslaver had remained loyal to the Union, having a relative such as a son or brother in the Confederate Army would not prevent them from receiving payment.

To ensure against fraud, the commissioners published each petition in district newspapers, along with a notice signed by the clerk stating, "All persons having knowledge of any facts going to show that the claims are in any respect ill-founded are requested to submit the same for the consideration of the Commissioners."[26] This allowed others in the community to raise objections and help ferret out any fraud or known disloyalty on the part of petitioners. Once the review process was complete, the commission determined how much enslavers should receive and sent their recommendations to the secretary of the Treasury.

Most enslavers received only a fraction of what they requested. This was unsurprising given that the Compensated Emancipation Act's $1 million allocation was estimated to cover about one-third of the real value of those enslaved. The act also allocated up to $100,000 (almost $3 million today) for any of the formerly enslaved who wanted to relocate to Haiti or Liberia. According to historian Kenneth J. Winkle, Thomas C. Sorensen Professor of American History at the University of Nebraska-Lincoln, "Almost no one chose to leave."[27]

The Compensated Emancipation Act was the first instance of the US government paying compensation for ending slavery—but the payment was made primarily to *white enslavers*. The process established by the act focused exclusively on the perpetrators of slavery and on what they were owed for giving up their "property," not on the actual human beings who had been enslaved and treated as less than human for generations. Moreover, those who were enslaved were subject to the whims of their enslavers. If their enslaver resisted the new law and refused to recognize that slavery had ended, then the enslaved had no legal proof of their freedom. The process was designed to begin with the filing of a petition, and enslavers could simply refuse to file, and the process to certify the enslaved person's freedom would not be completed. In other words, without action by their enslaver, enslaved people could not prove that they were free. And many enslavers did just that. They moved their enslaved workers outside district lines, engaged in other chicanery to evade the technical applicability of the law, or simply ignored the law.

At President Lincoln's urging, Congress approved a Supplemental Act on July 12, 1862, which empowered the enslaved to take control of their own destinies. As a result, they no longer had to wait for their enslavers to do the right thing. Instead, they could request emancipation by filing their own claim. Moreover, the Supplemental Act granted freedom to enslaved persons without any compensation to their enslavers, so it provided an additional financial incentive to enslavers to request compensation under the original act. Some enslavers, however, still chose slavery, either because they hoped the legislation would be declared unconstitutional or they were simply prepared to violate the law. The addiction to exploiting black labor is not easily shaken.

Enslaved self-petitioners were required to fill out a form and provide evidence to support their claims, which included written as well as oral testimony from witnesses who could verify their ownership, residency in the district, and other personal circumstances. If the petition process was hard for Margaret and other enslavers, imagine how much harder it was for the enslaved who had been denied an education and taught never to disobey their enslaver. Luckily, they had help in the form of white lawyers like George E. H. Day, "who specialized in challenging the Fugitive Slave Law by defending runaways."[28] The key to a successful petition for freedom was proving that they had been residents of the District of Columbia on April 16, 1862, the day the Compensated Emancipation Act became law. Alternatively, they could petition for freedom by citing their enslaver's disloyalty, but that was more difficult to prove.

One exception was the case of Philip Meredith. The thirty-year-old had been allowed to live as a free man in Washington, where he worked as a waiter and supported his wife and eight children. His former enslaver was none other than Robert E. Lee, general in chief of the Confederate Army, who in fact had given Meredith his blessing to leave his servitude. James Eveleth, a former legal agent of Lee's, testified on Meredith's behalf, explaining, "He has been here for years with masters knowledge—When Gen Lee went south he left servant in District." Eveleth added that in the past, he had "frequent conversations with Gen Lee in which Gen Lee expressed regret that he owned servant. Wished he was free." Meredith's petition against his enslaver on the grounds of disloyalty to the Union was easily approved.

By necessity, the Supplemental Act allowed black Americans to testify as both petitioners and witnesses in a formal judicial proceeding—an extraordinary occurrence. The Compensated Emancipation Act set a precedent that would ultimately become the law of the land in federal court. But in 1862, allowing black Americans to testify against white Americans was something truly remarkable. For the duration of the commission's proceedings, the testimonies of whites and blacks, free or otherwise, were given equal weight.

For example, white enslaver Mary R. Bibb tried to circumvent the law by moving most of her enslaved workers from her home in Georgetown to her farm in Maryland just as Congress concluded debate on the Compensated Emancipation Act.[29] Two of her enslaved workers, Charlotte Beckett and Harriet Williams, knew what she was up to and initially refused to relocate. As Williams later recounted, Bibb never told them the Compensated

Emancipation Act granted them freedom. Rather, she threatened to have them both arrested if they tried to leave. Bibb even hired a wagoner to move Beckett and her four children. As the wagon driver recalled, he got a lot of relocation work from enslavers like Bibb "just before [the] Emancipation Bill passed."[30]

Once Beckett learned the truth, however, she returned to the district with her children in early May and self-petitioned for her certificate of freedom in late July. Testifying in support of her petition were several white people as well as Harriet Williams, who said, "I know this woman. These are her children. I was raised with them. They with me belonged to Mrs Bibb."[31] Her petition was quickly approved. Roughly two months later Bibb asked the commissioners to reverse their decision. Beckett must have been terrified that she would fall back into slavery's hands when the commission agreed to reopen the case in mid-September.

Before the commissioners, Bibb testified that Beckett and her children were fugitive slaves, rather than emancipated, and she handed over "the warrant she had sworn out for their arrest."[32] In a 2–1 vote, the commissioners affirmed their earlier decision, and Beckett and her children remained free. They reasoned that Bibb had not really tried to enforce the warrant given that Beckett's whereabouts were well known. On October 1, 1862, Charlotte Beckett and her children were declared free once and for all.

If the enslaved managed to prove their case and win their freedom, as Beckett did, the Compensated Emancipation Act required them to pay twenty-five cents to secure a certificate of freedom from the federal government. That was also the case for those freed if their enslaver filed a petition. That's right. The enslaved, who were released without a penny to their name, had to pay a fee just to get papers declaring they were free. The enslaved, who were never compensated for their years and decades of labor, had to pay for their freedom. And while securing the twenty-five cents may have been no real barrier to their freedom, the requirement displays a level of cluelessness. In total, the commission evaluated 166 Supplemental Act petitions and denied 22.[33]

The commission issued its final report on October 1, 1862, and by the terms of the statute, each commissioner was paid $2,000 (almost $62,500 today). "By January 21, 1863, all accounts were figured, the books closed, claimants notified, and the report sent to the Secretary of the Treasury. Each claimant then walked up to the cage in Room 18, 'gave his name,'" as Noah Brooks, a correspondent for the *Sacramento Union*, recorded. "The commission clerk looked up the number of his claim, and the Sub-Treasury cashier produced a check which bore the same number. Thereupon the claimant signed a receipt, received this check, and went to General Francis Spinner, U.S. Treasurer, where he signed another receipt, and the check being duly counter-signed, was payable at the Sub-Treasury."[34]

Though slavery had legally ended in the District of Columbia, the spoils of the institution would continue to be a part of the financial futures of enslavers like Margaret Barber for many years to come. She lived a long and prosperous life and died of influenza on February 14, 1892, at the age of eighty-two, at a time when very few Americans, and certainly not enslaved people, lived so long.

Some enslavers in the district continued to ignore the 1862 Compensated Emancipation Act. In the summer of 1863, more than a year after the act was passed into law, Colonel William Birney discovered that "some unknown number of men, women, and children who were 'entitled to their freedom in the District of Columbia' . . . were being held" against their will "in slave pens in Baltimore."[35] These people were moved to another state where the district law could not initially be enforced. Colonel Birney ultimately released this group of enslaved people from their captors and recruited many of the men to serve in the Union Army.

But what about Peter Jenkins, Richard Williams, Susan Carroll, and the rest of the thirty-four people enslaved at Northview— what happened to them? The newly freed received nothing to compensate them for the wealth that Margaret Barber had stripped from them in the form of wages. Total wage theft from slavery is conservatively estimated to be $19 trillion. Now they were no longer enslaved, but lacking resources, they weren't truly free either.

Many of Margaret's enslaved workers remained on the Northview estate after gaining their freedom, "to tend the winepress orchards, raise the geese, and guard the livestock pens from pilfering soldiers."[36] Mary Jenkins, "No. 1 Cook," and her family took up residence on Kendall Green, an open-air hospital camp made up of tents pitched in a field, akin to modern-day refugee camps. The "cause of [her] destitution," as documented in the Freedmen's Bureau records, was "no work and large family." Ellen Jenkins, described in Margaret's petition as a "good cook," found work in the district as a nurse and lived another twenty years as a free woman until she passed in 1882.[37]

As a general rule, most of the formerly enslaved left their enslavers and found work in the district, joined the Union Army once they were allowed to serve, or moved north. In 1866 the Freedmen's Bureau reported that only seventy-seven people in the district were employed by their former enslavers.

The end of slavery in the District of Columbia did not lead to white enslavers generally supporting the end of slavery. In that respect, the experiment failed. Ending chattel slavery would take a civil war and the passage of the Thirteenth Amendment.

Becoming law on December 6, 1865, the Thirteenth Amendment provided: "Neither slavery nor involuntary servitude, except as a punishment for crime whereof the party shall have been duly convicted, shall exist within the United States, or any place subject to their jurisdiction."

Lynching's Targets

"Negroes with white skin."[38] That was how white Americans considered Italians, according to the historian Alan G. Gauthreaux. Why? Because Italians, in particular those from Sicily, broke all social and economic conventions when it came to living in the American South. It also did not help that their skin was considered darker than that of their fellow countrymen from northern Italy.

Sicilians who immigrated to the United States in the late nineteenth century were not interested in becoming Americans. They simply wanted to earn money, send it to family members back home, and save enough to live comfortably when they returned to Italy permanently. Unlike the northern Italians who wished to remain in the United States, Sicilians felt no need to learn about Southern culture, as they were not planning on staying there very long.[39] Some worked on the docks, others became business owners, and many worked on plantations. But while they were here, they worked, ate, and lived among black Americans on the plantations and other workplaces that employed both groups: "In certain regions of Louisiana and Mississippi their children were forced to attend segregated schools with blacks."[40]

Plantation owners treated Sicilians and blacks similarly—very poorly—which motivated Sicilians to strike, together with black Americans, in support of improved wages and working conditions. Sicilians established their own retail stores in the rural South and often accorded black customers the same dignity and respect they did white customers.[41] This didn't go over well with white community members.

Sicilian immigrants also made enemies of white American workers because they were willing to work for lower wages, which crowded white Americans out of the labor market.[42] The problem of low wages, of course, was created by former enslavers looking for the cheapest labor possible as a replacement for the free labor system of chattel slavery that had been outlawed. They thought the immigrant population would fill that need. They also hoped to get immigrant support for their political representatives, mistakenly assuming that all immigrants desired to assimilate and bought into the privileges of white supremacy.[43]

What happened instead was that the Sicilians' "social and economic status encouraged them to empathize with black people and support Republican and Populist candidates over their white supremacist rivals."[44] This would prove fatal for some. Although the overwhelming majority of victims of racial violence in the United States have been black, it might come as a surprise to find out that "of the [fifty-one] white men murdered by lynch mobs" between roughly 1890 and 1910, some 40 percent were Sicilians.[45] What is even more amazing is that the federal government paid compensation for sixteen of those deaths.

On a stormy night in October 1890, New Orleans police chief David Hennessy walked home under the shelter of his umbrella. He had no idea that the shadowy figure across the street presented any danger. But several minutes later that figure was joined by several others who opened fire on the chief, leaving him slumped on the ground with six gunshot wounds. His assailants fled into the cover of night. When asked if he could identify who shot him, he answered, "Dagos," a racial slur for Italians. Hennessy was taken to the hospital, and when asked again before surgery whether he knew his assailants, he repeated his earlier identification, stating, "The dagos shot me." By nine o'clock the next morning, Chief Hennessy was dead.

The response from city officials was swift.

The mayor ordered a search of the city's Italian neighborhoods, and the police obliged, arresting any Italians they could find. By noon, at least sixty Italians had been rounded up. Eleven were charged with Chief Hennessy's murder, and six proceeded to trial. None of the men were convicted. Three were acquitted, and a mistrial was declared for the remaining three, yet the judge ordered them back to prison to await trial on additional charges. Anti-Italian sentiment in New Orleans, however, increased after the jury verdicts failed to convict anyone. The next evening, on March 14, 1892, a mob broke into the jail and lynched all eleven Italians, including the three men who were acquitted, the three whom the jury did not convict, and five who never received a trial.

The Italian government was outraged when it learned of its citizens' murders abroad and "insisted upon a promise that reparation would be made."[46] It believed that a debt was owed because the victims were "Italian citizens in foreign countries [and as such] should be accorded the full measure of protection fixed by the laws of these countries." When the request was ignored, Italy recalled its ambassador to the United States, Baron Fava, which was followed by the United States withdrawing its ambassador from Rome. Italy "threatened military action unless the United States government paid reparations to the families of the murdered men."[47]

Diplomatic relations remained strained for several weeks

until President Benjamin Harrison ordered the secretary of state to withdraw almost $25,000 ($2,211.90 per family) from State Department funds (nearly $864,000 today) to compensate Italy and the families of the eleven men.[48] The payment marked the first of three times the federal government would compensate Italy for lynchings of its citizens in the South.

In August 1896 three more Italians were lynched at St. Charles Parish in Hahnville, Louisiana.[49] Their names were Lorenzo Saladino, Salvatore Arena, and Giuseppe Vontorelli.[50]

Saladino had been arrested for the murder of Jules Gueymard, a "wealthy planter and merchant" who was shot while waiting at the docks.[51] Arena and Vontorelli were arrested for the murder of a Spanish yardman working on the Ashton Place Plantation.[52]

Around 11 P.M. on August 9, a lynch mob formed outside the jail where all three men had been taken into custody.[53] "Hang the dago!" someone from the crowd shouted. After about ten minutes of attacking the jail doors, the crowd made its way inside and targeted its human prey. Saladino, according to reports, was found "cowering in a corner of his cell muttering prayers and pleading for mercy. He was dragged out," along with the two other prisoners, Arena and Vontorelli.[54]

According to press reports, the mob "decided to take them over to a shed near the courthouse and string them up. . . . The three Italians were lined up again and told to pray, as they would have but two minutes to live. They prayed, and then the ropes were adjusted around their necks, and one after another they were strung up the rafters."[55] When Hahnville residents awoke the next day, they found three bullet-riddled bodies still hanging. (After the lynchings, someone else confessed to killing the "old Spaniard," and other evidence casts doubt on Saladino's presumed guilt.)[56]

The Italian ambassador Baron Fava once again sought justice for his murdered countrymen. He wrote to secretary of state Richard Olney, asking for an explanation and demanding to know what was being done to keep Italians safe in America.[57] The Italian consul of Louisiana, Charles Papini, conducted an investigation and uncovered a case of mistaken identities. Arena had been misidentified originally as Decino Sorcoro and Vontorelli as Angelo Mancuso, the two men who had been suspected of killing the Spaniard.

Secretary Olney told Fava that a grand jury had been assembled to investigate the matter and was "unable to ascertain the offenders."[58] He claimed there was no proof that the victims were Italian citizens and therefore the United States did not owe reparations for their murders. Italy refused to back down.[59] Ultimately, the Italian government was able to prove that the three victims had been Italian subjects at the time of their deaths and that their families were entitled to an indemnity from the US government. And that is how for a second time the federal government compensated Italy to the tune of $18,000 (almost $675,000 today) for the lynching of its citizens—$6,000 to each of the victims' Italian families.[60]

Three years later in 1899, a series of events led to five more Italians being lynched in Louisiana, this time in Madison Parish in Tallulah. It began because of a dispute involving a goat.[61]

Madison Parish was home to several thousand black Americans, several hundred white Americans, and six Sicilians, including three brothers: Francesco, Giuseppe, and Carlo Difatta. The Difatta brothers were successful businessmen who owned two grocery stores in Tallulah. Their success brought with it a certain level of "animosity."[62]

On July 19, 1899, a goat belonging to Francesco Difatta wandered onto the property of Dr. J. Ford Hodge. It wasn't the first time, but as far as Dr. Hodge was concerned, it would be the last. He took out his revolver and shot the goat. Angered by the loss of his animal, Francesco got into an argument with the doctor but left it at that. His brother Carlo, however, was not willing to let it go as easily. When he encountered Dr. Hodge later that day, the two got into a heated exchange. Carlo punched Dr. Hodge, who then drew his revolver and fired, grazing Carlo's head. Carlo fell to the ground, and Dr. Hodge held him there by pinning him to the ground with his boot on his chest. Enter Giuseppe, who witnessed the entire incident from inside the family home. While Dr. Hodge worked on fixing his jammed revolver—presumably to shoot Carlo again—"Giuseppe fired upon Hodge from the balcony with a pistol loaded with birdshot."[63]

Gossip that "the Italians had killed Dr. Hodge" spread like wildfire through the town,[64] and the Difatta brothers were quickly arrested. Next, the sheriff rounded up Giovanni Cirano and Rosario Fiducia, two friends of the Difattas', also Sicilians, and charged them with conspiracy for allegedly being "in cahoots with the 'cold-blooded foreigners.'" Within hours, rumors circulated that Dr. Hodge had been shot between fifty and seventy-five times. A lynch mob soon gathered outside the jail and built a makeshift gallows.

With their weapon of choice constructed, the crowd stormed the jail three separate times and carried out three separate lynchings. They first dragged out Carlo and Giuseppe, then Francesco and Rosario, and finally Giovanni. According to the murderers, their actions were warranted to "teach the Italian and his gang a lesson."[65] One newspaper account went so far as to describe the mob as well-behaved: "not a shot was fired, and the crowd was orderly and quiet, but very determined."[66] As for Dr. Hodge, the reports of his death were greatly exaggerated. Three days later he "was declared 'out of all danger.'"[67]

In the aftermath, Tallulah residents announced that "all others of the [Sicilian] race within the parish lines had three days to leave under penalty of death." The single remaining Sicilian fled, and Tallulah "emptied their town of Italians."[68] Even though the members of the lynch mob were well-known and two witnesses, black brothers, provided a list of names to Italian diplomatic investigators, the Madison Parish grand jury concluded that they were unable to identify the perpetrators. Once again, Louisiana courts refused to provide justice for murdered Italians.

The *Times Democrat*, along with other newspaper reports, sought to justify the murders. "Citizens Plead Necessity for White Supremacy" ran the headline on one of the articles. As the historian Jessica Barbata Jackson, at Colorado State University, described it, the idea that the "lynching . . . was necessary for 'white supremacy'" was the substance of the paper's argument. "The native-born, white community in Tallulah felt 'obliged' to commit the lynching, since the 'complicity in the conspiracy . . . could never have been proven legally, and that to ensure white supremacy, no other course was possible than the course pursued.' The *Times* went on to explain that of the 'several lynchings' in Madison Parish in the past eighteen months, 'the result is that Madison Parish is never the scene now of any race troubles. The negroes have come to the realization of the fact that lawlessness on their part will not be tolerated.'"[69]

"Suggesting that 'white supremacy' would otherwise be in jeopardy, and identifying the reasons for the lynching of these five Sicilians as comparable with the motives behind the lynchings of African Americans," Jackson explains, meant "that Italians could be, when necessary, consigned outside a larger category of whiteness."[70] In other words, white supremacy was willing to sacrifice a few nonblack people in order to maintain the racially inferior status of black Americans.

In his annual address to Congress on December 5, 1899, President William McKinley brought up the need for federal legislation to contain mob violence. He asked Congress to give the federal courts jurisdiction over the "class of international cases where the ultimate responsibility of the federal government may be involved" (under the international rule of Full Protection and Security) in order to prevent such lynchings from happening again in the future.[71] At a time when black Americans were being lynched in far greater numbers, the president was more concerned about the federal government's responsibility toward foreigners. Why? Because he didn't want to keep writing checks to Italy.

Italy again pressed into service Ambassador Baron Fava, who demanded an indemnity from US secretary of state John Hay. Eventually, President McKinley asked Congress for relief funds payable to the families of the deceased. Once again, on March 3, 1901, Congress appropriated a sum of $4,000 (just under $150,000 today) to be paid "out of humane considerations, without reference to the liability thereof, to the Italian Government as full indemnity to the heirs of Joseph (Giuseppe) DiFatta and John (Giovanni) Cirano, Italian citizens lynched at Tallulah, on July 20, 1899."[72] The other three victims' families received nothing because a Department of Justice investigation found they were not Italian citizens.[73]

The anti-Italian sentiment that led white mobs to repeatedly lynch Italians was largely motivated by a desire for retaliation. As new immigrants, Italians did not behave like Southern white men in a most important matter: race. Italians did not come here with the view that black Americans were their inferiors. When they became merchants, they treated their black and white customers equally. Their children went to school with black children (not by choice but by law), and they were willing to work with and take the side of their fellow black workers—not their employers or plantation owners. White Louisianans aided by a complicit justice system used lynching to control Italians—just as white Americans used it to control black Americans, as we will see in Part II. But Italians had one significant advantage that black Americans did not: They had a country and government willing to fight for them.[74]

Land Grab

Tribal Nations have always had something the federal government wanted: land. "All land titles in the United States originate in Indian title," wrote the legal scholar Joseph Singer.[75] And the government was prepared to get it by any means necessary. Sometimes it bought the land outright, but as cheaply as possible, mind you, by entering into exploitative treaties with Tribal Nations. In other instances, the land was seized when the Supreme Court created new legal theories that deprived tribes of their rights.[76] The federal government was not above using violence, or the threat thereof, to take what it wanted in cases where it couldn't twist the law or bend a Tribe to its will.

In fact, government agents occasionally encouraged private white citizens to grab Tribal land by force: "The ink was hardly dry on the treaties before white settlers began their trek overland into Indian country, breaching the solemn promises of the United States."[77] Ultimately, this concerted effort to usurp all land that the government saw fit to occupy resulted in one of history's most significant wealth transfers, the ceding of land from Tribal Nations to white families.

In the eighteenth and nineteenth centuries, the US government repeatedly violated treaties that it had negotiated with Tribal Nations, resulting not only in the seizure of land but also in the loss of valuable rights included in landownership, such as the ability to sell timber and grazing rights. Such treaties, which were often negotiated against a backdrop of threats of starvation, resulted in "agreements" with unconscionable terms because tribes were left with little option but to agree or face certain death. As if the scales weren't already tipped in the government's favor, in *Johnson v. McIntosh* in 1823 the Supreme Court established a legal doctrine that stripped Tribal Nations of many of the landownership rights enjoyed by non-Indian landowners.[78] The Court codified the notion of "discovery," which enabled the United States to claim that it was the only entity that had a right to buy Native Tribal land. The law did not recognize the right of Tribal Nations to *own* property—only their right to occupy the land. That rule, of course, hastened the federal government's ability to strip Tribal land away. Even when bloodshed was avoided— and bloodshed was rarely avoided—the constant appropriation of more and more land amounted to a violent and hostile act.

Tribal Nations began filing claims with the US government as early as 1831, following the negotiation of numerous treaties that had been violated.[79] However, Congress barred the cases from being heard by the court of claims, as "the American right to buy always superseded the Indian right not to sell."[80]

In the spring of 1945, almost a century later, Congress held hearings on legislation that would enable Tribal Nations to have their claims against the US government heard due to their being formerly "denied equal access to the courts."[81] Many conservative members of Congress supported the bill because they thought it would hasten Tribal assimilation into white American culture. It was well known that the adjective often used to describe Tribal members was *savages*. In the Supreme Court decision announcing the new "discovery" rule, Chief Justice John Marshall stated in his opinion that "the tribes of Indians inhabiting this country were *fierce savages*, whose occupation was war. . . . To leave them in possession of their country, was to leave the country a wilderness; to govern them as a distinct people, was impossible, because they were as brave and high spirited as they were fierce, and were ready to repel by arms every attempt on their independence"[82] (emphasis added).

White Americans' racism toward Tribal Nations was very much out in the open. But for me, the most remarkable part of this history is that white Americans actually believed the country rightfully belonged to them. When you have unfettered power to strip people of *their own* land, you have no reason to lie about what you are doing. Tribal Nations were judged for how they used the land, and because they used it differently, it was argued they had forfeited the right to keep it. The chief justice correctly acknowledged that Tribal Nations would not go down without a fight, so the Supreme Court stepped in to make it legal to take whatever land the government wasn't able to take through war.

During the 1945 hearings, some members of Congress also believed cynically that Tribal Nation members were holding out on assimilating because they believed it would make them ineligible for any future reparations that Tribes might be awarded.[83]

Arguing in support of the Tribal Nations claims bill, Rep. Henry Jackson (D-WA) said, "Let us pay our debts to the Indian tribes that sold us the land that we live on. . . . Let us at least pay what we promised to pay . . . and let us see that the Indians have their fair day in court so that they can call the various Government agencies to account on the obligations that the Federal Government has assumed."[84]

President Harry Truman signed the Indian Claims Act into law on August 13, 1946, with the statement: "I am glad to sign my name to a measure . . . which removes a lingering discrimination against our First Americans and gives them the same opportunities that our laws extend to all other American citizens to vindicate their property rights and contracts in the courts against violations by the Federal Government itself." The legislation established the Indian Claims Commission, a panel of three appointed commissioners (later expanded to five) that was to hear claims, make decisions, and complete its business ten years from the date of the commission's first meeting.[85] The process set forth was the equivalent of holding mini trials over the course of a decade and initiating a fact-finding campaign, followed by the commission's review and final opinion announcing any monetary awards to be issued. Noticeably absent was the possibility of land being returned to Tribal Nations—the one thing Tribal Nations wanted.[86]

President Truman concluded his thoughts with the hope that "with the final settlement of all outstanding claims which this measure ensures, Indians can take their place without special handicap or special advantage in the economic life of our nation and share fully in its progress."[87] It wasn't the first time Tribal Nations had heard such a promise. Behind the scenes, the costs of the momentous compensation scheme had not provoked any real concern because federal officials believed that most of the claims would wind up being dismissed.[88]

The Indian Claims Commission eventually abandoned its mandate to complete its work in ten years, as numerous extensions dragged the process out across four decades; it remained in operation until September 30, 1978. There were problems from day one, not the least of which was that the Tribal Nations wanted land and not money, but the commission was empowered to award only monetary damages.

The first commissioners were not appointed until eight months after the bill was signed. Edgar E. Will, a former lieutenant governor of Texas, served as the first chief commissioner, along with Louis J. O'Marr and William Holt.[89] All were white men, and none had any experience in federal Indian policy or federal Indian law. (That would remain true for all the commissioners until the late 1960s, even after the commission was expanded to include five members.) Their offices were located in Washington, DC, far away from where most Tribal members lived, and only lawyers approved by the commission were allowed to represent the Tribes. The commissioners could have created and staffed an investigative division right away, as authorized by the 1946 legislation, to help them verify the facts of the claims brought forward. But they did not do so for several years.

Another failing of the commission was that it did not notify all eligible Tribes about their right to submit a claim and the process for submitting one. In accordance with the law, the commission was required to send out a written explanation to the "recognized heads of every Indian tribe and band or to any other identifiable group of Indians existing as 'distinct entities.'"[90] Only Tribal Nations, not individuals, were allowed to present claims to the commission, and they were initially given a five-year period in which to do so.[91] The act provided for several types of claims to be heard, but "the vast majority of claims processed were claims for compensation related to land."[92]

The Absentee Shawnee Tribe, for example, submitted a claim

based on two treaties they had entered into with the United States—one in 1825 and one in 1831—for more than one million acres of land located in what is now eastern Kansas. But by the 1850s, the federal government had decided it wanted white Americans to resettle in the territory. Therefore, on March 3, 1853, Congress authorized the president to take the land back. The government proceeded to "negotiate" with the Shawnee Tribe through the commissioner of Indian Affairs, who began by telling the Shawnee that they had no choice but to sell. The final price "agreed" upon was $829,000. When their claim was brought before the commission under the 1946 claims act, officials agreed that the amount the Tribe had been paid could be considered "unconscionable"—a term defined by the court of claims as "so much less than the actual value of the property sold that the disparity shocks the conscience."[93] In 1971 the commission awarded the Shawnee Tribe additional compensation of $300,000 (worth a little more than $2.3 million today) for two broken treaties and unconscionable contract terms.

In another claim, a group of tribes that had signed the Treaty of 1829 submitted their grievances as a bloc.[94] The tribes involved were spread out geographically, spanning the Midwest from North Dakota to Indiana, including the Potawatomi Nation; the Prairie Band of the Potawatomi Tribe; the Hannahville Indian Community; the Chippewa Tribe of Indians; the Red Lake, Pembina, and White Earth Band; and the Ottawa Tribe of Indians. Again, the commission determined that the price the government had paid for their land—$364,901 for land that was already worth $2,470,264 in 1829—was "unconscionable." On April 15, 1965, the commission awarded the Citizen Band of Potawatomi Indians of Oklahoma, the Prairie Band of the Potawatomi Tribe of Indians, and the Hannahville Indian Community a total cash award of $2,094,573.02.[95] The three tribes appealed to the court of claims and argued that the Indian Claims Commission excluded valuable mineral deposits from its judgment. Therefore, in 1973, the commission awarded an additional $4,104,818.98 (just over $29 million today) to the three Tribes.[96]

A total of 370 claims were filed on behalf of the Tribal Nations, numbering roughly 176, that had been recognized by the federal government by the summer of 1946, when the Indian Claims Commission was established. However, many claims included multiple allegations, and the commission treated each allegation as a separate matter, resulting in a total of more than six hundred claims.[97] While 204 claims were dismissed, 274 claims resulted in awards.[98] Some claims were still unresolved when the commission ended in 1978, and those were transferred to the US Court of Federal Claims. The final claim was resolved in 2006.[99] Justice moved at a snail's pace for Tribal Nations.

The total amount of claims that the commission paid to Tribal Nations through 1978 was $818 million. The cases transferred to the US Court of Federal Claims resulted in additional awards, bringing the total amount paid to roughly $1.3 billion.[100] If payments had been made as swiftly as they were to the former enslavers in the District of Columbia, within a year of their claims being filed, or to Italy for the lynching of Italians in New Orleans, then the total amount due to the Tribal Nations would have been paid in 1946 and would be worth almost $21 billion in 2024.

Criminalizing Race

Who is considered a criminal in our society is much more subjective than we like to believe. Innocent Italians, convicted of no wrongdoing, were arrested and lynched, while the white Americans who lynched them were never brought to justice. What happened to Japanese Americans not very long ago is one of the most glaring examples of a people being imprisoned solely because of their race. Simply being of Japanese ancestry was grounds enough for the arrest and imprisonment of more than 100,000 people during World War II, including the Masuda family.

The Masudas exemplified the hardworking immigrant family. In the early 1940s, they were part of a small and flourishing community of nearly two thousand Japanese Americans living in Orange County, California.[101] Gensuke Masuda had come to America as a boy from Wakayama, Japan, in 1898 to work on the railroads in Oregon. Several years later Gensuke met and married Tamaye, who was also born in Wakayama, and they settled in Orange County around 1906 or 1907.[102]

Gensuke and Tamaye remained there for almost three decades, farming beans, cabbage, and celery along Newhope Road.[103] They farmed on other people's land at first, but eventually they were able to buy a plot of their own in Orange County. They had ten children who attended the local public schools, played various sports, and were active in the Presbyterian church.[104] Every member of the family worked on the farm. Although the United States had not yet entered World War II, two of the Masuda sons, Kazuo and Takashi, were drafted into the US Army on October 17, 1941.[105]

But the Masuda family's American Dream quickly turned into a nightmare on the night of December 7, 1941, "a date which will live in infamy." On that day Japan attacked the United States at Pearl Harbor, destroying and damaging US battleships and killing or wounding more than 3,500 servicemen and civilians.[106]

It was soon open season on Americans of Japanese ancestry—whether they were citizens or not—because in the eyes of their fellow Americans, they represented the face of the enemy.[107]

That same night Gensuke and seventeen other first-generation Japanese immigrants were arrested. It was later revealed that he had been targeted because he was active in a local Japanese wrestling league that frequently held matches with sailors on leave from touring Japanese vessels.[108] He was accused of "subversive activity" and eventually incarcerated in Montana. There was no trial, no lawyer, and no opportunity to present a defense.

A short two months later, on February 19, 1942, President Franklin D. Roosevelt issued Executive Order 9066, which authorized the secretary of war to designate "military areas" across the country "from which any or all persons may be excluded." The executive order never mentioned Japanese Americans by name, but it delegated the power to imprison them to the US military.

By this time, more than two thousand Japanese residents like Gensuke had already been arrested.[109] But the federal government was not the only racist actor. In several instances, states, cities, and local governments also took action to harass or exclude Japanese Americans. For example, in the aftermath of Pearl Harbor, the State of California required its Japanese American employees to answer a long questionnaire, providing "whether they could speak Japanese, their citizenship status, their membership in Japanese or Japanese American organizations." None of the questions or criteria were relevant to their job performance.[110] They were all summarily suspended from their jobs without pay and eventually "dismissed from their jobs without any further paychecks or severance pay."[111]

Within a year of the Pearl Harbor bombing, more than 100,000 Americans of Japanese ancestry would be sent to one of nine "war relocation centers" solely on the basis of their race.[112] About 35,000 were eventually given permission to leave to join the army, attend college outside the West Coast, or take up private employment. But they were allowed to leave only after their loyalty was reviewed and confirmed. By December 1944, around 85,000 people remained in "government custody."[113] The president's executive order was challenged in the courts all the way to the US Supreme Court—and was upheld.[114]

Initially the federal government urged Americans of Japanese ancestry—those they hadn't already arrested—to voluntarily relocate themselves out of the designated military areas and resettle east. Accordingly, the Masuda family packed up their ten-acre homestead in Fountain Valley, which they had newly purchased in the name of one of their citizen children, and moved to Fresno, where one of their married daughters lived and maintained a vineyard. The only reason they were able to move so readily was that they owned a new car, a truck, and farm equipment in good condition, all of which they took with them to Fresno. Before too long, Gensuke was released from the Missoula, Montana, prison camp and reunited with his family, likely due in part to the fact that he had two sons serving in the US Army. Kazuo had also written a strong letter in support of his father's loyalty to the US government.[115]

What began as voluntary resettlement turned into mass incarceration of the remaining Japanese population in America, residents and citizens alike. First, they were sent to temporary "assembly centers" located up and down the West Coast, and then they were moved to permanent "relocation centers," situated mostly in remote corners of the Interior West, like Manzanar,

California, and Poston, Arizona. These camps were basically prisons with armed guard towers, barbed-wire fences, and around-the-clock surveillance.[116]

Despite having already relocated to Fresno of their own accord, the Masudas were ordered to move to the Fresno County Fairgrounds in October 1942. They remained there for nearly two months before being transferred to the forested, rattlesnake-infested Jerome Relocation Center in Arkansas, where temperatures soared above 100 degrees in the summer and dipped below 20 degrees in the winter.[117]

The conditions at the prisons were dire. Masato Uyeda, one of those imprisoned who later testified before a government commission, remembered that the camps made their occupants feel like criminals. "Internees had to wear uniforms similar to prison garb and had numbers on their backs," he said. "The camp was surrounded by barbed wire fences and the US Army patrolled the fences with machine guns mounted in jeeps."[118] Food shortages and overcrowding were common. "Upon our arrival we were told to stuff our mattresses with straw. . . . We lived in bare tar-papered barracks that were hastily constructed," Grace Watanabe Kimura recalled. "We even had to share a room with another couple."[119] Another survivor, Shuzo Chris Kato, later testified, "The government destroyed the important family structure of the Japanese families by forcing them to eat in the mess halls and use communal showers and lavatories. . . . Everyone was forced to use out-houses since the sewer system had not been built."[120]

On occasion, this poor state of affairs led to unrest. In the summer of 1942, a riot broke out at the Santa Anita Assembly Center because of overcrowding and insufficient food. The following year the army deployed tanks and soldiers to the Tule

Lake Segregation Center in northern California to put down protests over food shortages and unsafe conditions, which had led to an accidental death. Meanwhile the Masudas now had two more sons serving in the US Army: Masao and Mitsuo (though Mitsuo would be medically discharged in 1943).[121] While the Masuda family were prey to white supremacy at home, their sons were enlisted to fight Nazis abroad.

During World War II, Kazuo served in the 442nd Regimental Combat Team, which fought across Italy and southern France. It was one of the war's most decorated units, composed of second-generation Japanese Americans. In July 1944, Kazuo was awarded the Distinguished Service Cross for repelling a German counterattack. But he didn't live long enough to receive the medal. He was killed on August 27, 1944, while "leading a night patrol across the Arno River in Italy." In a cruel turn, the Masudas received the news of Kazuo's death by Western Union telegram at the Gila River Relocation Camp in Arizona.[122] By this time, they had been relocated from Arkansas, where they stayed for almost twenty months, to the scorching hot desert of Arizona. The Masuda family remained there for the rest of their imprisonment.

On December 18, 1944, the Supreme Court ruled that the government could no longer detain Japanese American citizens whom it had conceded were loyal to the United States.[123] But it wasn't until 1946 that the last prison camp was closed.

In the spring of 1945, Mary Masuda was able to leave the Gila River camp and travel back to the family home on Newhope Road. When she got there, she found a white family living in *her* family's home, farming *their* land without permission or compensation. The wholesale theft of the Masudas' home was unforgivable, but the physical threats she would soon receive proved unforgettable.

While staying at a friend's house, an unidentified caller asked for Mary. She answered the phone and was told "she'd better go back to the concentration camp because Japanese Americans weren't welcomed in Orange County." Later that night she was confronted by four or five people who said they represented the Native Sons of the Golden West, an all-white fraternal order known for its anti-Japanese mindset. These "patriots," as they called themselves, told her she would be better off if she left town. One of the men, Mary recalled, said "he would get me a taxi to go back to Los Angeles in, but that maybe I wouldn't get there alive." Mary's friend warned her there were "more men waiting outside down the road."[124]

The intimidation did not work. Home for the first time in nearly three years, Mary lay wide awake with one nagging thought: "I came this far, I must fight for what Kazuo and all of the rest of the soldiers fought for." The next day she called the sheriff. When the sheriff offered no help, she talked to a reporter at the *Santa Ana Register*. A week or so later Walter Winchell, the well-known newspaper columnist and radio broadcaster, saw the *Register*'s coverage and publicized the incident on his radio show: "Five hoodlums recently terrorized a Japanese American girl."[125]

Winchell was estimated to reach "fifty million Americans— out of an adult population of roughly seventy-five million" who either listened to him on the radio or read his newspaper column.[126] It wasn't long before her story reached the highest levels of government. Interior secretary Harold Ickes called the situation a "shameful spectacle" and denounced the "Nazi tactics" used to harass Mary Masuda, which put public pressure on local sheriffs to take the case seriously.[127]

In September 1945, in spite of the threats of violence she faced on her last visit, Mary moved her family back to Newhope

Road in Orange County.[128] And while the Masudas were able to return home, most prison camp survivors were not. Only one out of four prewar farm operators were able to reclaim their property.[129]

Mary's courage and determination did not go unnoticed. On the morning of December 8, 1945, Joseph Stilwell, a four-star general, saluted the Masuda family in a simple ceremony on the porch of their family home. "It is an honor to be delegated to make this award," General Stilwell said. He pinned Kazuo's Distinguished Service Cross medal on Mary, who in turn pinned it on her mother. The ceremony was broadcast nationwide by the War Relocation Authority, who hoped that Mary Masuda's bravery would convey the high price Japanese Americans paid during the war in order "to safeguard democracy." (I can't help but think the government was also trying to get some positive press given that their targeting of American citizens and residents of Japanese ancestry had led to such hate-filled actions.) It was an attempt to signal that moving forward, anti-Japanese harassment "would not be tolerated."[130]

Following the medal presentation, General Stilwell spoke at a United America Day rally staged in his honor at the Santa Ana Bowl by the Council for Civil Unity and Santa Ana civic organizations. A smattering of Hollywood celebrities, including Louise Allbritton, Robert Young, and Will Rogers, Jr., were featured in the programming as part of the event's "American-All" theme. After being introduced by Rogers, Stilwell declared: "Who, after all, is the real American? The real American is the man who calls it a fair exchange to lay down his life in order that American ideals may go on living. And judging by such a test, Sgt. Masuda was a better American than any of us here today."[131]

Another featured speaker at the rally was an actor and army

captain who capitalized on the theme of racial unity, world peace, and domestic harmony in his speech: "Blood that has soaked into the sands of a beach is all of one color, America stands unique in the world, the only country not founded on race, but in a way an ideal. Not in spite of, but because of our polyglot background, we have had all the strength in the world. That is the American way."[132] The army captain was right about blood being only one color but, of course, woefully wrong about our country not being founded on racial identity.

Of the more than 100,000 people of Japanese ancestry imprisoned during World War II, two-thirds were US citizens, and almost all of the remaining one-third were permanent residents. They were imprisoned solely because of their race, because they looked like the people who bombed Pearl Harbor. They were innocent and had done nothing to suggest disloyalty. And yet they were still rounded up and sent to prison without so much as a hearing. The government justified this abuse of power as necessary to protect national security in a time of war.

After the war, the federal government passed several pieces of legislation to try to atone for this shameful history. The most important was the Japanese American Evacuation Claims Act in 1948. Passed by Congress and signed into law by President Truman, it awarded people of Japanese ancestry the right to be compensated for real and personal property losses as a result of their exclusion and evacuation during the war. However, the act did not permit claims for loss of income or pain and suffering. Roughly $37 million was paid out, far below the actual losses.[133] The awards were intentionally low because the requirement of proof was so onerous that claimants were incentivized to settle quickly for lower amounts. In the end, the Evacuation Claims Act did not come close to fairly compensating survivors and their families for the badge of racial inferiority that had been stamped upon them by the federal government.

Subsequent efforts included amending the Social Security Act in 1972 so that Japanese Americans over the age of eighteen were treated as though they had earned an income and contributed to the system during their incarceration.[134] Similarly, in 1978, federal civil service retirement provisions were amended to give credit to Japanese Americans for the time they spent in detention after age eighteen.

Once the incarceration of Japanese Americans ended, most survivors did not want to talk about the trauma. "I could deal with hardships," one survivor later explained, "but I could not deal with the psychological assault of being in a prison without being guilty of any crime. . . . I can understand why some Japanese Americans have never shared this episode with their offspring. One does not share a shameful experience very easily."[135]

By the 1960s, with a growing national civil rights movement, things began to change. Children and grandchildren of Japanese Americans who had been imprisoned during the war began a grassroots campaign for the government to redress the harms done.[136] In 1970 the Japanese American Citizens League (JACL) adopted a resolution that demanded "federal legislation to provide tax-free monetary 'reparations' to Japanese Americans (or their heirs) who were excluded and incarcerated during World War II and a $400 million fund for community projects."[137] However, progress stalled because there still wasn't widespread support even in the Japanese American community for reparations.

According to one estimate, at that time about one third of Japanese Americans supported a national campaign, one third were against it, and one third were neutral.[138] Some believed that looking backward would only cause more pain. Others thought that even if they were to get an apology and restitution, no amount of money could compensate them for the true harm they had experienced. But those in support persevered. Their compelling narrative quickly gained traction among non-Japanese Americans.

In the late 1970s, several Japanese Americans had been elected to Congress, and the JACL successfully lobbied them to put their support behind the redress movement. The Congressional Black Caucus, including Rep. Ronald Dellums (D-CA) and Rep. Mervyn Dymally (D-CA), also proved to be helpful allies. Eventually in August 1979, Senators Daniel K. Inouye (D-HI), Spark Matsunaga (D-HI), Samuel I. Hayakawa (R-CA), and Ted Stevens (R-AK) agreed to co-sponsor Senate Bill 1647. Meanwhile in the House of Representatives, Norman Mineta (D-CA), Robert Matsui (D-CA), and James Wright (D-TX), along with 114 other representatives, introduced House Resolution 5499 on September 28, 1979. In response, Congress proposed the creation of the Commission on Wartime Relocation and Internment of Civilians (CWRIC), and President Jimmy Carter signed it into law on July 31, 1980.[139]

The legislation charged CWRIC with accomplishing three tasks: to review "the facts and circumstances surrounding Executive Order Numbered 9066" as well as the impact it had on American citizens and permanent residents; to assess the "directives of United States military forces" that led to the detention of American citizens in "internment camps"; and finally to propose "appropriate remedies" for any wrongs committed by the US government as a result of Executive Order 9066.

The commission began with seven commissioners: Arthur Flemming, chair of the US Commission on Civil Rights and former secretary of health, education, and welfare under President

Dwight D. Eisenhower; Joan Z. Bernstein, former general counsel of the Department of Health and Human Services; Judge William Marutani, the only Japanese American to sit on the commission; Arthur J. Goldberg, former ambassador to the United Nations and former US Supreme Court justice; Rep. Daniel Lungren (R-CA), from Long Beach, a sitting member of Congress who asked to be appointed; Edward W. Brooke, an African American Republican and former US senator from Massachusetts; and Hugh B. Mitchell, former US Democratic senator and representative from Seattle. Bernstein was selected as chair and Lungren as vice-chair.[140] Just as progress seemed imminent, there was a major setback.

Before the commission could hold any hearings, President Carter was voted out of office and California governor Ronald Reagan was sworn in as president on January 20, 1981. President Reagan opposed everything associated with the former president, including the commission. Early on in his first term, he remarked to his cabinet that "he had little use for 'left-over Carterisms like the CWRIC.'"[141] But because the Democrats controlled the majority of the House, and the Republicans the Senate, President Reagan could not repeal the legislation. Within a month of taking office, he signed into law a bill that expanded the commission to nine members.[142] Rev. Robert F. Drinan, a Jesuit priest, Georgetown Law professor, and former Democratic congressman from Massachusetts, and Father Ishmael Vincent Gromoff, an Aleutian Russian Orthodox priest, were added.[143]

The CWRIC commissioners held twenty days of public hearings across the country, from July to December 1981 in Washington, DC, Los Angeles, San Francisco, Seattle, three cities in Alaska, Chicago, New York City, and Cambridge, Massachusetts.

More than 750 witnesses testified. Most were survivors of the prison camps. Witnesses included scholars as well as a few apologists. In addition to these testimonies, the commission and staff reviewed archival documents.

Meanwhile action was going on at the state level in California. Priscilla Ouchida, whose parents were imprisoned during World War II, was a legislative aide to freshman state assemblyman Patrick Johnston. She suggested that Johnston introduce legislation to address the state's role in this episode of history. Johnston took up the charge and proposed a bill that would pay the wrongfully terminated state government workers $5,000 each, the minimum amount of documented losses actually suffered, over five years.[144] The bill was signed into law by Gov. Jerry Brown on August 17, 1982. Of the original 314 employees who were fired by the state, 280 received redress payments. Most of the remaining received payments later through subsequent legislation. The following year several other local governments followed suit, including the City of Los Angeles, the County of Los Angeles, the City and County of San Francisco, the County of Sacramento, the County of Santa Clara, and the State of Washington.[145]

In December 1982, and June 1983, the CWRIC issued a damning 467-page report entitled *Personal Justice Denied,* which concluded that the decision to imprison Japanese Americans was a result of "race prejudice, war hysteria, and a failure of political leadership."[146] Not only that, but their close examination of the facts had failed to reveal a single instance where an ethnic Japanese posed a security or military threat[147] that would justify "all American citizens of Japanese descent and all Japanese resident aliens [to be] excluded from the West Coast."[148]

The imprisonment of Japanese Americans was implemented

"without individual review." By contrast, "individualized, selective action" was taken against resident aliens from other enemy nations. As the report argued, "No mass exclusion or detention, in any part of the country, was ordered against American citizens of German or Italian descent. The ethnic Japanese suffered a unique injustice during these years."[149]

Executive Order 9066 had enacted true and irrevocable harm on the Japanese American community. When those incarcerated were released after the end of the war, many left the prison camps with nothing but the twenty-five-dollar allowance given to them by the government.[150] The homes and businesses they had been forced to leave behind years before had fallen into disrepair or worse—they were now in the hands of people who refused to return their ill-gotten gains. The Masuda family took their property back, though it is not at all clear how they managed to do that. Many others were not as "lucky."

At the outbreak of war with Japan, Masato Uyeda lost his bottling store in Seattle's Pike Place Market and twelve years' worth of savings to arson; as a survivor, he received a mere $200 in compensation in 1957 under the Japanese American Evacuation Claims Act.[151] Shuzo Chris Kato's family owned a forty-five-room hotel, restaurant, and several other businesses that they were forced to sell at a loss before being relocated. "I believe my parents received only about $7,000 total for all the businesses mentioned above," Kato later testified. "The true value must have been ten times as much."[152]

Similarly, in Florin, California, Masaru Yamasaki's family was forced to sell off their farm just before harvest time. "Negotiations were made through the Farm Security Administration [FSA] to then sell the crop and all farm equipment to a Caucasian," Yamasaki stated. A white man named George Faris agreed to buy the farm for about $2,000 and took out a loan from the FSA to pay for it. Before the loan arrived, however, the family was called away to the Walerga Assembly Center. Faris returned the loan to the FSA and assumed ownership of the farm without payment. "To this day, my dad never received a penny from that particular sale," Yamasaki said.[153]

Thus, the commission acknowledged "the enormous damages and losses, both material and intangible," that Japanese Americans suffered. "To the disastrous loss of farms, businesses and homes must be added the disruption for many years of careers and professional lives, as well as the long-term loss of income, earnings and opportunity," the report added. In fact, Japanese Americans were late to the postwar boom in America precisely because of all the losses they had sustained during the war.[154]

A study performed for the commission estimated that Japanese Americans lost between $108 million and $164 million (in 1945 dollars) in income and between $41 million and $206 million in property as a result of their "exclusion," which does not include property that was compensated for as a part of the Japanese American Evacuation Claims Act.[155]

Of the intangible injuries Japanese Americans experienced, none was bigger than the stigma that "marked the excluded," the badge of inferiority they were forced to wear. The report rightly noted that "the deprivation of liberty is no less injurious because it wounds the spirit rather than the body. . . . Two and a half years behind the barbed-wire of a relocation camp, branded potentially disloyal because of one's ethnicity alone—these injustices cannot neatly be translated into dollars and cents."[156]

Presciently, just before making its final recommendations, the commission put forth this warning:

The belief that we Americans are exceptional often threatens our freedom by allowing us to look complacently at evil-doing elsewhere and to insist that "it can't happen here." Recalling the events of exclusion and detention, ensuring that later generations of Americans know this history, is critical immunization against infection by the virus of prejudice and the emotion of wartime struggle. "It did happen here" is a message that must be transmitted, not as an exercise in self-laceration but as an admonition for the future. Among our strengths as a nation is our willingness to acknowledge imperfection as well as to struggle for a more just society. It is in the spirit of continuing that struggle that the Commission recommends several forms of redress.[157]

The commission outlined five recommendations, the first of which was that Congress should apologize on behalf of the nation for the "acts of exclusion, removal and detention" and enact a joint resolution, to be signed by the president, acknowledging that a "grave injustice" was done.[158]

Second, the president was to issue pardons for all those convicted of violating laws related to the relocation and exclusion of ethnic Japanese, such as curfews and orders to report to specific assembly areas. Any other wartime convictions of ethnic Japanese should also be reevaluated by the Department of Justice and pardoned by the president since their "offenses were grounded in a refusal to accept treatment that discriminated among citizens on the basis of race or ethnicity."

Third, Congress was to direct executive agencies to identify which Japanese Americans were eligible to "apply for the restitution of positions, status or entitlements lost in whole or part because of acts or events between December 1941 and 1945." For example, the commission suggested that the Department of Defense should review World War II cases where Japanese Americans received anything less than an honorable discharge.

Fourth, in "recognition of the injustice done to American citizens of Japanese ancestry and Japanese resident aliens during the Second World War," Congress was urged to appropriate funds for a special foundation. The purpose of this body would be "to sponsor research and public educational activities so that the events which were the subject of this inquiry will be remembered, and so that the causes and circumstances of this and similar events may be illuminated and understood."

The final and perhaps most significant recommendation, supported by every commissioner except Congressman Lungren, was that Congress establish a fund of $1.5 billion for the "personal redress" of Japanese Americans. The fund was intended "to provide a one-time per capita compensatory payment of $20,000 to each of the approximately 60,000 surviving persons excluded from their places of residence pursuant to Executive Order 9066." As part of the terms of reparations payments, anyone could renounce their claim to "any monetary recompense either direct or indirect" and Commissioner William M. Marutani did.

More important, as had not been the case with the DC Compensated Emancipation Act, the commission stressed that the burden of locating survivors should fall on the government, claimants should not be required to pay any fees in order to submit their applications, and the oldest survivors should be the first to receive payments. A board made up of a majority of Japanese Americans, appointed by the president and confirmed by the Senate, would ultimately administer the fund. And whatever money was left over after reparations payments would be redirected to pay for the foundation outlined in the fourth recommendation.[159]

What started out as an impossibility—the idea of "reparations" pushed for by the JACL for survivors of Japanese imprisonment—had gained significant traction by the publication of the commission's report. Those who had been wronged were so close to the finish line—but not nearly close enough. To get reparations, they first had to get legislation through Congress. It would not be easy. Indeed, from the issuance of the commission report, it took almost five years—and Democratic control of both the House and the Senate with the 100th Congress (1987–88)—to get the actual legislation passed.

Japanese Americans understood better than most the herculean task that lay ahead, and some pursued a different strategy. The National Council for Japanese American Redress (NCJAR) was formed in May 1979 to organize "a national effort to obtain redress for people of Japanese descent who had been imprisoned in United States concentration camps during World War II." The NCJAR broke with the JACL over its commission approach and instead went the class action lawsuit route against the US government for "damages caused by the wartime exclusion and incarceration."[160]

Their lawsuit was filed against the government on March 16, 1983, for "$27 billion for injuries suffered as a result of the World War II exclusion and imprisonment of Japanese Americans in U.S. concentration camps."[161] The lawsuit addressed not only property losses but also the value of constitutional and civil rights violations. As the lawsuit made its way through our slow judicial system, reparations legislation was being debated in Congress.

On September 17, 1987, the House passed H.R. 442 (named

after the heroic army unit of Japanese American soldiers) by a bipartisan vote of 243–141, with a majority of Democrats (180) and a minority of Republicans (63) voting in favor. During the House debate, Rep. Barney Frank (D-MA) brought up the NCJAR lawsuit, stating: "So this might well save the Government money. Nobody can be sure. I would not bet on the success of that lawsuit but there is a lawsuit, and what we are saying is that here is an offer of a settlement, and if you accept that, then you are out of the lawsuit. It is an absolute bar to people pursuing the lawsuit, where if they are allowed to sue the Government and the Government is admittedly at fault, the damages would be far greater than anything in here."[162] The NCJAR's lawsuit provided tailwinds of support for H.R. 442.

This was followed on April 20, 1988, by a vote in the now-Democratic-controlled Senate, again with a bipartisan majority of 69 in favor (44 Democrats and 25 Republicans), 27 opposed (20 Republicans and 7 Democrats), and 4 members not voting. Then the bills moved to a conference committee, where they would be reconciled for a final vote, and then onto the president's desk, where the final legislation would face its biggest obstacle: Ronald Reagan.

In 1984, President Reagan had been reelected in a land-slide, receiving 525 Electoral College votes, 49 states, and almost 60 percent of the popular vote. His opposition to all things CWRIC continued.

One week before the House vote, the Reagan administration released a "Statement of Administration Policy" that declared unequivocally that his "administration opposes H.R. 442, and the President's senior advisers will recommend that the President veto the bill, should it be presented to him."[163] Several reasons were given; chief among them was the belief that the 1948

Japanese American Evacuation Claims Act was in reality a "comprehensive and reasonable program of restitution for injuries brought upon persons of Japanese ancestry who were interned." The administration also objected to the projected cost "in excess of $1 billion." It concluded that no "further payments . . . [were] warranted." And yet the commission's report documented how inadequate the payments under the Japanese American Evacuation Claims Act had been.

Immediately after the House passed H.R. 442, the Office of Management and Budget (OMB), the Domestic Policy Council, and other White House staff recommended that President Reagan veto the bill—making good on the administration's statement.[164] The White House had already committed to funding a costly "war on drugs," and it did not want redress payments to get in the way.[165] But the redress campaign had an unknown ally in Republican Gov. Thomas Kean of New Jersey.

Governor Kean was no stranger to advocating for the rights of racial minorities. In June 1985, he signed a bill divesting the state's "pension funds from firms that do business in South Africa" because of apartheid.[166] He was also cued into the redress movement. The editor of his 1988 memoir *The Politics of Inclusion* was Grant Ujifusa, the legislative strategy chair on the JACL Legislative Education Committee between 1982 and 1992.

Ujifusa had strong views on how to push the redress legislation across the finish line. In his opinion, it had to be framed as "something conservative Republicans could buy into as consistent with their values and principles." Thus, Ujifusa argued, "the thing not to do was to define our bill as a piece of traditional civil rights, ethnic, special-interest legislation. Instead, we defined it as a piece of general-interest legislation consistent with the most conservative, even original-intent reading of the Constitution."[167]

What it boiled down to was a single commonality: equality of opportunity. Republicans were generally skeptical of government intervention, but like their Democratic counterparts, they still believed in equality of opportunity. According to Ujifusa, "That is precisely what Japanese Americans in camps were denied. . . . In 1942, what we really wanted was something contemporary conservatives extol—to be left alone by the government."[168]

Ujifusa understood that President Reagan would be more receptive to hearing this message from allies and asked Governor Kean to advocate on the cause's behalf. Kean happened to be hosting the president on a visit to New Jersey on October 13, 1987, less than one month after H.R. 442 passed the House of Representatives.

During a private limousine ride with President Reagan and deputy chief of staff Ken Duberstein, Governor Kean learned that the president had been counseled to veto the bill by one of his main advisers, S. I. Hayakawa, himself a Japanese American and former US senator from California who was a co-sponsor of the legislation establishing the CWRIC. Undeterred, Governor Kean made his case to the president: "I told him that I thought Hayakawa was wrong, and that members of the community felt very differently about the bill. I told him that it was a blot on the nation, that he had a great opportunity to purge. And he said to me, 'You know I kind of felt that way . . . I was getting all this advice, but before I got it all I was inclined to sign it.' He said he was glad that I was making another argument."[169]

Governor Kean followed up with a letter to President Reagan on February 6, 1988, and again urged him to sign the bill.[170] Included with his letter were two other letters: one from Grant Ujifusa and another from Jane Masuda Goto, whose family was incarcerated during World War II. The governor's letter reminded Reagan "of his participation in the wartime medal ceremony for a dead Nisei soldier from the 442d R.C.T. who was awarded the Distinguished Service Cross," that is, for Kazuo Masuda.[171] Yes, the previously unnamed actor at the 1945 Distinguished Service Cross ceremony had been Captain Ronald Reagan.

Jane Masuda Goto, one of Kazuo's sisters, had been present at the ceremony in Santa Ana all those years ago. Her letter to President Reagan, which included a photograph of the ceremony, recalled his remarks as an army captain: "Our family feels that what you and General Stilwell said in 1945 are as true and important as ever: the ideals for which all good Americans should be willing to fight and die. My brother did both, even though his parents and family were stripped of all their American rights, and placed in an Arizona internment camp."[172]

The letters must have made an impact on Reagan. By mid-February 1988, Duberstein indicated to Ujifusa that the president had changed his mind—he was going to sign the bill. Conservatives such as education secretary William Bennett and chief domestic policy adviser Gary Bauer also expressed their support.[173] On March 28, 1988, an OMB memo questioned whether the threat of a veto was "appropriate," and the very next day chief of staff Howard Baker sent a memo to President Reagan recommending that he "withhold any further threat of a veto and explore with Congress the possibility of reducing the potential costs."[174]

Senator Hayakawa remained opposed to redress.[175] On May 5, 1988, he sent a handwritten note to Baker that described Japanese Americans as "just rolling in prosperity."[176] His note continued: "They are a damn sight better off than whites, but they play on the widespread assumption that non-whites are all more-to-be-pitied than whites. Makes me damn sick to listen to those skillful hustlers. I crawl with embarrassment at their gimme/gimme attitude towards government."[177]

All this occurred against the backdrop of the 1988 presidential campaign. Leading candidates Vice President George H. W. Bush, Gov. Michael Dukakis, and Rev. Jesse Jackson all endorsed the redress legislation.[178] Their unified support boxed in the Reagan administration, which still had concerns about the bill's price tag. They wanted redress payments to be spread out over a longer period, from five to ten years, as well as a provision that restricted anyone who took payments from retaining any claims against the federal government. They also wanted to limit annual appropriations to $500 million.

The conference report that reconciled the difference between the House and Senate bills and took President Reagan's concerns into account was filed on July 26, 1988. As a result, on August 1, 1988, President Reagan sent a letter to House Speaker Jim Wright expressing his support for the "substantially improved" bill. He added, "The enactment of H.R. 442 will close a sad chapter in American history in a way that reaffirms America's commitment to the preservation of liberty and justice for all. I urge the House of Representatives to act swiftly and favorably on the bill."[179]

Congress subsequently passed H.R. 442, and it was sent to the president for signature on August 5, 1988. The legislation did not mention the word *reparations* but rather spoke of "restitution to those individuals of Japanese ancestry who were interned."[180] The bill signing occurred five days later in the Old Executive Office Building. After the customary salutations, President Reagan opened the proceedings with this statement: "We gather here today to right a grave wrong. . . . More than forty years ago . . . 120,000 persons of Japanese ancestry living in the United States were forcibly removed from their homes and placed in makeshift internment camps. This action was taken without trial, without jury. It was based solely on race."[181]

He spoke of the loyalty of Japanese Americans, including those who had fought for the United States during World War II while their families were imprisoned in camps back home. He explained that although the bill would provide for a restitution payment to each of the sixty thousand survivors—for losses that could never be repaid—the legislation was less about property than about honor and the government admitting its mistake.

Before the president closed, he shared a story:

I wonder whether you'd permit me one personal reminiscence, one prompted by an old newspaper report sent to me by Rose Ochi, a former internee. The clipping comes from the Pacific Citizen and is dated December 1945. "Arriving by plane from Washington," the article begins, "General Joseph W. Stilwell pinned the Distinguished Service Cross on Mary Masuda in a simple ceremony on the porch of her small frame shack near Talbert, Orange County. She was one of the first Americans of Japanese ancestry to return from relocation centers to California's farmlands." "Vinegar Joe" Stilwell was there that day to honor Kazuo Masuda, Mary's brother. You see, while Mary and her parents were in an internment camp, Kazuo served as staff sergeant to the 442d Regimental Combat Team. In one action, Kazuo ordered his men back and advanced through heavy fire, hauling a mortar. For 12 hours, he engaged in a singlehanded barrage of Nazi positions. Several weeks later at Cassino, Kazuo staged another lone advance. This time it cost him his life.[182]

President Reagan told the story of the Masuda family, a story that he himself had been reminded of by Jane Masuda Goto not that long ago, and he recalled the words once spoken at that ceremony:

> After General Stilwell made the award ... other show business personalities paid tribute—Robert Young, Will Rogers, Jr. And one young actor said: "Blood that has soaked into the sands of a beach is all of one color. America stands unique in the world: the only country not founded on race but on a way, an ideal. Not in spite of but because of our polyglot background, we have had all the strength in the world. That is the American way." The name of that young actor—I hope I pronounce this right—was Ronald Reagan. And, yes, the ideal of liberty and justice for all—that is still the American way.[183]

President Reagan signed H.R. 442 and finally made good on his own words. The actual payments, however, would not be sent out for almost two more years due to appropriation battles—with President Bush's signature.

Of course, H.R. 442 had its fair share of critics who thought the compensation paid to the survivors of internment was unfair. A little over six months later a lawsuit was filed challenging the act's constitutionality. On March 9, 1989, a white plaintiff of German ancestry sued the government alleging the unconstitutionality of the act because it did not award payments to white people.[184] The challenge was heard on appeal by the US Court of Appeals for District of Columbia Circuit.

In its decision, the court began by acknowledging the racism that informed the mass incarceration of Japanese American citizens: "Fifty years ago, President Roosevelt authorized his Secretary of War to send Japanese Americans to internment camps solely because of their race."[185] The plaintiff, on the other hand, had been incarcerated after his father, who was suspected of espionage, had an individual hearing and was found guilty after all the evidence was presented. It is unclear whether the plaintiff was taken into custody with his father out of a wish to keep the family together. But the important distinction is that his father received an individual hearing before he was incarcerated, which meant his circumstances were not comparable to those of Japanese Americans who were summarily incarcerated without any due process. The plaintiff lost because the court found he suffered no discrimination when he was excluded from receiving any payments.

The court gave deference to congressional decision-making here because it had conducted extensive hearings and found that "Japanese Americans were the victims of prejudice, while German Americans were not," a conclusion that was "amply supported by historical evidence." The court ruled that Congress "had clear and sufficient reason to compensate interns of Japanese but not German descent; and the compensation is substantially related (as well as narrowly tailored) to Congress's compelling interest in redressing a shameful example of national discrimination." The case never reached the US Supreme Court because it declined to hear it.[186]

What these four case studies tell us is that the federal government, through a variety of different mechanisms, has paid cash compensation for the end of slavery, for the racial violence of lynching, for economic exploitation and land theft, and for mass incarceration because of race. The government faced steep opposition to making each of these historic payments, yet it still got done. Calculations on the harms done and who was owed what were complicated, yet it still got done. It was incredibly expensive, yet it still got done. What has never been done, however, is paying compensation *in any form* to black Americans for similar harms. The next section focuses on the history of the harms done to black people *after* the end of chattel slavery. Not only does it document their suffering, but it also demonstrates how their suffering has harmed us all.

PART II

EVERYTHING, EVERYWHERE, ALL AT ONCE

Not everything that is faced can be changed, but
nothing can be changed until it is faced.

—JAMES BALDWIN, 1962

After chattel slavery, black people were hit with every kind of oppression and degradation imaginable. There was nowhere they could hide, nowhere they could escape the grip that white supremacy had on this country. And as hard as it will be for you to read, imagine what it was like to experience.

There were times while researching this part of the book that I had to walk away. I had to stop what I was reading and metaphorically change the channel. At various points, I considered walking away for good—but I didn't. Why? Because *they* couldn't walk away. Black people had to endure it all.

What I learned was that there was nothing that black people could have done to forge a safe path to economic freedom and self-sufficiency. There was nothing they could have done to fulfill Reverend Frazier's dream of sustaining themselves with a little something extra to spare. Everything they did would eventually put a target on their backs. There would be no underground railroad to aid their escape this time around—because there was no escape. They were largely on their own.

I eventually came to realize that as awful as this history is, it also tells a story of hope, about a people who never gave up. Their abuse led not to resignation but to resilience and a determination that they would make a way out of no way. Why? Because they were a people who had survived the degradation and daily indignities of enslavement. Freedom's setbacks did not break their spirits, and neither would I let it break mine. I pray that it does not break yours.

Their story begins with the optimism that the Thirteenth Amendment produced because it was designed to provide fertile soil for black success and landownership. That, however, was followed by an immediate white supremacist backlash from the executive branch, which was later fueled by an all-white, all-male

Supreme Court (whose justices included former enslavers). Together, the executive and judicial branches encouraged the spread of antiblack racism throughout the country. No matter where black people went, or what they did, their blackness placed targets on their backs.

The Promise of Freedom

From the outset, the Thirteenth Amendment was designed to be breathtaking in vision and scope.[1] It reads simply:

> Section 1. Neither slavery nor involuntary servitude, except as a punishment for crime whereof the party shall have been duly convicted, shall exist within the United States, or any place subject to their jurisdiction.

> Section 2. Congress shall have power to enforce this article by appropriate legislation.

This was a radical break from the doctrine of states' rights: It meant Congress and the federal government—not the states—would be in control of the newly freed. It was a departure so revolutionary that it could only have been accomplished through a civil war. In many ways, the Thirteenth Amendment is the hero of the story. *Breathtaking* seems too mild a word.

The debate around the Thirteenth Amendment in Congress reveals how legislators thought about it. Rep. Isaac N. Arnold (R-IL), for example, believed it would create "equality before the law" and become "the great cornerstone" of our government.[2] Rep. John Bingham (R-OH) reinforced that sentiment by stating the Thirteenth Amendment was "designed . . . to accomplish . . .

the abolition of slavery in the United States, and the political and social elevation of Negroes to all the rights of white men."[3] Sen. John Sherman (R-OH) went one step further and added that the amendment was "an express grant of power to Congress to secure . . . liberty by appropriate legislation."[4] Rep. Thomas T. Davis (R-NY) argued that equality could be attained only "by removing every vestige of African slavery from the American Republic."[5]

Of course, not every member of Congress agreed with this expansive interpretation. Sen. John B. Henderson (Unconditional Union–MO) insisted that "in passing this amendment we do not confer upon the Negro the right to vote. We give him no right except his freedom, and leave the rest to the States." Sen. James McDougall (D-CA) opposed the amendment in part because of his "understanding" of science: "It may not be within the reading of some learned Senators, and yet it belongs to demonstrated science, that the African race and the Europeans are different, and I here now say it as a fact established by science that the eighth generation of the mixed race formed by the union of African and European cannot continue their species. Quadroons have few children; with octoroons reproduction is impossible. It establishes as a law of nature that the African has no proper relation to the European, Caucasian blood."[6]

Opponents also argued that the Thirteenth Amendment, if ratified, "would fundamentally alter the balance of power between the states and the federal government, so much so that the amendment itself was unconstitutional."[7] For example, Rep. William Holman (D-IN) regarded the amendment as "fatal to the fundamental principles of the Republic, the right, the irrepressible right of the states to domestic government."[8] That argument, however, crystallizes an important feature of the amendment: "unlike any previous amendment, it expanded federal power at the expense of the states, injecting the federal government into the regulation of 'domestic relationships' like that between master and slave.'"[9] For the first time, the federal government was telling states what they could or could not do when it came to slavery. Such a development was anathema to those who believed that states had the right to make these types of decisions for themselves.

The Thirteenth Amendment was passed by the Senate on April 8, 1864, by the House on January 31, 1865, and signed by President Abraham Lincoln the very next day. By December 18, 1865, enough states had ratified it (three-fourths) to make it the law of the land. Regardless of which side they were on, the views expressed in Congress show just how wide-ranging legislators imagined the amendment's impact would be. They "expected the constitutional change to provide sweeping power to protect civil rights."[10] Indeed, the first piece of legislation enacted by Congress under the Thirteenth Amendment demonstrated that sweeping power by authorizing the country's first civil rights statute. Yet dark clouds appeared on the horizon, because by now President Lincoln had been assassinated and Vice President Andrew Johnson had become president. And Andrew Johnson was no Abraham Lincoln. But Congress persisted.

The Civil Rights Act of 1866 was passed by Congress, vetoed by President Andrew Johnson, and subsequently overridden by Congress with a two-thirds majority. Johnson "fear[ed] it would 'establish for the security of the colored race safeguards which go infinitely beyond any that the General Government has ever provided for the white race.'"[11] Further, he argued that "the bill [is] made to operate in favor of the colored and against the white race."[12] Barely a year out of slavery, Johnson was afraid that mandating black people receive rights equal to those of white people was somehow antiwhite (or reverse) discrimination. That can make sense only if you believe that white Americans are superior to their black peers.

The act declared that all people born in the United States are considered citizens, and more important, that "such citizens, of every race and color, without regard to any previous condition of slavery or involuntary servitude, except as a punishment for crime whereof the party shall have been duly convicted, shall have the same right, in every State and Territory in the United States." This idea was revolutionary given the fact that the formerly enslaved had been beaten, maimed, or murdered with impunity by their enslavers because they were considered property under the law. The legislation continued, making it clear that this newfound citizenship was to include the right "to make and enforce contracts, to sue, be parties, and give evidence, to inherit, purchase, lease, sell, hold, and convey real and personal property, and to full and equal benefit of all laws and proceedings for the security of person and property, *as is enjoyed by white citizens*" (emphasis added).

It is hard to imagine broader, more radical language in the post–Civil War era than "all persons . . . shall have the same right . . . as is enjoyed by white citizens." This legislation was possible only because we fought a civil war that the Confederacy lost. The act was completely consistent with the views spoken by Senator Sherman and Representative Arnold during the Thirteenth Amendment debates. No speech demonstrates this more clearly than the words uttered by Rep. William Lawrence (R-OH), a member of the House Judiciary Committee who voted in support of the 1866 Civil Rights Act. "There are certain absolute rights which pertain to every citizen, which are inherent, and of which a State cannot constitutionally deprive him," Lawrence argued.

"Every citizen, therefore, has the absolute right to live, the right of personal security, personal liberty, and the right to acquire and enjoy property. These are rights of citizenship."[13]

Congress continued to act on behalf of the newly freed. In 1866 it passed the Fourteenth Amendment over President Johnson's veto; it was ratified in 1868 by the states. In 1869 it passed the Fifteenth Amendment, again over Johnson's veto; it was ratified by the states in 1870. Together with the Thirteenth Amendment (the trilogy is often referred to as the Reconstruction Amendments), they were designed to free the enslaved, provide them with rights equal to those of white Americans, and give black men the vote.

Congress passed several additional pieces of legislation during this period to afford greater protections to black Americans. The Southern Homestead Act, passed on June 21, 1866, and signed by President Johnson, set aside 46 million acres of public land in Alabama, Arkansas, Florida, Louisiana, and Mississippi for purchase as 80-acre plots, then later as 160-acre plots.[14] The intended beneficiaries, at least in the beginning, were to be freedmen without land. In June 1876, however, before much of the land was distributed, the program was repealed.[15] And what explains President Johnson's support? Likely his belief that poor white Americans would benefit.[16]

Congress then passed the Civil Rights Act of 1875, which guaranteed all citizens equal access, regardless of race, to accommodations, theaters, and public schools, among other places.

The legislative branch also extended the support of the Freedmen's Bureau, which was originally created under the president's war powers and designed to assist the newly freed. (As W.E.B. Du Bois stated, if the Freedmen's Bureau had "been made a permanent institution, given ample funds for operating schools and purchasing land, and if it had been gradually manned by trained civilian administrators," it could have had enormous power to improve the lives of black people.[17] "All this was clear when President Johnson vetoed the Freedmen's Bureau bill in 1866.")[18]

Progress was made with these historic laws. For the first time, black Americans were elected to Congress and state legislatures. They opened their own businesses and started families. Some even thrived and secured a small piece of the American Dream for themselves. They literally pulled themselves up by their bootstraps.

The most obvious hurdle for the newly freed was the reality that the end of slavery had left them without capital. They received no reparations for the end of slavery. The promises made by General Sherman were quickly dashed after President Lincoln's assassination. President Andrew Johnson stopped the operation of Field Order No. 15, repossessed the forty acres of land given to newly freed black men, and returned it to their white former enslavers.

Nevertheless, black Americans, in the decades following emancipation, overcame incredible odds to build black wealth from the ground up. Driven by what W.E.B. Du Bois described as "land hunger—this absolutely fundamental and essential thing to any real emancipation of the slaves,"[19] black Americans began acquiring land through hard work, perseverance, and a little luck. Du Bois estimated that "Black families owned 3 million acres in 1875, 8 million in 1890, and 12 million in 1900. By 1910, African Americans had acquired more than 16 million acres."[20]

Why did the freedmen thirst for land? Because they knew what Reverend Frazier spoke of, that it would be through land that they would have true freedom. Owning their own land would mean black Americans were no longer economically dependent on white people for their survival. Through determination and diligence, many black people succeeded in obtaining land. Despite the many obstacles, many were thriving. That became a problem for white supremacy.

As the historian Paula Giddings, Elizabeth A. Woodson Professor Emerita of Africana Studies at Smith College, explains, "By the 1880s and 1890s, a significant number of blacks began to do very well in terms of entrepreneurship and landownership, and it simply couldn't be tolerated."[21] With President Johnson, black people did not have a friend in the White House. According to the historian and law professor Annette Gordon-Reed, Carl M. Loeb University Professor at Harvard Law School, "Black empowerment and participation in the American system was a nightmare scenario for Andrew Johnson." He described America as "a country for white men, and by God, as long as I am President, it shall be a government for white men."[22] Black people, however, did have an ally in the legislative branch and *initially* a friendly judiciary.

At first, court challenges to the Civil Rights Act of 1866 were largely unsuccessful, allowing the legislation to work as it was intended. In one case, a black female apprentice was offered an employment contract that did not include teaching her how to read, even though state law required that white apprentices be taught to read. Chief Justice Salmon P. Chase, on circuit, found that her white employer had violated the act when he treated her differently than he would have treated a white apprentice.[23] In another case, the act provided the basis for the court to uphold the right of a black woman to buy a ticket and ride in the first-class car.[24] But those storm clouds on the horizon were gathering steam, and soon black people would have no protection and nowhere to hide.

Slavery 2.0

According to the sociologist Heather O'Connell, after slavery ended, it was replaced by "coercive systems of social and economic control in the U.S. South, such as sharecropping, lynching and Jim Crow laws, developed in response to the social and economic void created by the abolition of slavery."[25] Thus white supremacy continued to provide white Americans with social and economic control over black Americans long after slavery was declared illegal.

Once chattel slavery ended, slavery *shape-shifted,* first into sharecropping and convict leasing, with the threat of lynching as the enforcement. As John Hope Franklin quoted from the Joint Congressional Committee on Reconstruction's Report, there was "a disposition on the part of [white] citizens to secure, as far as possible, the same control over the freedmen by contracts which [the whites] possessed when they held them as slaves."[26] Some freedmen were forced to sign sharecropping agreements that allowed them to cultivate other people's land in exchange for a share in the profits after the crops were sold and expenses deducted. More often than not, there were no profits after their landlords—who were usually white and oftentimes former enslavers—completed their creative bookkeeping.

Sharecropping was designed to produce a "system of debt peonage" in which "insolvent croppers unable to repay debts from one year to another were required by law to work indefinitely for the same unscrupulous planter."[27] If a black farmer questioned what they were owed, they could wind up dead. But they would not wind up with more money. If a farmer left before the end of their annual contract, they would forfeit any right to future profits. Meanwhile, those who were able to get work in town as domestic servants and janitors—jobs white people generally avoided—were paid measly wages. Hiring black workers who could be paid less than their white peers benefited white employers. These contracts were unfair but legally valid.

Convict leasing served a similar purpose. During slavery, black incarceration was rare to nonexistent because plantation owners were solely responsible for disciplining and punishing enslaved people. They generally did not send their enslaved workers to prison because they did not want to lose valuable labor. As a result, prisons held mainly white Americans.[28] But the Thirteenth Amendment included a loophole. If a person was convicted of a crime, the law allowed convicts to be imprisoned in slavery-like conditions. And that loophole was exploited by all those who wanted to create a legal form of slavery.

The end of the war saw a crumbling South, both literally and figuratively. Southern state budgets were broken along with their infrastructure and buildings.[29] In need of cheap labor, convict leasing—an institutional practice whereby states leased prisoners to private companies and plantations—played an important role in rebuilding the South. W.E.B. Du Bois described convict leasing as "a new slavery and slave-trade."[30] According to Eric Foner, DeWitt Clinton Professor Emeritus of History, at Columbia University, what began small before the war quickly expanded afterward into a widescale system to "provide employers with a supply of cheap labor."[31]

Which behavior constitutes a crime in our society often has racialized roots. It was once a crime to teach an enslaved person to read, but not to enslave, buy, or sell that very same individual.[32]

What happened to Japanese Americans during World War II is one of the most glaring examples in recent history of a people being imprisoned solely because of their race, but this practice has a long history in our country. Black Americans, once freed, were also criminalized because of their race, for both economic and social reasons, and have never received cash compensation for their loss of liberty.

Convict leasing presented a seamless transition from slavery: "The same men who built railroads with thousands of slaves . . . were also the first to employ forced African American labor in the 1870s."[33] In Texas in 1867, for example, black Americans made up roughly one-third of those in the state penitentiary but almost 90 percent "of those leased out for railroad labor."[34] The threat of an arrest for vagrancy would hang over the head of any who did not want to enter into restrictive, one-sided sharecropping agreements.

Douglas Blackmon, author of the Pulitzer Prize–winning book *Slavery by Another Name*, describes how "revenues from the neo-slavery poured the equivalent of tens of millions of dollars into the treasuries of Alabama, Mississippi, Louisiana, Georgia, Florida, Texas, North Carolina, and South Carolina where more than 75 percent of the black population in the United States then lived."[35] Convict leasing played another important role—it helped maintain antebellum relationships between whites and the newly freed. According to Walter Wilson:

the prison population rapidly became black workers and peasants. Negroes convicted of minor "crimes" were hired out to private businessmen under slavery conditions. It was undoubtedly a deliberate move by the ruling class to secure forced labor on a large scale as a partial substitute for chattel slavery.[36]

Convict leasing relied on a subjective, often corrupt criminal justice system. The so-called crime that ensnared more black people than any other was that of "vagrancy." If a person could not prove they were employed, they were guilty of vagrancy. In other words, being unemployed was a crime. However, this law was applied selectively and almost never used to arrest white men: "In a time of massive unemployment among all southern men, [vagrancy] was reserved almost exclusively for black men."[37] Free black people were controlled through "vaguely worded laws (e.g., vagrancy, loitering, etc.) which, by merely being on the books, meant that just about any black could be arrested for committing just about any form of behavior and summarily sentenced to prison."[38]

This travesty happened only because the judicial system was weaponized on behalf of white labor needs. The end of slavery meant white business owners could no longer extract free black labor, "so they turned to mass arrests making convict leasing popular and profitable."[39]

In 1908 assistant US attorney general Charles Wells Russell declared convict leasing "a system of involuntary servitude—that is to say, persons are held to labor as convicts under those laws who have committed no crime."[40] But that did not help twenty-two-year-old Green Cottenham.[41]

On March 30, 1908, Green Cottenham, a black man, was arrested in Alabama and charged with vagrancy. He was found guilty before a county judge and immediately sentenced to thirty days of hard labor. His sentence was later extended to almost a year because he could not afford to pay the considerable fines that came with his conviction. The next day he was "sold" to a subsidiary of U.S. Steel and sent to work in a mine. In exchange, they paid the county twelve dollars a month ($415 today) to pay off Cottenham's fines. Cottenham worked long hours digging and loading coal, and at night he was chained inside a long wooden barrack. Failure to perform to the company's satisfaction resulted in whippings. He wasn't alone, as hundreds of men just like him worked in the mine. And while Cottenham was born free, the son of formerly enslaved people, this had to be as bad as anything his parents experienced.

Vagrancy wasn't the only crime that ensnared black people. Mississippi, in 1921, made "social equality" a crime, punishable by fines up to $500 and prison time "not exceeding six [6] months" at the court's discretion. The law provided that: "any person, firm or corporation who shall be guilty of printing, publishing, or circulating printed, typewritten or written matter urging or presenting for public acceptance or general information, arguments or suggestions in favor of social equality . . . between whites and negroes, shall be guilty of a misdemeanor."[42]

Convict leasing by prisons eventually led to the return of private forms of slavery. Individual actors began illegally detaining black people and putting them to work, while evading the criminal justice system, with the complicity of the federal government. For instance, two sheriffs in Mississippi in 1929 reported receiving between $20,000 and $30,000 each for "procuring black laborers and selling them to local planters." In 1932 police in Macon, Georgia, arrested "sixty black men on 'vagrancy' charges" and turned them over to J. H. Stroud, a plantation owner. A *New York Times* exposé reported a similar story in Helena, Arkansas, a cotton town.[43] Those sheriffs and policemen acted with impunity, seemingly beyond the reach of the criminal justice system. In an unusual case in Mobile, Alabama, in 1941, criminal charges were actually filed against Charles E. Bledsoe, who pleaded guilty in federal court to a charge of peonage for holding a black man named Martin Thompson against his will. Bledsoe's sentence: $100 fine and six months' probation.[44]

What if a black person through some miracle was fortunate enough to build a successful business? One might assume they would be beyond the reach of slavery's shape-shifting traps. They could not be arrested for vagrancy, and they would not be subject to restrictive, wealth-depleting sharecropping agreements. But their very success put a target on their back. In actuality, these were the people most at risk of succumbing to the deadliest consequences of Slavery 2.0: the lynching noose.

"Killing and maiming large numbers of enslaved people had been unprofitable," the historian Kidada E. Williams asserts, "but doing the same to *free* Black people, especially those actively trying to act on their new rights and privileges, was . . . nobody's loss."[45] The annual number of lynchings in the United States reached its peak in 1892, with 230 killings, 161 of which were of black people.[46] That amounts to "almost one every other day."[47] The lynchings of Italians in Louisiana does not compare, yet no black family ever received cash compensation for the losses of black Americans who were lynched. One of those lynched in 1892 was Tommie Moss.

Thomas Henry Moss, Sr., who took his first breath in Mississippi in 1853, was among the last black Americans to be born enslaved. But within the span of a generation, he was a free man and reaching for his share of the American Dream. He eventually moved to Memphis, Tennessee, married Elizabeth Milliken—or Betty, as he called her—and started a family. Betty gave birth to a baby girl named Maurine. Not too long after her arrival, the Mosses had another child on the way. Tommie, as his friends knew him, was a successful businessman who worked hard at two jobs and saved up enough money to purchase a home. In

1890, 87 percent of black workers were either in farming (56 percent) or domestic service (31 percent).[48] Most were employed in the South. Only 1 percent were in professional service. Tommie Moss was in that 1 percent.[49]

Tommie Moss was one of the first black postal workers in Memphis. In 1891 he earned $850 per year.[50] At that time, "Negro skilled labor" earned three dollars a day on the high end, $1.10 at the lowest, and $1.75 on average.[51] He made a good living with steady work, and it showed. The Mosses owned their own home at a time when only one in five black Americans were homeowners. He was a man of great faith and volunteered at Avery Chapel's Sunday school. He served his country as a member of the Tennessee Rifles, a black military organization that helped protect Memphis during the outbreak of yellow fever in the 1870s. Tommie was determined to build a life for his children that was better than the one he was born into, and he was well on his way.

Tommie and Betty Moss were two of Ida B. Wells's best friends in Memphis.[52] Ida, an emerging black journalist and activist, knew Tommie at least as far back as 1885, and the Mosses made Ida the godmother of their daughter Maurine. By this time, Ida was working at the Free Speech office on Beale Street, which was part of Tommie's mail route. As she put it, "whatever 'Tommie knew in the way of news we got it first.' "[53]

In 1889, after saving up enough money, he started a cooperative grocery store with nearly a dozen other black people. They called it the People's Grocery and opened it right outside Memphis. By day, Tommie continued to work as a mail carrier for the postal service, and by night, he put his heart and soul into the People's Grocery. The new enterprise was aptly named because it served as a haven for the black community in Memphis.

Previously, the only option for their daily shopping was the grocery store directly across the street, owned by a white man named William Barrett. Shopping there as a black customer was often an unpleasant experience. Black shoppers didn't feel safe there, as Barrett had received several tickets from the police for illegal activity in the store. The People's Grocery, on the other hand, was a community-oriented business that employed black people and treated its customers with the respect and dignity they deserved. Tommie hired Will Stewart to be his clerk and Calvin McDowell, a fit twenty-one-year-old private in the Tennessee Rifles, to act as manager.

Tommie was doing well by doing good. He believed that blacks should focus on practical and business matters rather than politics. For example, he made sure people in his community could provide for themselves and helped numerous people become postal carriers. Tommie Moss was seemingly the perfect black man. His expression of his newfound freedom eventually hit the brick wall of white supremacy, because not even his perfection could protect him.

Trouble was quietly brewing in Memphis. Tommie's prominence as a successful black businessman placed him on a direct collision course with white supremacy. William Barrett, the owner of the grocery across the street, was opposed to the People's Grocery from the very beginning as he did not like the competition—especially from a black-owned business. The historian Terence Finnegan, at William Paterson University, states that "the autonomy and independence of black men were the greatest threats to the reimposition of white male supremacy, which is why most lynching developed from conflicts between black males and white males."[54]

On an ordinary day at the beginning of March 1892, an innocent game of marbles near the People's Grocery between two boys—one white, one black—turned into a brawl. No one knows who threw the first punch. But the black child was winning when the white child's father rushed to his son's aid and started beating up the black child. Tommie and his clerk Will Stewart saw what was happening, broke up the fight, and stopped the white father from attacking the black child.

This intervention did not sit well with the white father, who immediately stirred up a group of white men to destroy the People's Grocery in retaliation. One of the men who readily joined the mob was William Barrett. He had been waiting for such an opportunity and didn't hesitate to seize it.

Barrett went to a judge and got an order for Moss's and Stewart's arrests, but neither was at the People's Grocery when the mob came. The manager Calvin McDowell had to face them on his own. Rather than leave because the arrest warrant couldn't be carried out, Barrett lashed out at Calvin, and a struggle ensued, knocking Calvin to the ground. In the heat of the moment, Calvin managed to take Barrett's gun and shot at him as he ran out of the store.

Later that day, the mob made a second approach, this time with the police in tow. By now, Tommie and Will had rejoined Calvin at the store. Tommie and Calvin stood their ground and shot at their attackers, not knowing that some of their targets were police. Several police officers were shot and injured but managed to escape with the crowd to Barrett's store. Tommie, Calvin, and Will, along with several other black men, were swiftly arrested and taken to the Memphis jail.

The first two nights the Tennessee Rifles stood guard at the jail, to ensure that no one tried to lynch the men locked up inside while they awaited word on whether the injured officers were going to live or die. If the officers died, the three men knew there would be trouble. But if they lived, they assumed they would eventually be set free. Perhaps naïvely, they believed in the justice of the law, that its principles would be applied to them fairly whether they were black or white. On their second night in jail, they were told that the officers would survive their wounds. The Tennessee Rifles left, believing the prisoners were out of danger. They were wrong. Ida B. Wells later observed that the officers' survival "was actually a catalyst for violence, for the black men could not now be 'legally' executed for their 'crime.'"[55]

A band of white people went back to the judge and claimed they had information on a group of black people preparing an attack. The judge accordingly ordered law enforcement to take away the Tennessee Riflemen's guns and prohibited the one white store owner who was sympathetic to the black community from selling guns to them. On March 9, 1892, a horde of seventy-five to one hundred masked men stormed the jail, dragged out Tommie Moss, Calvin McDowell, and Will Stewart, and lynched them. In death, they became known as the Memphis Three.

Their bodies were so badly brutalized that they could be identified based only on physical descriptions of what had been done to them. The details of the lynching were painstakingly documented, leading many to believe that those who organized it had alerted the press in advance, so that they would be sure to record it. No one was ever brought to justice for the murders of the Memphis Three, as was often the case with lynchings.

However, their murders and the explosive dissolution of the People's Grocery sent a strong message to the black community— they were not welcome in Memphis. Tommie's reported last words before his death hung in their memory like an ominous warning: "Tell my people to go west. There is no justice for them here." More than two thousand blacks left the city for good. Part of the terror was the lack of accountability and lawlessness of the act. In practice, the law did not protect black Americans.

Betty Moss gave birth to their second child about a month before Tommie was lynched. They named their newborn son Thomas Moss, Jr. With Tommie Moss dead, his creditors took what was due them and sold the People's Grocery to William Barrett for one-eighth of its value. Betty took the family and moved to Indianapolis, where they had to start all over again. The wealth that the Mosses had worked so hard to build for Maurine and Tommie Jr. was violently stripped away with the help of the state. Ida B. Wells put it this way: "Thus, with the aid of the city and county authorities and the daily papers, that white grocer had indeed put an end to his rival Negro grocer as well as to his business."[56]

In her reporting, Wells fearlessly attacked those who participated in, encouraged, or simply ignored the lynching. Her unrelenting journalism denouncing the lynchings would eventually lead her to flee Memphis, the place she had called home for nearly a decade, for her safety.[57]

A recent study conducted by Shytierra Gaston at Georgia State University reinforces the idea that lynching was used as a tool to instill fear, seize property, and reinstate white supremacy. The study found that of a subset of twenty-two lynching victims who were killed in the South between 1883 and 1972, most of their families, like Betty Moss and her children, and Ida B. Wells, were forced to leave "behind their social capital, support systems, resources, and wealth."[58] White Americans like William Barrett, who were responsible for such lynchings, more often than not wound up taking possession of their victims' property. Because the victims' families had been forced to flee "with little other than the clothes on their backs," their ability to build wealth was disrupted.

They were forced to start over from scratch, plunging them further behind their white peers financially.

"If you are looking for stolen black land," Ray Winbush, director of Fisk University's Race Relations Institute, told AP reporters, "just follow the lynching trail."[59] During the 1880s, 82 percent of all lynchings occurred in the South. By the 1920s, the rate increased to 95 percent.[60] Most black Americans lived in the South after slavery ended, which meant lynchings were a message to black people to behave themselves and not get too uppity (read: too financially successful or too self-confident) if they did not want to get killed. Stewart Tolnay, an emeritus sociologist at the University of Washington, suggests that "the success of black people was a threat to white supremacy." As he states, "There were obvious limitations, or ceilings, that blacks weren't supposed to go beyond."[61]

As we have seen, the violent act of lynching didn't just affect immediate family members of the victims; it also impacted extended communities. Many families had no choice but to move in with other relatives, who in turn saw their wealth-building capacity decline as they stretched their income to feed, clothe, and sustain more people. This included many children who had a parent lynched. While the lynching victim's family lost wealth through violence, their extended family lost wealth through caring for those suffering the consequences of the violence. All the while, white American wealth continued to grow.

Of the twenty-two lynching cases surveyed, Gaston found that more than half of the victims had owned land as well as other assets like businesses, livestock, and equipment.[62] When she interviewed descendants of these victims, she learned of the economic toll caused by their family member's lynching. In one case, when a woman's father was lynched, "the responsibility of the family was abruptly placed on her mother (the victim's wife), who ended up 'taking on several jobs' and becoming 'the sole provider of the family' of seven children with the help and support of 'her parents and my father's father.'" As that same survivor put it: "We went from prosperity to poverty overnight. All the resources my father had owned, the white man just came and took them away and there was nothing we could do about it."[63] Another descendant described how his family's land was sold in the wake of his great-grandfather's murder and was now the site of "the biggest, most opulent house in the town."[64]

Racial violence like lynching was designed to strip black Americans of their citizenship rights, including the right to own property, vote, and live peaceably, but it also manifested in other forms, such as land grabs and race riots, where black Americans were attacked by large mobs, as in Tulsa in 1921. Although the number of lynchings peaked in the 1890s, similarly brutal attacks continued well into the twentieth century. In 2001 the Associated Press (AP) conducted an eighteen-month investigation of black land loss in America "over the last 150-plus years" and recorded fifty-seven instances of land grabs.

At the turn of the twentieth century, a movement of white farmers known as the Whitecaps began terrorizing black farmers in the South. These white vigilantes, according to the historian George Wright, "were intent on driving blacks from their land and discouraging other blacks from acquiring it." More often than not, their attacks on black farmers were aided by local law enforcement. Like the Ku Klux Klan, the Whitecaps used whatever methods were at their disposal, including intimidation tactics like nailing "notes with crudely drawn coffins to the doors of black landowners, warning them to leave or die."[65] Lynchings were often a part of whitecapping (designed to enforce white supremacy's "community norms"), which became "a quick and easy way to illegally deprive Blacks of their land."[66] During the 1880s and '90s, at least 239 whitecappings were recorded, with the largest number occurring in Mississippi.[67]

Eli Hilson of Lincoln County, Mississippi, was a target of a whitecapping. On November 18, 1903, hours after his latest child was born, Whitecaps fired several shots at his house. Eli did not heed the warning. Within a month he was dead. His wife, Hannah, discovered him in his buggy with a bullet in his head—the horse had pulled the carriage with his lifeless body all the way home. Their eleven children were now in Hannah's sole care, and she scrambled to provide for them while also managing the seventy-four-acre farm. In the end, the devastating loss of her husband proved to be too much. Hannah couldn't keep up with the mortgage payments and lost the land to foreclosure in 1905. According to the AP report, the farm was purchased by S. P. Oliver, a member of the county board of supervisors, for $439. In 2001 the property was valued at $61,642.[68]

In another instance, on the night of October 4, 1908, a group of fifty white men wearing hoods encircled the home of black farmer David Walker in Hickman, Kentucky. They demanded that Walker come out so they could give him a whipping. Walker shot at them instead, and in retaliation, the crowd set his house on fire. When Walker and his family finally came running out, the men shot at them, injuring three children and killing everyone else. Walker's oldest son was burned alive inside the house. Again, no one was ever brought to justice, and Walker's two-and-a-half-acre farm was subsumed into the property of a white neighbor, who subsequently sold it to someone else, "whose daughter owns the undeveloped land today."[69]

One day in 1916, Anthony Crawford, a black farmer in Abbeville, South Carolina, drove to town to sell his cotton harvest at the local mercantile. The white store owner, W. D. Barksdale, offered Crawford eighty-five cents a pound for his cotton, but Crawford, being one of the most successful farmers in the county, knew better and said he could get a higher offer. This ordinary business transaction quickly devolved into a physical altercation. Barksdale accused Crawford of lying, Crawford in turn called Barksdale a cheat. Three clerks threatened Crawford with ax handles and pushed him out into the street, where the sheriff arrested him for cursing a white man.

As soon as Crawford was released on bail, fifty white people cornered him and beat and stabbed him. The sheriff threw him back into jail, but not long after, a deputy handed the keys to Crawford's cell over to the angry crowd. They dragged Crawford out and strung him up at a baseball field on the outskirts of town. In a letter to *The Abbeville Press and Banner*, one Mrs. J. B. Holman wrote that Crawford "seems to have been the type of Negro who is most offensive to certain elements of the white people. . . . He was getting rich, for a Negro, and he was insolent along with it."[70] No one was ever brought to justice for his murder.

In the wake of this savage lynching, members of the Crawford family and many hundreds of black people fled Abbeville. According to the AP report, two white men were named the executors of Crawford's estate, one of whom was Andrew Ferguson, a cousin of the mob's two ringleaders. Ferguson sold off most of Crawford's property and walked away with $5,438. Although Crawford's children inherited their father's farm, they each received only $200 from the liquidation proceeds. They tried to keep the farm but ultimately forfeited the property when they couldn't settle a $2,000 balance on a bank loan, even though the farm was valued at $20,000. A white man won the property at a foreclosure auction for $504.[71]

Similarly, an attack on Election Day 1920 sent the black community of Ocoee, Florida, packing. A group of white Americans "went hunting for a black man who had dared approach the ballot box in the 1920 presidential election."[72] Their attack on him resulted "in the single bloodiest day in American political history."[73] Eighteen black families owned property in the town, making up 330 acres and forty-eight city lots. They had no choice but to sell their land, whether the amount offered was fair or not. Valentine Hightower, for instance, sold his fifty-two acres for a piddling $10 in 1926. In 2001 the land ceded by those eighteen families was worth more than $4.2 million. And that figure doesn't take into consideration that property assessments are typically lower than market value or that they include buildings that were later erected on the property.[74]

In Yazoo County, Mississippi, the twin brothers Norman and Homer Stephens ran a trucking business "hauling cotton pickers to plantations." When a white farmer couldn't get workers delivered to his field quickly enough, because the Stephenses had other commitments to attend to first, he sent the sheriff after them. The two brothers wound up in jail that night and overheard the sheriff "talking about where to hide their bodies." The year was 1950. Luckily, Norman and Homer crawled out a window and escaped from their cell on the second floor of the county jail. They ran home, immediately packed their bags, and took the first bus out of town, headed to Ohio. Norman's wife and five kids joined him there a year later. The family continued to pay the mortgage and property tax on their house back in Mississippi but were too afraid to ever return. In the 1960s, they stopped making payments and lost the house for good.[75]

Another strategy for stealing land and capital from black Americans was to destroy official documents and create "gaps in the public record."[76] In Paulding, Mississippi, on the evening of September 10, 1932, more than a dozen whites set fire to the city courthouse. The property records for half of Jasper County, a predominantly black area, went up in smoke overnight. Once it was no longer clear who owned title to much of the property, Masonite, a company specializing in wood products, swooped in and won legal ownership of more than 9,500 acres of land in the area. The AP pieced together information from the limited property records that survived the fire and "document[ed] that at least 204.5 of those acres had been acquired by Masonite after black owners were driven off by the Klan." Masonite has since reaped millions of dollars in revenue from the land in the form of natural resources like gas, timber, and oil.[77] As soon as black Americans began to pull themselves up by their bootstraps, their feet were cut off.

For this book, I interviewed Sherrilyn Ifill, holder of the inaugural Vernon Jordan Endowed Chair in Civil Rights at Howard University, a law professor, former executive director and counsel of the NAACP Legal Defense Fund, and the author of *On the Courthouse Lawn: Confronting the Legacy of Lynching in the 21st Century.*[78] She shared with me her thoughts about the need to understand the lynching of black people in America:

We must never underestimate the role that lynching and the pervasive threat of lynching played in policing the boundaries of Black citizenship in the first half of the 20th century. The poll tax, the "understanding clauses" and literacy tests used at registration to bar Blacks from registration, the removal of polling places, all had their intended effect on suppressing Black suffrage. But the threat of the unimaginable horror of lynching—torture and murder—cheered on by white crowds, and for which there would be no recourse, was critical to discouraging Blacks who might be inclined to try and navigate the legal and administrative hurdles to try and vote. Lynching most powerfully ensured that expansive ideas about Black citizenship would be abandoned. As a result, Black people understood that in their interpersonal relations with whites, in how they carried themselves in public spaces, how they responded to slights and insults, and even whether they could protect themselves against sexual and other kinds of assault, they had to weigh the possibility that lynching might be the price to be paid for the assertion of their rights as citizens and human beings.

Physical violence was not the only thing black Americans needed to be frightened of. Economic violence perpetrated by the government was cause for serious concern. In 1940, the Federal Housing Administration (FHA) insured a loan to only one black American in Greensboro, North Carolina, despite the city having roughly thirteen hundred black homeowners.[79] The FHA was established by the National Housing Act of 1934 to insure mortgages made by private sector banks and to support new construction projects that were deemed "economically sound."

The insurance was designed for low-down-payment, low-interest-rate, long-term mortgages, which meant banks had to include those terms if they wanted their mortgages insured—and they did. The FHA worked with developers to ensure that prospective buyers would be eligible for FHA-insured mortgages, but they also required developers to include racially restrictive covenants in their documents. The FHA determined that "economically sound" meant blacks need not apply, such that "by the end of the 1950s, only 2 percent of the homes built with FHA support since World War II were occupied by blacks and other minorities."[80]

The federal government, through the Veterans Administration, also discriminated against black veterans through the Servicemen's Readjustment Act of 1944 (the GI Bill). According to the historian and political scientist Ira Katznelson, "No other New Deal initiative had as great an impact on changing the country as the [GI Bill]."[81] Through the GI Bill, millions purchased homes, went to college, started businesses, and found high-paying jobs.[82] What it did not do, by and large, was help the over one million returning black veterans and their families to the same extent that it helped returning white veterans. Why? First, colleges could still legally refuse to admit black students, which limited most black veterans to historically black colleges and universities, which simply could not accommodate the entirety of the demand. More than half of black veterans applying to Southern black colleges were "turned away due to lack of space."[83] Second, the GI Bill failed to help black Americans because "Congress placed day-to-day decisions about eligibility and policy in the hands of local district offices."[84] That harmed black Americans in two distinct ways: It discouraged them from even applying for the bill's benefits, and even if they did, it guaranteed that they would receive separate and unequal treatment.

Take the case of E. A. Crawford, a black veteran honorably discharged, who returned to Corpus Christi, Texas, in 1946. He tried to access the GI Bill's mortgage benefits but was "repeatedly denied a mortgage."[85] Believing himself to be the victim of race discrimination, he went to the banker and asked, "Why is it a Negro veteran cannot obtain aid under this provision same as white" GIs? In response, the banker frankly admitted, "It is almost impossible for a Colored man to get a loan."[86] When race discrimination is legal, you can say the quiet part out loud.

The obstacles that black Americans had to overcome in the South led many to leave in search of better economic opportunities. However, they soon discovered that wherever they went—to the West, the Midwest, or the North—their blackness made them a target for physical and economic violence similar to what they experienced in the South. There was truly no escape, no safe haven for them. Across the country, black Americans faced barriers to landownership through devices such as sundown towns, racially restrictive covenants, and federal governmental discrimination. If they managed to overcome these hurdles and become property owners, then they faced tactics designed to strip them of their property, such as state exercise of eminent domain powers. When all else failed, white Americans could fall back on the tried-and-true method of lynching.

In the following section, we'll see exactly how black Americans fared when they left the South in search of a brighter future across the country.

Post-Slavery Discrimination Travels

The West: "Tell my people to go west. There is no justice for them here."

Those were Tommie Moss's last words before his lynching. And black Americans should have found greener pastures out west because the federal government was giving land away. While they struggled to buy land, the federal government was helping white citizens and white immigrants who would soon become citizens acquire land through the Homestead Act.

Passed by Congress and signed by President Abraham Lincoln on May 20, 1862 (a month after the vote to compensate white enslavers), the Homestead Act provided that white men and women who were "heads of household, military veterans, and those over 21 years of age" were entitled to 160 acres of land in the West and Midwest as long as they had not "borne arms against" the federal government.[87] White women, as long as they were unmarried, were eligible to receive land under the act. Homesteaders either had to be US citizens or white immigrants who had filed their intention to become one.

But who owned the land out west? Tribal Nations. The Homestead Act allowed white men to take property that didn't belong to them and build lives on the dashed hopes and dreams of others. Which is partly why Tribal Nations later received cash compensation through the Indian Claims Commission for the land that white Americans took from them, sanctioned by the federal government.

Black Americans, unlike their white peers, had little or no access to the federal government's 160-acre-plot land grab. They were not considered citizens in 1862, thanks to an 1857 Supreme Court decision that held that black people were ineligible for citizenship, whether free or enslaved, because they were "so far inferior, that they had no rights which the white man was bound to respect."[88]

"Ironically, black men who served on the Union side during the war and even remained enlisted as Buffalo Soldiers to help protect settlers on the frontier from outlaws and Indian attacks,"

Dr. Trina Shanks explains, "were denied the opportunity to make land claims in some of the very communities they fought to defend."[89] Once the 1866 Civil Rights Act was passed, black Americans became citizens and so were now eligible to participate in the Homestead Act, but they were often unable to overcome the barriers of racial discrimination.[90]

Those who applied for land under the Homestead Act were required to attest that the property was for their own use and for "cultivation and settlement" purposes, at which point they were given six months to move onto the land and make improvements. In order to own the land outright, they could either pay the minimum price per acre or wait a period of five years, after which they would be eligible to obtain title by paying the requisite land office fees.[91] They could accomplish all this with very little money down, and by becoming landowners, they gained the financial freedom to make a better life for themselves and future generations.

One of the few black Americans who received land under the act was Henry Burden. Born enslaved, he escaped and later joined the Union Army. After the end of the war, he went to Nebraska and "in 1870 filed a homestead claim in Saline County."[92] He was the first black American to get land under the act in Nebraska, where he lived with his family until he died in 1913.

Against this backdrop of federal largesse for the benefit of white people and to the detriment of Tribal Nations, black freedmen, who started with nothing and had to buy land without a helping hand, were generally forced to struggle in ways their white peers did not. Which seems more than a little unfair, if for no other reason than the fact that freedmen had significantly more experience farming. Many had spent their entire previous lives as enslaved people tilling the land of white folks, growing crops and reaping harvests without compensation. Who was more qualified to farm than those who had formerly done the farming?

The federal government excluded the most qualified workers from the benefits of property ownership, while reserving the land for those with merely a single qualification: their whiteness. Such preferential treatment by the federal government did not always lead to successful outcomes, and many white homesteaders predictably failed.

Of course, I am not arguing that stealing land from the original landowners, the Tribal Nations, would have been fine as long as it was made available to black Americans. Tribal Nations and black Americans were victims of white supremacy in different ways. One racial group does not win when they are used to oppress a different racial group. The only winner in that instance is the system of racial subordination that led to mostly white Americans being awarded almost 246 million acres of land.[93]

There were other methods of keeping black Americans off desirable land. We've all seen photos of "whites only" drinking fountains. Well, imagine a WHITES ONLY sign hanging over an entire town or a whole neighborhood. That's what a sundown town is: an area where black people had to be out by sundown or risk their lives. They were allowed to work there but not live there. James Loewen, the author of *Sundown Towns: A Hidden Dimension of American Racism,* describes them as "any organized jurisdiction that for decades kept African Americans or other groups from living in it and was thus 'all-white' on purpose."[94] He puts "all-white" in quotes because in some instances towns allowed a single black household as an exception.

Sundown towns were the original opportunity hoarders: They limited the ability of black people to buy property inside city limits and take advantage of amenities available to white Americans.[95] For the most part, sundown towns were not found in the South, with its historical ties to slavery. You see, in the South black people knew their place and knew that the hanging noose awaited their next misstep. Instead, sundown towns appeared throughout the nation, primarily during the period following Reconstruction between 1890 and 1940, when white people were once again looking for ways to exert their control over black Americans.[96]

In 1890 there were only 119 counties in the United States outside the "traditional South" (Virginia, North Carolina, South Carolina, Georgia, Florida, Alabama, Tennessee, Mississippi, and Louisiana) that had no black residents, but by 1930 that number had almost doubled to 235 counties. Why did black people disappear from these counties? The answer is, they became sundown towns. Loewen estimates that more than half of all the cities in Oregon, Indiana, Ohio, eastern Kentucky, Tennessee, and the Ozarks, among other regions, were sundown towns. There were also sundown suburbs in places like La Jolla, California. By Loewen's count, California at one time had more sundown towns "than all parts of the traditional south put together."[97]

I was surprised (but shouldn't have been) to see that sundown towns proliferated in western states that today have very small percentages of black Americans, like California (5 percent), Montana (0.6 percent), Oregon (3 percent), and Utah (2.1 percent). Honestly, California especially surprised me because I thought the black population there today was much larger. For the other states, I assumed black people never wanted to go there in the first place.[98] (Oregon, in fact, was admitted to the Union with laws in place that specifically excluded black people from settling there.) But if you look at their demographics, you see that the states became whiter *over time* because black people left in droves. Sundown towns are a part of what made them leave. And I can't leave this section without nominating Montana for the Hall of Shame.

SUNDOWN TOWNS IN THE WEST[99]

State	# of counties with < 10 black people in 1890	# of counties with < 10 black people in 1930
Arizona	1	1
California	4	8
Colorado	19	28
Idaho	9	33
Montana	2	41
Nevada	6	8
New Mexico	9	11
Oregon	16	24
Utah	16	22
Washington	16	20
Wyoming	5	11

[Table 3]

Another example is Glendale, California, where local officials and ordinary citizens found a variety of ways to make it clear that black people had no place in the community. Although there is "no official record" of a sundown law in Glendale, there is ample evidence that the city functioned as a de facto sundown town.[100] In 1938 the Los Angeles city park commissioners "refused to allow the Civilian Conservation Corps to house a company of African American workers at Griffith Park because the bordering cities of Glendale and Burbank had ordinances which prohibited Black people from remaining after sun down."[101]

Another reason the number of sundown towns rapidly increased was because majority white communities did not want to bear the expense of building separate schools when black Americans with school-age children moved into town. This was during segregation, before *Brown v. Board of Education* declared segregated schools unconstitutional. The law required separate but equal schools, which meant states had to spend the resources to create "blacks only" school districts. The white officials who were responsible for building and overseeing these districts "sometimes encouraged threats or violence against a black family to avoid the expense of setting up a new black school for them."[102] Opportunity hoarding is never clearer than when we see what white parents are willing to do in order to give their children a leg up on everybody else.

One additional way black people have had their wealth stripped from them in order to benefit their white peers is eminent domain. When a state or local government decides it wants to take land currently owned by a private citizen and use it for a "necessary" government purpose, it can force the owner to sell their property and exercise a wide latitude in determining what to pay for it.

In 1912 Charles and Willa Bruce purchased beachfront property on Manhattan Beach in southern California for $1,225. They eventually turned their plots into a popular resort destination called Bruce's Lodge, for black families who were denied access to other beaches because they were black. When Willa and her husband became property owners, they emboldened other black families to buy land and build cottages by the beach. The white residents of Manhattan Beach, however, did not welcome this change. To them, the black Americans moving into their neighborhood were part of a "national problem" that was abruptly brought to their doorstep. The white residents in Manhattan Beach were determined to solve it by any means necessary. "Visitors' tires were frequently slashed, phony '10 Minute Only' parking signs were erected to cause inconvenience, and the Ku Klux Klan set a fire on the Bruces' property and burned a cross near the house of a Black neighbor."[103]

In 1915 City Clerk Lewellyn Price complained that the Bruces held "a coon picnic . . . attended by about seventy-five to one-hundred-and-fifty coon pullman porters and their friends" and that it was "quite a detriment to the neighborhood." NO TRESPASSING signs were put up on properties surrounding the beach, "forcing Black beachgoers to traipse a half mile out of their way to reach the water." Undaunted, the Bruces were determined to remain on their slice of paradise. "Wherever we have tried to buy land for a beach resort we have been refused, but I own this land, and I am going to keep it," Willa Bruce told the *Los Angeles Times* in 1912.[104] She likely understood that if she was chased away from Manhattan Beach, she probably wouldn't be able to purchase another beach property like it. She would be running for the rest of her life. Bruce's Lodge was something worth fighting for—a sanctuary and "a little breathing space" for black Americans to enjoy the beach. But room to breathe was not what she received from her white neighbors for experiencing a little black joy.

In 1924 the Manhattan Beach Board of Trustees accomplished what the Ku Klux Klan could not. They drove out the Bruces by using eminent domain to seize all their property. Four other black families who owned property in Manhattan Beach saw it taken away from them as well, along with "twenty-five other properties owned by White property owners."[105] It wasn't just black families who lost their property through eminent domain, but white families too. White supremacy does not mind sacrificing the financial futures of several white families if that's what is required to achieve the greater goal of creating all-white spaces.

City officials said that they needed it for a park—a park that was not built for almost thirty years. The Bruces did not take the city's eminent domain assault lying down. They sued and asked for $120,000 in compensation. But the legal case dragged on for five years, and finally they had no choice but to agree to a ridiculously low settlement of $14,500 in 1929.

The Bruces were broke and spiritually depleted from the fight. In an interview, one of the family's descendants, Duane Yellow Feather Shepard, explained that "having spent their final pennies fighting eviction, the Bruces left California destitute the same year. Willa suffered a nervous breakdown and died in 1935, and Charles passed away two years later."[106] Shepard obviously believed that what happened to his ancestors was more than unfair. You know who agreed with him? A member of the Manhattan Beach Board of Trustees, the same board that was responsible for the legal theft of the Bruces' land. Board member Frank Daugherty wrote in 1945 that "it was a mean trick to make them leave their homes, but it was the only way out." Daugherty described how "white residents believed 'the Negro problem was going to stop our progress.'"[107] No consideration was given to what taking their land would do to Willa and Charles Bruce. This was opportunity hoarding on steroids.

What happened to the Bruces was quite common among black Americans. Research shows that between 1949 and 1973, almost one thousand cities used eminent domain to displace "one million people, two-thirds of them African American," under the Federal Housing Act of 1949.[108]

Glendale real estate records also reveal racially restrictive covenants, another barrier imposed to stop black people from buying property. "In the 1910s and 1920s, racially restricted housing was noted in advertisements for Glendale homes, and by the 1940s, Glendale was noted as a model for other communities that wanted to racially restrict housing."[109] Through covenants, white homeowners agreed not to sell their property to black people or "Negroes," as most of the provisions referred to them, in legally binding documents. Apparently, even in a sundown town where black people were not welcome after dark, the white residents felt it was necessary to take a belt and suspenders approach.

In 1940 the California Real Estate Association (CREA) cited Glendale "as being worthy of singular praise in its utilization of measures to keep it a '100% Caucasian Race Community.'" CREA was able to keep black homebuyers out of Glendale by encouraging white homeowners to make the pledge: "I will not sell or rent to any person or groups other than the Caucasian Race." Within a few years, the Glendale CREA chapter established a Race Restriction Committee in order "to establish perpetual race restrictions on all parcels of property in Glendale."[110] Racially restrictive covenants like this one operated across the country to prevent black Americans from becoming homeowners, and it was all perfectly legal, until the 1968 Fair Housing Act was passed in the wake of Martin Luther King, Jr.'s assassination.

Of course, there were also informal methods of keeping Glendale all white, which included violence or the threat of violence and harassment. Hate crimes affecting black people who moved into Glendale or who visited Glendale have been documented from the 1900s through the 1990s. The list includes accounts of black workers who consistently experienced "hostility and discrimination." And if that wasn't enough, Glendale was home to white supremacist organizations like the Ku Klux Klan, which was "active in Glendale as early as the 1920s" through the 1960s. The group was considered to be "a 'strong' organization including many of the business' men of the suburban city [as] members of the masked brotherhood."[111]

But the federal government also discriminated against black Americans to prevent their wealth building through the Department of Housing and Urban Development and the Department of Veterans Affairs. Redlining prevented prospective black homeowners from acquiring property with FHA insurance. White immigrants did not face similar obstacles. Recall how white immigrants were afforded access to land under the Homestead Act, while black Americans were denied the same access.

When two Norwegian immigrants arrived in America in 1954, they quickly acquired an eighteen-hundred-square-foot home in Glendale for $8,500. Soon afterward their children came from Norway to join them, and the house became a place of refuge for their large family, which ultimately included four children and two great-grandchildren. One of those great-grandchildren was Paul Thornton, an editor for the *Los Angeles Times* who shared his story in 2022. Because they owned their home, his immigrant family was able to survive off the earnings of a furniture mover.[112] Thornton's grandparents sold the house in the early 1990s, significantly improving their balance sheet. Today the house is worth approximately $1.4 million. As immigrants, they might argue that they were never involved in the slave trade in the United States and should not be held responsible for any future reparations. Yet they still benefited from slavery's legacy and Glendale's racially restrictive covenants because they were white. Today's descendants of white immigrants benefit from an antiblack system that draws its roots from chattel slavery.

That's how two white Norwegian immigrants could become homeowners in this country with relative ease, while the descendants of black people who had lived here for centuries were barred from spending a single night in town as residents, much less buying a home there. Oh, and you couldn't die there either because only white people were allowed to be buried in Glendale's Forest Lawn Memorial Park until the 1960s.[113]

John C. Cannon was a black veteran who had earned the distinction of "a 2nd lieutenant's commission" while serving in the US Army Medical Corps. Upon his return to civilian life, he received three employment options: "one as a bus boy, one as a porter, and one as a car washer." By failing to recommend him for a health department position, the Los Angeles office violated governmental policy. By 1946 this type of employment discrimination resulted in an "11 percent higher" unemployment rate for African American veterans nationally than for their white counterparts.[114] The discrimination was not limited to job placement benefits under the GI Bill. In 1947 when Veterans Administration officials surveyed black veterans nationwide, they discovered that only 5 percent "were enrolled in courses and programs under the GI Bill's educational benefit."[115] As one returning black soldier observed: "This nation throughout its history has been more willing to fight a war for democracy than to actually practice it."[116]

Although the Fair Housing Act of 1968 made redlining illegal, other schemes have been engineered to take its place. On January 12, 2023, the Department of Justice announced that it had entered into a $31 million settlement agreement to resolve allegations that City National Bank, the largest bank headquartered in Los Angeles and among the fifty largest banks in the United States, "engaged in a pattern or practice of lending discrimination by 'redlining' in Los Angeles County."[117]

The Midwest: "The Negro problem has spread from [the] south."

Black families who harbored the dream of owning their own homes and building something they could pass on to future generations met with similar obstacles in the Midwest. When the Great Migration began in earnest in the 1910s, many black Americans left the South, either to escape white racial violence or to look for better opportunities.[118] What they didn't know yet was that wherever they went, their blackness would follow them.

A 1916 newspaper editorial published in Beloit, Wisconsin, warned its white readership:

> The Negro problem has moved north. Rather the Negro problem has spread from south to north. . . . With the black tide setting north, the southern Negro, formerly a docile tool, is demanding better pay, better food, and better treatment. . . . It's a national problem now, instead of a sectional problem. And it has got to be solved.[119]

Some white people were fine with black Americans gaining equal rights—as long as they didn't live on the same street. But as soon as black Americans attempted to move into white neighborhoods and demanded to be treated with the same respect afforded to their white peers, black Americans became a "problem" that needed to be solved. The Reconstruction Amendments had been designed to do exactly that: to bring the formerly enslaved into equal status with white Americans. Under slavery, white communities in the South had come up with "the original sundown rule: to be out after dark as a slave required written passes from owners."[120] This carried over into the post-slavery era, as white communities threatened freed black Americans who showed up in all-white towns after sundown.

Sundown towns increased between 1890 and 1930 for all midwestern states, some dramatically. Black people did not live there then—and they live there now only in small percentages, because the states liked it that way.

SUNDOWN TOWNS IN THE MIDWEST[121]

State	# of counties with <10 black people in 1890	# of counties with <10 black people in 1930
Illinois	6	17
Indiana	14	20
Iowa	28	38
Kansas	20	23
Michigan	23	26
Minnesota	57	61
Missouri	8	28
Nebraska	41	64
North Dakota	26	42
Ohio	1	2
South Dakota	37	52
Wisconsin	27	42

[Table 4]

The historian and sociologist James Loewen estimates that more than half of all the cities in Illinois, Indiana, Ohio, and Kansas, among other regions, were sundown towns.[122]

Six Nebraska counties recorded between twenty and fifty black Americans among their residents in 1890, but by 1930 those same counties had only one to eight black residents.[123] Cities that did not expel their black residents after 1890 often "concentrated them into a few neighborhoods."[124] During the same period, the black populations in Omaha and Lincoln, Nebraska, doubled.

Racial violence followed black people to the Midwest. For example, on August 18, 1901, an armed white mob killed four blacks and torched five black-owned houses in Pierce City, Missouri. There were a thousand white Americans against the town's 129 black Americans. Within four days of the attack, every single black person left town. They never returned. Of the nine black property owners, all were forced to sell their land, which made up thirty acres of farmland and ten city lots, to whites, at below-market rates. Eviline Brinson, who lost her husband and her house in the onslaught, "sold her lot for $25 to a white woman." Brinson had paid nearly four times as much when she bought the property in 1889.[125]

The Northeast: "For white purchasers only"

Just as it did in the West and Midwest, racial discrimination followed black Americans to the North. Sundown towns proliferated there, too. In 1890 every county in the state of Maine, except for two, counted at least a dozen or so black residents.[126] But by 1930, we see a different Maine. Five counties no longer had any black residents at all, while several other counties showed significant decreases in the black population.

SUNDOWN TOWNS IN THE NORTHEAST[127]

State	# of counties with <10 black people in 1890	# of counties with <10 black people in 1930
Maine	2	5
New Hampshire	0	2
New York	0	1
Pennsylvania	3	4
Vermont	3	4

[Table 5]

Connecticut, Delaware, Maryland, Massachusetts, New Jersey, and Rhode Island had no counties with fewer than ten black people in 1890 as well as 1930. There were also sundown suburbs in places like Darien, Connecticut, and Chevy Chase, Maryland, which was "one of our first sundown suburbs."[128] In 1909 the Chevy Chase Land Company filed suit against the developer it had sold land to, claiming fraud because the developer was "offering to sell lots . . . to negroes."[129] The land company reacquired the property, the development was never built, and the land remained vacant for decades.[130]

Governmental discrimination also followed black people north. In 1940, the FHA insured 2 percent of black homeowners in Baltimore (representing twenty-five FHA-insured loans) compared with 8 percent of white homeowners. The story of one neighborhood of black homeowners in Baltimore is especially telling. As you will see, it was the "perfect" black neighborhood.

Morgan Park was developed around 1916 by Morgan College, a historically black college now known as Morgan State University. From what I can tell, the neighborhood was developed for black people as a defensive measure—to provide decent and safe housing for black faculty and other black Americans connected to the college who were unable to live in other parts of

Baltimore because of their race. One factor that likely gave these homeowners an advantage in the eyes of the FHA was that the development included a racially restrictive covenant (though not the typical one): Only black people could buy property in Morgan Park. Its residents were financially well off, and many were faculty at the college and so could easily satisfy FHA income requirements. Neighborhood lore described Morgan Park as a place "occupied by the upper crust of Black society in Baltimore, including famous residents such as W. E. B. Du Bois." Most important, Morgan Park was geographically isolated in northeastern Baltimore and was surrounded on three sides by a small stream that separated it from nearby white neighborhoods, ensuring that it would remain all-black. Even the streets were deliberately built without any connection to the white neighborhood to its east, Lauraville. As a result of checking all the FHA's boxes, in 1940, eleven out of twenty-six black homeowners received FHA support.[131]

The Veterans Administration also hit northern black Americans. In 1945 Hollis L. Metz was a returning black veteran and had been honorably discharged. He sought a VA-guaranteed loan in New Rochelle, New York. Employed by the federal government, his annual income ($3,250) was above that of the average FHA mortgage insurance recipient ($3,118), with a median monthly mortgage amount of $39.21. Metz also had $500 in savings. Yet he was denied the same no-money-down mortgage guarantee that the GI Bill made available to returning white servicemen. By August, he had been rejected by three different banks. As a result, Metz, his wife, and their two children "were ultimately unable to purchase the home of their dreams because of racial discrimination."[132]

By 1957, Levitt and Sons had built "Levittowns" in New

York and Pennsylvania, and William Levitt was planning to construct a third one in New Jersey.[133] On June 5, 1958, he described that project as one that "would be for white purchasers only."[134] As late as February 1960, he was fighting in court for his right to "exclud[e] Negroes from homes supported by FHA mortgage insurance."[135] It took Congress to fix what the Supreme Court had wrought twenty years earlier, when it declared private racial discrimination in housing constitutional. Not until 1968, with the passage of the Fair Housing Act, did Levitt have to stop discriminating against would-be homebuyers on the basis of race.

But denying black Americans access to homeownership did not begin with the purchase contract. Lack of access to credit markets also created problems for black Americans, preventing them from even getting to that stage. While FHA insurance had been like the wind at the backs of white homeowners, the exact opposite was true for black homeowners. FHA insurance can be credited for the significant growth in white homeownership rates, with a majority of white Americans (57 percent) owning homes by 1950. Just ten years earlier, only 46 percent of white Americans had been homeowners. Despite being denied access to FHA insurance, homeownership among black Americans increased from 23 to 34 percent during that same period. They bought homes with costlier mortgages and navigated racially restrictive covenants, yet somehow they still increased their homeownership rate by 10 percentage points—similar to their white peers, but without the preferential treatment.[136] And by 1950, black Americans were paying income taxes to a federal government that continued to deny them equal access to government services like VA benefits and FHA-insured mortgages, since racial discrimination in housing was still 100 percent legal.

Broken Promises: The Judicial Backlash Against Black Americans

I know what you're thinking. Why didn't the Reconstruction Amendments fix all this? Why didn't they prevent sharecropping, convict leasing, lynching, sundown towns, racial covenants, and FHA and GI Bill discrimination from happening in the first place? Yes, they were supposed to.

But one group that looked for an opportunity to halt black progress was the majority of the nine white justices on the US Supreme Court. In fact, following the end of chattel slavery, it was the all-white, all-male Supreme Court that eventually stripped the Reconstruction Amendments—the Thirteenth, Fourteenth, and Fifteenth—of their power to transform the nation.

The Supreme Court found its opportunity in the *Civil Rights Cases,* a group of five cases, consolidated into one, that each challenged the constitutionality of the first two sections of the 1875 Civil Rights Act. Two cases arose out of incidents in which black Americans were denied access to hotel accommodations. Two additional cases dealt with black people being denied admission to theaters. And a fifth case involved a train conductor who refused to allow a black woman to ride in "the ladies' car" because "she was a person of African descent," for which he was fined a penalty of $500.[137]

Applying the letter of the law should have made it an easy case. Section 1 of the 1875 Civil Rights Act provided that all persons were "entitled to the full and equal enjoyment of the accommodations, advantages, facilities, and privileges of inns, public conveyances on land or water, theaters, and other places of public amusement . . . applicable alike to citizens of every race and color, regardless of any previous condition of servitude." Likewise, Section 2 stipulated that anyone who violated the rights of a citizen, as stated in Section 1, would be legally obligated to "pay the sum of $500 to the person aggrieved thereby" and would be liable to additional consequences if found guilty of this misdemeanor. Congress understood that victims of race discrimination should be compensated for their harm.

When the *Civil Rights Cases* reached the Supreme Court in 1883, however, the Court not only declared that the Thirteenth Amendment did not prohibit race discrimination in public accommodations—it also went further by resolving that "mere discriminations on account of race or color were not regarded as badges of slavery."[138] As the noted legal scholar George A. Rutherglen, Justice Thurgood Marshall Distinguished Professor of Law at the University of Virginia, put it, "Only the rights that free blacks had before the Civil War, and that the slaves did not, constituted the necessary incidents of slavery that could be remedied under the Thirteenth Amendment. Since free blacks were subject to pervasive discrimination before emancipation, the same would also be true of the newly freed slaves."[139]

Thus, discrimination against black Americans, recently freed or not, was declared legal and therefore not worthy of compensation. The Supreme Court held that under the Thirteenth Amendment, Congress was powerless to prevent it. As the majority ruling explained: "It would be running the slavery argument into the ground to make it apply to every act of discrimination which a person may see fit to make as to the guests he will entertain, or as to the people he will take into his coach or cab or car, or admit to his concert or theater, or deal with in other matters of intercourse or business."[140] By that logic, ending slavery had been enough, and black people should be grateful and stop complaining and being overly sensitive. In other words: Get that chip off your shoulder!

Supreme Court justice John Marshall Harlan was the lone dissenter. He believed that the Thirteenth Amendment was intended to do more than just end slavery—it was to establish freedom. As he saw it, "The power of Congress under the Thirteenth Amendment is not necessarily restricted to legislation against slavery." Rather, the amendment was also a legal mechanism for "protecting the liberated race against discrimination, in respect of legal rights belonging to freemen, where such discrimination is based upon race." The Thirteenth Amendment gave Congress the power to address racial discrimination, plain and simple.

As a result of the Court's decision in the *Civil Rights Cases,* federal law allowed slavery to continue in different forms.

If the Thirteenth Amendment was not being used to help the newly freed, neither was the Fourteenth. Passed by Congress to bolster the rights of this vulnerable group, the amendment provides: "the states are forbidden from making or enforcing any law which shall abridge the privileges or immunities of citizens of the United States, or shall deprive any person of life, liberty, or property without due process of law, or deny to any person within their jurisdiction the equal protection of the laws." Yet the Supreme Court proved to be a significant obstacle in securing basic rights for black Americans under the Fourteenth Amendment as well.

One of the Court's most disastrous opinions, in this regard, was in the 1896 case *Plessy v. Ferguson.* This test case had been designed to seek a declaration from the Supreme Court that segregation was illegal. Homer Plessy was a light-skinned black man and Louisiana citizen who purchased a first-class ticket on the East Louisiana Railway. The train required segregated cars for the "white and colored races" on account of a Louisiana statute that stated: "No person or persons shall be permitted to occupy

seats in coaches, other than the ones assigned to them, on account of the race they belong to."[141] Plessy was one-eighth black
and perhaps as much as seven-eighths white, and he appeared
white. That was why he was chosen as a plaintiff, to try to demonstrate the absurdities of Jim Crow. It is likely also the explanation for why he was allowed to buy a first-class ticket.

Plessy, who was in on the test case, ignored the new COLORED
ONLY sign and sat down in the section reserved for whites. The
train had barely set out from the station when the conductor ap-
proached Plessy and asked, "Are you a colored man?" Plessy answered yes. The conductor told him he had to "retire to the
colored car." Plessy responded that he was an American citizen,
had paid for his ticket, and was not going to move. The conductor again asked him to leave, and when Plessy refused, he told the
train engineer to stop. A private detective, who was also part of
the plan, told Plessy, "If you are colored you should go into the
car set apart for your race. The law is plain and must be obeyed."
Plessy refused and was taken off the train and arrested. The test
case had begun.[142]

The Supreme Court opinion opened by citing the *Civil Rights
Cases* as precedent that denying someone access to a theater or
inn "cannot be justly regarded as imposing any badge of slavery."[143] The majority agreed that "a statute which implies merely a
legal distinction between the white and colored races . . . which
must always exist so long as white men are distinguished from
the other race by color—has no tendency to destroy the legal
equality of the two races, or re-establish a state of involuntary
servitude."[144]

To explain its position, the Court added that the plaintiff's
argument was founded on a mistaken notion, principally "the assumption that the enforced separation of the two races stamps

the colored race with a badge of inferiority." Even if such a thing were true, the opinion claimed, "it is not by reason of anything found in the act, but solely because the colored race chooses to put that construction upon it."[145]

Another flaw, as the Court saw it, was that "the argument also assumes that social prejudices may be overcome by legislation, and that equal rights cannot be secured to the negro except by an enforced commingling of the two races. We cannot accept this proposition." The Court went on to provide its view on how racial equality would be won for black Americans: "If the two races are to meet upon terms of social equality, it must be the result of natural affinities, a mutual appreciation of each other's merits, and a voluntary consent of individuals."[146] The decision concludes with a final observation: "If one race be inferior to the other socially, the constitution of the United States cannot put them upon the same plane."[147] As a result, the Supreme Court legally validated the "separate but equal" doctrine that held that separate facilities for black Americans were constitutional and therefore legal.

Jim Crow would prove expensive for black Americans in ways large and small. It became a driving force behind sundown towns, and one small example comes from the Coca-Cola company. If you visit the International Civil Rights Center and Museum in Greensboro, North Carolina, you can see a Coca-Cola dispenser that was used in segregated waiting rooms. One side dispensed soda in the white waiting room for five cents, while the other side sold the same soda in the colored waiting room for *twice* the price—ten cents.[148]

Not surprisingly, Justice Harlan dissented. He argued that the expansive nature of the Fourteenth Amendment granted black citizens the right to be free from "unfriendly legislation" that tar-

EVERYTHING, EVERYWHERE, ALL AT ONCE   117

geted them because of their color, implied their inferiority, and threatened "the security of their enjoyment of the rights which others enjoy." In his eyes, these methods of legal discrimination were "steps towards reducing them to the condition of a subject race."[149]

Justice Harlan called out the majority's de-contextualized reasoning when it claimed the legislation treated both races equally. "Every one knows that the statute in question had its origin in the purpose, not so much to exclude white persons from railroad cars occupied by blacks, as to exclude colored people from coaches occupied by or assigned to white persons," Harlan wrote, challenging his peers on the Court. "Railroad corporations of Louisiana did not make discrimination among whites in the matter of commodation [sic] for travelers. The thing to accomplish was, under the guise of giving equal accommodation for whites and blacks, to compel the latter to keep to themselves while traveling in railroad passenger coaches. No one would be so wanting in candor as to assert the contrary."[150]

Justice Harlan didn't pull any punches. Instead, he said the thing none of the other judges would admit out loud: "What can more certainly arouse race hate, what more certainly create and perpetuate a feeling of distrust between these races, than state enactments which, in fact, proceed on the ground that colored citizens are so inferior and degraded that they cannot be allowed to sit in public coaches occupied by white citizens? That, as all will admit, is the real meaning of such legislation as was enacted in Louisiana."[151]

In Justice Harlan's view, allowing states to regulate civil rights on the basis of race was "cunningly devised to defeat legitimate results of the war" and would lead to "no other result than to render permanent peace impossible, and to keep alive a conflict of races, the continuance of which must do harm to all concerned."[152] Referring back to the Thirteenth Amendment, he concluded that separating citizens on the arbitrary basis of race while they're on a public highway, for example, was "a badge of servitude wholly inconsistent with the civil freedom and the equality before the law established by the constitution." He added, "The thin disguise of 'equal' accommodations for passengers in railroad coaches will not mislead any one, nor atone for the wrong this day done."[153] Harlan predicted that the Court's decision in *Plessy v. Ferguson* would have a profound effect on the country. It would encourage "separate but equal" to spread to other areas of public life, not just on railroads. He wasn't wrong. Racial segregation remained the law of the land well into the 1960s.

You may be wondering, as I did, how did Justice Harlan come to view the rights granted to the newly freed differently from his Supreme Court brethren? Was it that he was raised in an abolitionist family? No, just the opposite—he was born into a family of enslavers.[154] John Marshall Harlan was born on June 1, 1833, into a wealthy slaveholding family in Kentucky, and he himself was an enslaver. Although he had fought for the Union in the Civil War, he opposed the Emancipation Proclamation. He was appointed to the US Supreme Court in 1877. What set him apart, I believe, is that he saw the humanity in black Americans because he reportedly had a black half brother.[155]

In 1824 in Kentucky, an enslaved woman and her eight-year-old son showed up on the doorstep of James and Eliza Harlan, John's parents. The boy's name was Robert, and he was born enslaved in Mecklenburg County, Virginia. His determined mother had taken "her precocious son on a journey across hundreds of miles of wilderness. She wanted her talented boy to meet his father, believing that a reunion would lead to better opportunities."[156] Stories differ on whether James Harlan was actually Robert's father or, for unknown reasons, stepped in to raise the boy. The former was a possibility because James Harlan's extended family owned plantations near Mecklenburg County. It was therefore conceivable that he was Robert's father. In any event, James took a keen personal interest in Robert and purchased him, but not his mother, who was sold down south.[157]

When John Marshall Harlan was born in 1833, Robert would have been seventeen. Robert developed into "a strapping young man with a golden smile" and "confidently sallied forth into the world around Harlan's Station." Even though Robert was technically enslaved, James had a soft spot for him and "gave him a position of trust within the family."[158] John likely grew up hearing stories about or witnessing the challenges his half brother faced. For instance, when James enrolled Robert in school, he was later sent home because the school discovered he was part black.[159] Thereafter Robert was educated by the older Harlan sons.[160]

Consequently, Robert had to lead a different life from his stepbrothers, who were all groomed to study law. Although he was extremely intelligent, he had to pursue different activities on account of his race, like training and racing horses.[161] In his midteens, he began collecting cash by "gunning and selling coonskins." He became a barber because it was one of the few acceptable occupations for a black man.[162] While doing all that, he also had to steer clear of slave catchers. "His light skin and literacy provided a bugger of sorts—he didn't look or act like a runaway—but he risked trouble every time he left Harlan's Station."[163]

John Harlan saw his half brother "as a man of action, intrepid where his other brothers were bookish, unafraid of the sometimes violent world outside Harlan's Station, and eager to participate in the rough-hewn rituals of frontier life."[164] By the age of twenty-four, Robert had been racing his own horses for five years, and his business as a barber provided him with regular income. Eventually he opened a grocery store, got married, and had children.[165]

However, as with many other prosperous black people, Robert Harlan's mixed-race family was constantly at risk of being attacked by local gangs of white vigilantes who targeted black businessmen and white abolitionists. In the summer of 1848, when news of the gold discovered in California reached Kentucky, Robert decided to take his chances out west. Brimming with self-confidence, he believed he could make a success of it, but he could not "risk a long journey without proof of his freedom." Despite his special privileges, he had lived his thirty-two years to date as an enslaved man. In September 1848, Robert asked James if he could purchase his freedom. James obliged and petitioned for a deed of emancipation, and Robert was thereafter declared free. In exchange, Robert signed a $500 promissory note that he planned to repay when he returned from California.[166]

In San Francisco, Robert connected with several other Kentuckians, and with the experience he had gained from running a grocery, he opened a new establishment to cater to the thousands of miners who came looking for gold. By the time he returned to Kentucky, he'd amassed "a fortune that was the envy of most of his contemporaries; news reports counted his wealth at between $45,000 and $90,000—or between $1.4 million and $2.8 million in 2021 dollars." He had more than enough money to pay back the promissory note he had pledged to James.[167]

Robert Harlan overcame slavery, occupational segregation, and white vigilantes in order to build wealth for his family. But we can't ignore that his success was partially due to the fact that a white enslaver took him into his home, saw to it that he was educated, treated him with dignity and respect, and allowed him personal agency. The Supreme Court justice John Marshall Harlan observed his stepbrother's travails up close and personal. We can see the effect Robert might have had on Justice Harlan when we read his dissents.

When we are thinking about the plight of black Americans, we can celebrate Robert Harlan's success, but it is not to be used as a model, because it was not of his own making. He succeeded in a system that thought of him as property because of a powerful white man, a tenacious mother, and sheer luck. Robert didn't need the Thirteenth Amendment because he could rely on his white benefactor. The overwhelming majority of black Americans did not have that kind of family connection. They needed the protection of the law and the Thirteenth Amendment, especially the part that empowers Congress to pass legislation enabling a pathway to success for all black Americans. Justice Harlan likely understood that too: that most black people, unlike his exceptional stepbrother, needed the protection of the Thirteenth and Fourteenth amendments in the face of hostile innkeepers, train conductors, and white vigilantes.

Hodges v. United States was another important case that came before the Supreme Court at the turn of the twentieth century.[168]

The claimants were eight black men who had been working in a sawmill in Arkansas when a group of at least a dozen armed white men threatened them with physical violence if they did not quit their jobs. Ruling on the case in 1906, the Court established that the Thirteenth Amendment applied only to slavery and involuntary servitude. Although the men were unable to work and were threatened with physical harm, that was not the same thing as being enslaved. In the Court's words, "A freeman has a right to be protected in his person from an assault and battery. He is entitled to hold his property safe from trespass or appropriation; but no mere personal assault or trespass or appropriation operates to reduce the individual to a condition of slavery."[169]

Once again Justice Harlan dissented from the majority opinion.[170] He would have ruled in favor of the black workers because the Thirteenth Amendment was designed to end not just slavery itself but all "incidents or badges" of slavery. The eight workers, in his view, were victims of a conspiracy of white men who wanted to rob them of their right to work, which was a clear badge of slavery. Inhibiting these black workers from making valid contracts for services solely because of their race, he recognized, was an incident of slavery that "the 13th Amendment destroyed." The threat of violence, like those faced by the men in the Arkansas sawmill, had been omnipresent since slavery ended.

It would take almost six decades for another Supreme Court to pick up where Justice Harlan's dissent left off. In the 1954 landmark case *Brown v. Board of Education*, the civil rights attorney Thurgood Marshall, who was also director-counsel of the NAACP Legal Defense Fund (LDF), argued that *Plessy v. Ferguson*'s doctrine of "separate but equal" was inherently prejudicial under the equal protection clause of the Fourteenth Amendment. In the LDF brief, Marshall not only cited Justice Harlan's dissent in *Plessy* but was inspired by it. Marshall had reportedly read passages from Harlan's dissent to his staff as they brainstormed ways to legally attack segregation.[171] And for once, a majority of the Supreme Court agreed. As a result, all legislation mandating racial segregation in education was finally overturned. But only in education.

Not in other areas, however. That would take a little longer. The Court did not declare that antiblack discrimination was subject to a heightened level of scrutiny but focused instead on the harm that racial segregation caused in black schoolchildren by "causing powerful feelings of 'inferiority as to their status in the community.'"[172] As a result, it would take until 1955 for segregation in municipal golf courses,[173] 1956 for intrastate buses,[174] and 1958 for public parks and golf courses to be declared unconstitutional.[175]

In this phase of shape-shifting, antiblack discrimination could no longer hide in plain sight with WHITES ONLY signs. It would have to become subtler and more duplicitous. That's how you got racially restrictive covenants folded into real estate contracts until 1968, when Congress passed the Fair Housing Act, making it illegal. In the meantime, private white homeowners could prevent sales to prospective black homebuyers through privately enforced covenants. The Supreme Court made that clear in 1948, through its decision in *Shelly v. Kraemer*, when it ruled that while courts could not enforce racially restrictive covenants, private parties certainly could. Lenders could discriminate against black borrowers until Congress passed the Equal Credit Opportunity Act of 1974. But even after 1974, the federal government through the US Department of Agriculture (USDA) continued to discriminate against black farmers when it came to access to credit. Since the 1950s, about 15 million acres of black land has been lost, most commonly by being "seized by the US Department of Agriculture to settle debts accrued by black farmers as a result of the department's racist lending practices."[176] Ninety percent of black-owned farmland was simply repossessed by the government. (Nineteen-ten was the high-water mark for black ownership of land in this country.)[177] When the US Commission on Civil Rights convened in 1965, 1968, and 1970, it found that the USDA had discriminated against black farmers in providing loans and other payments. Nothing was done to reverse these harmful policies, however. Meanwhile the population of black farmers fell from 6 percent in 1964 to 2 percent in 1982.

In 1990 a congressional committee once again found the USDA at fault for discrimination against black farmers. Just five years later the Government Accountability Office published a report charging the USDA with failing to address discrimination against black farmers. A group of black farmers filed suit but ultimately settled out of court for an undisclosed amount. But the black farmers were not paid nearly enough, and the settlement excluded all losses that occurred before 1982, which were significant.

Black farmers also faced discrimination from banks in their lending decisions.[178] Most banks were happy to lend money to white farmers, but they did not extend the same generosity to black farmers. Therefore white farmers received bank loans on favorable terms, while black farmers did not, and this was perfectly legal until 1974.

That brings us to yet another way that black farmers continue to lose their land, which for once is not because of the USDA but due to developers who use sketchy legal rules to force the sale of black farmland in desirable locations. What's more, when a black farmer dies without a will, the law allows for something called "partition sales," which enables a third party to buy one heir's interest and force a sale of the entire property. This generally results in a nonblack developer taking over the property for other purposes.[179]

Mass Incarceration and Criminalizing Blackness

While most of the discrimination against black Americans that we have read about in this chapter would seem to constitute crimes, it was usually not considered in that light. Even instances that were overt crimes were never prosecuted. The law's judgment of who is a criminal has always had a thumb on the scale for blackness. And while "widespread convict leasing" may have ended during World War II,[180] criminalizing black people did not. Instead of vagrancy statutes, it was reincarnated in "tough on crime" drug laws.

In 1971 President Richard Nixon launched his infamous War on Drugs, which unleashed the next wave of mass incarceration. Nixon's close aide John Ehrlichman reportedly admitted the campaign was racially motivated: "We had two enemies: the antiwar left and black people. . . . We knew we couldn't make it illegal to be either against the war or black, but by getting the public to associate the hippies with marijuana and blacks with heroin, and then criminalizing both heavily, we could disrupt those communities. We could arrest their leaders, raid their homes, break up their meetings, and vilify them night after night on the evening news. Did we know we were lying about the drugs? Of course we did."[181]

Under Ronald Reagan, the War on Drugs went into overdrive.

In the 1980s, Congress passed several laws under the guise of fighting this so-called war. First, the 1984 Comprehensive Crime Control and Safe Streets Act eliminated parole in the federal system. Two years later the 1986 Anti-Drug Abuse Act established mandatory minimum sentencing for drug offenses, including the hundred-to-one ratio between crack and powder cocaine sentences. In other words, the amount of crack cocaine required to trigger the minimum sentencing guidelines was one hundred times less than the amount of powder cocaine required for a minimum sentence. A report from the Sentencing Project, a nonprofit dedicated to criminal justice reform, provides a very clear illustration of the impact of the 100-to-1 disparity:

> A dealer charged with trafficking 400 grams of powder, worth approximately $40,000, could receive a shorter sentence than a user he supplied with crack valued at $500. Crack is also the only drug that carries a mandatory prison sentence for first offense possession. A person convicted in federal court of possession of 5 grams of crack automatically receives a 5 year prison term. A person convicted of possessing 5 grams of powder cocaine will probably receive a probation sentence. The *maximum* sentence for simple possession of any other drug, including powder cocaine, is 1 year in jail.[182]

If you set out intentionally to design racially discriminatory laws, you could not do much better. From 1986 to 1990, a congressional report showed that "both the rate and the average length of imprisonment for federal offenders increased for Blacks in comparison to Whites." What's more, it concluded, the increase was largely due to the mandatory minimums applied to crack versus powder cocaine cases.[183] According to the US Sentencing Commission, black Americans "accounted for 88.3 percent of federal crack cocaine distribution convictions in 1993, and [w]hites 4.1 percent."[184] Does that statistic mean black Americans were more likely to deal drugs than white Americans? Or were they just more likely to get caught while dealing drugs?

A *Los Angeles Times* investigative report revealed that between 1988 and 1994, "not a single white . . . has been convicted of a crack cocaine offense in federal courts serving Los Angeles and six Southland counties since Congress enacted stiff mandatory sentences for crack dealers in 1986." Instead, white crack offenders were prosecuted by California's state court, where they often received significantly shorter sentences—up to eight years less for the same crime.[185]

According to surveys conducted by the National Institute on Drug Abuse, white Americans were "more likely than any other racial group to use crack." Yet "the U.S. Sentencing Commission reports that about 96% of the crack defendants in federal court are nonwhite. And, records show, the majority are low-level dealers, lookouts and couriers rather than drug kingpins."[186]

In addition, the *Los Angeles Times* discovered that the federal government had failed to prosecute any white crack offenses across seventeen states and in many cities, such as Chicago, Boston, Denver, Dallas, Miami, and Los Angeles. "Out of hundreds of cases," the newspaper reported, "only one white was convicted in California, two in Texas, three in New York and two in Pennsylvania."[187]

When a former white crack dealer, who also happened to be

the daughter of an oil company executive, spoke to the newspaper reporter, she told them how she blew through a $200,000 trust fund in half a year to pay for her drug use. Later, she became a dealer with "an elite clientele on the Westside." "You wouldn't believe the customers I had," the woman said. "Doctors, lawyers, business executives . . . all of them were white. I'd cook up crack and take it to their homes. No one ever suspected we were base-heads."[188]

In spite of such stories, black Americans are more likely to be convicted when they use crack cocaine and to receive longer sentences than white Americans. It turns out, the same President Reagan who apologized and approved redress payments for the imprisonment of Japanese Americans during World War II saw no contradiction in enforcing discriminatory laws that imprisoned drug users for longer sentences when they were using or dealing while black.

In 1996 the War on Drugs targeting black Americans got an assist from the Supreme Court when it declared open season on black drivers in *Whren v. United States*.[189] The Court declared that the police could pull over any motorist anytime they violated the rules of the road. Given the frequency with which *all* drivers do not follow traffic laws, that decision legalized the racial profiling of black motorists. The crime of driving while black was created by a unanimous Supreme Court opinion written by the late Justice Scalia. (The Supreme Court continues to write antiblack opinions.)

If a police officer could pull any driver over as a pretext to search the car, and if they assumed black drivers were more likely to have drugs in their cars, then predictably, more black drivers would be subject to traffic stops. Subsequent research showed that black motorists are more likely to be pulled over than white motorists even though white drivers were more likely to have drugs than black drivers.[190]

Black people are arrested, convicted, and sent to prison more not because they are prone to criminal activity but because the law *criminalizes* black behavior more than it does the behavior of their white peers. In 2010 President Barack Obama signed into law a bipartisan bill to reduce the disparity from 100-to-1 to 18-to-1.[191] The Fair Sentencing Act increased the amount of crack cocaine required for mandatory minimums for drug trafficking and eliminated the mandatory minimum sentence for first-time possession. That meant black Americans holding small amounts of crack cocaine would no longer be subject to such long sentences as they previously were.

It also doesn't help that the media emphasize race more when reporting on black perpetrators than on white ones.[192] Recall Ehrlichman's goal to "vilify [Black people] night after night on the evening news." Police routinely target inner-city neighborhoods but ignore places where white Americans do drugs, like Los Angeles's affluent Westside and the fraternity rows at prestigious universities across the country. Mass incarceration in America is a function of who is *seen* as a criminal—not a function of crime.

When it comes to black Americans, criminals are made—not born—and nowhere is that more accurate than in the school-to-prison pipeline. Criminalizing black children did not begin with the twenty-first century but has a long and storied past.[193] However, the goal is the same today as it was yesterday: arresting black youth.

Schools staffed with police—euphemistically referred to as "school resource officers"—make "three and a half times more arrests than in schools without police," according to Kristin

Henning, my Georgetown colleague, Blume Professor of Law, director of the Juvenile Justice Clinic and Initiative, and author of *The Rage of Innocence: How America Criminalizes Black Youth.* Since 2016, lawmakers in twenty-two states and numerous cities have enacted laws "making it a crime to disturb or disrupt the school."[194] But what actually qualifies as a "school disturbance" is up to the discretion (and biases) of teachers and administrators. Until it was repealed in 2018, a South Carolina law allowed students to be arrested for "disturbing the school if they . . . acted in an obnoxious manner."[195] What teenager can go a day without violating that law?

In the 2015–16 school year, black students "were almost four times more likely than White youth to be deemed criminally responsible for disturbing schools." In McKinney, Texas, where black students were merely 13 percent of the school population, they somehow constituted "43 percent of the disruption of class offenses charged." In Florida, black girls constituted 22 percent of the total state female population, yet "they accounted for 74 percent of female students arrested for disorderly conduct."[196]

Henning writes, "There is something particularly efficient about treating Black children like criminals in adolescence. Black youth are dehumanized, exploited, and even killed to establish the boundaries of Whiteness before they reach adulthood and assert their rights and independence."[197] Once again laws vaguely worded with phrases like "disruption of class," "willful defiance," and "disorderly conduct" are inherently discriminatory and designed so that "just about any black [can] be arrested." It was an efficient strategy during convict leasing, and it remains one today.

The costs these policies inflict on black families have not been fully accounted for. They include bail, being evicted from public housing due to the child's arrest and having to move, and fees for probation, supervision, evaluation, testing, expunging a record, and electronic monitoring devices, just to name a few.[198] Henning adds, "When families fail to pay the fines or fees, the state can send collection agencies after them, tack on interest, garnish their wages, seize their bank accounts, intercept their tax refunds, suspend their driver's licenses, or charge them with contempt of court."[199]

Today almost 60 percent of prisoners are white, according to the Federal Bureau of Prisons.[200] Yet a report from the Brennan Center for Justice states that after their release, "white people who have a prison record see their earnings trend upwards, while formerly imprisoned Black . . . people experience a relatively flat earnings trajectory."[201] A white job applicant with a criminal record is more likely to receive a job callback than a black applicant with no criminal history.[202] Black Americans with no criminal record earn less than their white peers with a record.[203] Mass incarceration impacts not just those who are incarcerated but also the people they have left behind. The Prison Policy Initiative estimates the annual cost of mass incarceration borne by family members is almost $3 billion, a disproportionate amount of which impacts black Americans.

In the same way that wartime incarceration caused Japanese Americans to lose their livelihoods and property, mass incarceration has also taken money from black families, making it harder to build generational wealth. An emotional toll, too, comes with imprisonment, the loss of dignity, and the badge of inferiority that "criminals" are forced to wear. And while compensation has been paid for the mass incarceration of other groups, like Japanese Americans, it has never been paid for black Americans and their affected loved ones.

The Presence of Post-Slavery Discrimination in the Twenty-First Century

If you are thinking that we need to get over all this history, as terrible as it was, because things are so much better now—think again. Yes, things are better now; however, many of us are still lugging around baggage forced on us by the systems of oppression instituted after slavery was abolished. Ending slavery did not end its legacy. It simply transformed slavery into different methods of oppressing black Americans. And the repercussions of this system fueled by white supremacy have continued to bleed into the present and to negatively affect black Americans and others. (The Italians lynched in Louisiana were also victims of white supremacy along with the white landowners in Bruce's Beach who also lost their property through eminent domain.)

To start with, our history of lynching black Americans has had economic consequences that still reverberate today. Lynchings led to a decline in black politicians and policymakers, which in turn led to greater economic insecurity for black Americans. All that came "at a cost to the broader society and includes starkly higher levels of modern-day poverty and unemployment in the population."[204] Looking at the data, we can start to understand why black Americans in the twenty-first century have higher poverty rates.

Even more startling, research shows that states with historically higher levels of black lynching have higher levels of poverty today, for both black *and* white Americans.[205] Nationwide, almost 21 percent of black Americans live in poverty compared with just over 9 percent of white Americans.[206] Yet the numbers are significantly greater across both groups in Southern states with the highest rates of lynching.[207]

STATES WITH THE MOST BLACK LYNCHINGS, 1877–1950[208]

Black Lynchings, 1877–1950	Mississippi	Georgia	Louisiana	Arkansas	Alabama	Texas	Florida	Tennessee
	654	589	549	492	361	335	311	233

[Table 6]

POVERTY RATES OF STATES WITH THE MOST BLACK LYNCHINGS

Poverty Rates of	Total Across US	Mississippi	Georgia	Louisiana	Arkansas	Alabama	Texas	Florida	Tennessee
White, Non-Hispanic Americans	9.4%	11.5%	9.5%	13.2%	12.8%	10.9%	8.3%	9.3%	11.5%
Black Americans	20.8%	27.5%	18.9%	29.1%	28.2%	26.0%	18.3%	18.0%	22.6%

[Table 7]

Higher levels of poverty result from lower levels of investment in aid programs that benefit the poor because aid programs disproportionately benefit black Americans. For example, when those high-poverty states receive block grants from the federal government for welfare funding, their governments are more likely to allocate the grant money to noncash benefits, rather than to cash that would go directly into the pockets of those most in need. Noncash benefits are a kind of loophole and can include

things like programs on "fatherhood or two parent family forma-
tion" that pay people, sometimes as much as six-figure salaries,
to give motivational speeches in schools about being a good student, behaving "right," and making good decisions.[209] Policy
choices like these result in increased poverty rates for black
Americans, but they also lead to higher poverty rates for white
people. Refusing to invest in anti-poverty programs hurts black
and nonblack citizens alike.

In the same way, stories of racial violence spanning 150 years
of American history reveal that many black Americans have
been prevented from building generational wealth, and they
shed light on our current racial wealth gap. According to the
Federal Reserve of St. Louis, for every dollar of wealth that white
families possessed in 2022, black families held only twenty-five
cents.[210] What's more, the fact that black Americans had to aban-
don homes they owned for fear of losing their lives provides context for the black-white homeownership gap. It also helps explain
the dearth of black-owned businesses.

The terror of racial violence hasn't disappeared; it continues
into the twenty-first century. One form it takes is the upholding
of citizen's arrest laws, which allow white Americans to make "arrests" of black men, who eventually wind up dead or lynched. A
recent example is the murder of Ahmaud Arbery in Georgia. On
February 23, 2020, Arbery was doing what he loved to do: He
went out for a jog. The twenty-five-year-old former high school
football player liked to stay in shape. Without thinking much
about it, he went for a run through Satilla Shores, a predominantly white community. As one black resident put it, "They're
not used to seeing a lot of black faces around here."[211]

Arbery lived in the nearby black community of Fancy Bluff.
While he was on his jog, two white men, Gregory and Travis

McMichael, a father and son team, spotted Arbery and assumed he must be a burglar, despite having no evidence. They grabbed two guns and hopped into their pickup truck to chase after Arbery. An altercation ensued. The McMichaels attempted to cut Arbery off with their car, then accosted him with their guns brandished. Arbery, who was unarmed, naturally fought back against his attackers. He was shot three times with a twelve-gauge shotgun and was killed.

When police arrived at the scene, Gregory McMichael, a former Glynn County police officer and investigator for the local district attorney's office, and his son Travis were allowed to go free. They claimed they had attempted to make a citizen's arrest and that their actions were justified based on an 1863 law still in effect. As was typically the case, the white perpetrators were initially exonerated. However, a third white man, William Bryan, a neighbor, had filmed their encounter with Arbery. Bryan joined in the chase against Ahmaud Arbery by jumping in his truck and following the McMichaels. The videotape of the murder was leaked, and within two days following the public outcry, the McMichaels and Bryan were arrested.

In a rare instance of justice obtained, the McMichaels were convicted of murder and aggravated assault by a jury of eleven white Americans and one black American and sentenced to life in prison. Bryan was also convicted and sentenced to thirty-five years. All three men were subsequently found guilty of hate crime charges in federal court.

The lynching of Ahmaud Arbery is a horrible reminder that our past is still with us. Even the simple act of going for a run can cost you your life when you are black in America. In truth, we never closed the book on that chapter of our history. While Ahmaud Arbery's family may have found some peace with the conviction of his murderers, countless other black families like the Mosses, who fled Tennessee because Tommie Moss was lynched; the Brinsons, who fled Missouri because of racial violence and were forced to sell their home for a fraction of the value; the Hilsons, who fell prey to whitecapping in Mississippi; the Walkers, who were murdered in Kentucky and lost their farm; the Crawfords, who lost their farm in South Carolina after Anthony was lynched; and the Stephens brothers, who fled Mississippi and eventually lost their home, are still waiting to see justice served.

Yesterday's racially restrictive covenants and FHA discrimination resulted in today's residentially segregated neighborhoods. Being born into neighborhoods that were previously redlined by the federal government decreases a black child's future *annual* earnings by $15,000.[212] In addition, today's home values are based on the percentage of black homeowners in the neighborhood.[213] The smaller the percentage, with zero being the optimal number, the higher the home value. The high property values associated with white neighborhoods benefit their white residents today with additional net worth, equity that has been denied to black Americans.

Our government's history of denying FHA-insured mortgages to black homeowners has led banks to target prospective black homeowners with high-interest subprime mortgages today. Keeanga-Yamahtta Taylor, the Leon Forrest Professor of African American Studies at Northwestern University, calls this "predatory inclusion."[214] Because black Americans have been denied access to the housing market on the favorable terms that white Americans received, their inclusion has come at a cost. When they do get access, it is on unfavorable, high-risk terms that have the power to strip them of all the wealth they have built up.

We have never seen a day when a majority of black Americans are homeowners, whereas a majority of white Americans have been homeowners since 1950, because of government subsidies. And homeownership remains out of reach for over a quarter of white Americans.

The Homestead Act, described as "the most comprehensive form of wealth redistribution that has ever taken place in America," has had a long afterlife.[215] One estimate has it that 25 percent of the current adult population, or 46 million people, are the living legacy of ancestors who owned property because of the virtually whites-only Homestead Act of 1862.[216] As noted by historian Kari Leigh Merritt, "these beneficiaries, of course, were overwhelmingly white." Merritt continues by noting that because black Americans were "largely denied these wealth entitlements, blacks were essentially left landless after years (and generations) of unpaid, coerced, and brutalized labor."[217]

In *Repair: Redeeming the Promise of Abolition,* Katherine Franke, formerly the James L. Dohr Professor of Law at Columbia University, describes how an "estimated $59 trillion . . . will be transferred from 93.6 million American estates from 2007 to 2061, in the greatest wealth transfer in US history."[218] Surely some of that wealth is slavery-tainted.

While black land loss can be partially explained by lynching, it was also the result of plain old antiblack discrimination by the federal government, which denied black farmers access to the Homestead Act. Meanwhile the USDA failed to provide access to credit for black farmers on the same terms as their white peers, leading to the staggering statistic that black people make up less than 2 percent of all farmers. But it gets worse. Governmental discrimination against black farmers is not behind us. In

2021 the Government Accountability Office found that black and minority farmers have less access to credit than do white farmers.

Stephanie Hagans should be a wealthy woman today. Her great-grandmother, Ablow Weddington Stewart, owned thirty-five acres of land in Matthews, North Carolina, a suburb of Charlotte. Black people like Stewart found a way to acquire land through their own tireless efforts and ingenuity. Unfortunately for Stephanie, her great-grandmother lost her property more than eighty years ago. In 1942 a white lawyer refused to accept payment from Stewart for a $540 debt and proceeded to foreclose on her property. The lawyer's actions meant that generational wealth would forever be foreclosed to Stewart's heirs. Decades later Stephanie asked the question anyone would ask in her shoes: "How different would our lives be, if we'd had the opportunities, the pride that land brings?"[219]

But Ablow Stewart's story is anything but unique. It is representative of black land loss and the unfulfilled dreams that linger because of it. A conservative estimate of the decline in black-owned farmland over the better part of the twentieth century calculates the loss at $326 billion.[220]

The legacy of sundown towns is still with us. Remember Glendale, California? Today fewer than 2 percent of the city's residents are black. Likewise, other sundown towns continue to look as they did in the past. Maine's black population is 2 percent, North Dakota has less than 4 percent, and Nebraska has just under 5 percent. Research shows that counties adjacent to counties that were once sundown towns tend to have a higher-than-average disparity between black and white poverty rates, resulting in higher black poverty rates and lower white poverty rates. Black poverty is understandably higher because being surrounded by a cluster of sundown towns limited black mobility and led to fewer economic opportunities for black people in the area. As the sociologist Heather McConnell has stated, "This large-scale segregation within and across counties could directly benefit whites through the protection or hoarding of resources." The financial winners were the privileged white Americans (and later their descendants) who lived in these towns and benefited from the decreased competition for jobs and homes.[221] The financial losers were the black Americans who were not allowed to live there.[222]

Eminent domain, which stripped property away from black Americans, did not end with the twentieth century. An analysis of 2000 census data revealed that "eminent domain project areas include a significantly greater percentage of minority residents (58%)."[223] In 2010 Columbia University used eminent domain to acquire property "in the predominantly black Manhattanville neighborhood."[224] Not-for-profit colleges and universities ensconced within black and brown communities are exempt from paying property taxes to fund the schools that neighborhood children attend.[225] Underresourced schools make it virtually impossible for graduates to be able to attend those colleges and universities.

According to the Brookings Institution, black Americans comprise 14 percent of the US population today, yet black businesses account for only 2.2 percent of all US businesses with more than one employee. A White House Council of Economic Advisers analysis suggests that "differences in business ownership account for 20 percent of the wealth gap" between white and black households.[226] The limited number of black-owned businesses traces its roots directly to the aftermath of slavery, when lynching and other forms of racial violence were carried out with the intention of preventing black Americans from building wealth, securing economic stability, and attaining a middle-class status. Tommie Moss was able to build a successful business even though he was born enslaved, but his white competitor, jealous and addicted to white supremacy, stopped at nothing—even murder—to take his business away.

Most black Americans have not received any measure of justice. They never received the land they were promised at the end of the Civil War, for one thing. Instead, they were systematically denied the right to acquire property, thwarted in their attempts to purchase property, and stripped of the property they held legal title to. The story of wealth in America is a story of black wealth being converted into white wealth. That conversion often occurred invisibly, which makes it easier today for white beneficiaries to claim ignorance. Black people were prevented from purchasing homes in sundown towns, so that white people could build wealth there. Black homeowners' land was taken away through eminent domain. Black farmers struggled to work with a discriminatory USDA to operate their farms, only to have future generations lose everything when their property got purchased by developers because they died without a will. All this has led to an intergenerational black deficit.

The legacy of slavery is that it continued to generate wealth for people like Margaret Barber and her descendants through the investment of her Compensated Emancipation Act payment, just as it resulted in the wage theft, loss of freedom, and generations of trauma inflicted upon enslaved Africans and their heirs. In 1983 the historical economist Dr. James Marketti estimated that enslaved black workers produced anywhere from $7 billion to $40 billion in income for their enslavers.[227] That number is somewhere between $20 billion and $114 billion today. Even if we were to settle on $40 billion, that is still a conservative estimate. Once you add interest to that sum, the monetary value increases dramatically to between $13 trillion and $36 trillion.[228]

Slavery didn't just drain enslaved people of the fruits of their labor. It also resulted in the loss of their bodily autonomy and freedom. They had no decision-making power over their own lives or how they spent their time. Loss of freedom is a difficult concept to measure, but experts estimate that the value of the hours lost to slavery is cumulatively between $35 trillion and $16 quadrillion.[229]

Enslavers in the South like Margaret were not the only people to benefit from slavery—far from it. The institution contributed an estimated $50 billion to $55 trillion annually to the national economy. Take cotton for example. Cotton picked in the South was processed by factories in the North. Once processed, cotton was sold to consumers across the developing world. In 1831 the United States supplied nearly half the world's raw cotton crop. "Southern white elites grew rich," Matthew Desmond explains, "as did their counterparts in the North, who erected textile mills to form an 'unhallowed alliance between the lords of the lash and the lords of the loom.'"[230]

Slavery's tentacles reached far beyond the plantation to financial institutions across the country. Southern banks that financed the business of slavery made loans using black people as collateral. They raised capital by issuing debt backed by mortgages on enslaved workers. Bondholders included foreigners from abroad as well as Americans in cities like Boston and Philadelphia.[231] When the price of cotton plummeted because of overplanting, among other things, investors and creditors called in their debts. That meant enslaved workers were taken and sold by courts.

In the North, there was J. P. Morgan & Co., which made loans secured by enslaved black bodies, and New York Life Insurance, which made money from insurance policies purchased by enslavers. Railroad lines, including Canadian National, CSX, Norfolk Southern, and Union Pacific were also built on the backs of enslaved laborers.[232] Whatever their stated ideological beliefs, North and South, plantation owners, banks, and the judicial system were all involved in ensuring that slavery continued.

Institutions of higher learning were implicated, too. As the historian Craig Steven Wilder, Barton L. Weller Professor of History at MIT, points out in *Ebony & Ivy: Race, Slavery, and the Troubled History of America's Universities,* Harvard, Dartmouth, and Yale, among others, were "major beneficiaries of the African slave trade and slavery."[233] Many campuses, in fact, were built by enslaved labor or founded with wealth generated by slavery. What's worse is that some of the most prestigious universities in the United States employed white supremacists, who taught the virtues of slavery, "portraying Africans and Native peoples as 'savage' and subhumans who were 'inferior to whites.'"[234]

Take my current employer, Georgetown University, for example. It sold 272 enslaved persons in order to remain financially viable and become the institution it is today. And it paid no reparations to the descendants of the 272 enslaved people.[235] Today Georgetown University provides an admissions preference for the descendants, but it offers no scholarships for them,[236] a relatively straightforward and easy thing to do. A student referendum in 2019 supported a tuition increase that would benefit the descendants of the 272, whom the Jesuit university had sold "to secure its financial future."[237] In response, Georgetown created a Reconciliation Fund that awards $400,000 annually to community-based projects.[238] My former employer, Emory University, publicly announced the creation of a Descendants Endowment to "award scholarships for descendants of enslaved persons with ties to Emory." It represented that two full scholarships would be awarded to support undergraduate students annually, beginning in the fall of 2022.[239] However, Emory has not publicly acknowledged that any such scholarships have *actually* been awarded.[240]

No American alive today can outrun slavery's taint. Remember that proposed development in Chevy Chase, Maryland? It currently houses "an office building, the Chevy Chase Center shopping strip and Saks Fifth Avenue," where I have on occasion shopped.[241]

Margaret Barber's wealth, which included her Compensated Emancipation Act payment, was passed down from generation to generation. And yet those she enslaved never received any financial compensation that they could invest and leave for their descendants. Slavery in America is never just about the past; it inevitably seeps into our present and our future.

The past is never dead. It's not even past.

The fact that enslaved people built the White House is widely known, but something that is less commonly known is that our first black vice president lived on land that was once tilled by the hands of enslaved workers.

In 1878 Congress established a commission to find a new site for the US Naval Observatory and invited District of Columbia landowners to submit proposals. Seventy-eight proposals came in, including one from the financially shrewd Margaret Barber. Northview's ample acreage and secluded locale made it an ideal site, and the commission settled on purchasing it from Margaret on April 25, 1881, for the price of $63,000 (a little over $1.8 million today). The Barbers' elaborate mansion was torn down and the house at One Observatory Circle was erected to house the superintendent of the Observatory. The home would later become the official residence of the vice president, when Gerald and Betty Ford briefly lived there in 1974 before moving into the White House when Ford became president. Every vice president since Walter Mondale has lived in the Naval Observatory and is a direct beneficiary of enslaved labor. This important piece of history has been hiding in plain sight. How is that possible? Who tells the story, it turns out, matters a great deal.

When Anita Ravenscroft Henry von Selzam, great-granddaughter of Margaret Barber, penned her memoirs, she wrote fondly of her great-grandmother. "The days of my great-grandmother must have been fabulous," she speculated. "Her country house was what is now the Naval Observatory. She was forced by the government to sell 'North View' as it was called, as they needed it. They tore it down of course." Anita recalled how the grand house had been defiled: "During the Civil War the portraits were slashed and the mirrors stolen. By great luck after General Grant died of drink, we got some of the mirrors back. Unfortunately, these were lost in the Blitz in London."

Anita rewrote her family's history by ignoring the fact that her great-grandmother, Margaret Barber, was an enslaver. While *her* days might have been fabulous, you know who did not live a fabulous life? Her enslaved workers. Anita didn't even bother to mention them. Yet her grandmother's wealth was possible only because of unpaid enslaved labor. The crystal chandeliers, multiple ballrooms, and gilded mirrors were all paid for with profits earned from the system of slavery. Anita also misremembered her great-grandmother being forced to sell the property; in reality, Margaret was the one who proposed the sale of her land to the federal government, from which she benefited immensely (although her son thought she sold it for too little).

I am reminded of something President Joe Biden once said: "Great nations don't ignore their most painful moments. They embrace them."[242] The day was June 17, 2021, and President Biden was in an exuberant mood as he presided over the signing ceremony for the bill that made June 19—better known as Juneteenth—a federal holiday. The president explained that a Union Army general, Major General Gordon Granger, had to march down to Galveston, Texas, in order to "enforce the Emancipation Proclamation" and free Texans "from bondage." Although Biden was only a few months into his term, he predicted that the bill would "go down, for me, as one of the greatest honors I will have had as President."

We have made tremendous progress in this country. It is nothing short of awe-inspiring to witness a nation that once enslaved black Americans transform itself, in less than two centuries of freedom, into a country where it is possible to elect our first black president, who lived in a house built by enslaved hands, and then our first black woman vice president, who lived on land once tended by enslaved hands. This is an achievement to be acknowledged and celebrated.

At the same time, this history has been too easily forgotten, and its erasure is symbolic of our failure to talk about our painful past, whether out of shame or ignorance. The result is that we cannot fully come to grips with its wider impact in the present moment. The remnants of slavery and white supremacy remain with us today, as does Margaret Barber's legacy. Our failure to hold ourselves accountable for it has not lessened the severity of the impact. A debt is owed to black Americans. When will it be repaid?

While other groups have been compensated for similar harms, no other group has experienced all the harms that black people have. This is the story of the persecution and oppression of an entire race of people. No one was allowed to escape from their blackness. It is also a story of how discrimination against black people became systemic, targeted all black Americans, and became entrenched in how we build wealth in this country. The quest for the American Dream therefore has never taken place on a level playing field, but rather on one where the dream of financial and economic security was elusive for most black Americans. This is a collective problem that requires a collective solution to dismantle those unjust systems.

Post-slavery, black people had to fight for their financial lives, in every institution, in every part of the country, all . . . at . . . once. I think of their daily struggle for freedom as an extraordinarily brave act of drinking water from a firehose each and every day. On the merits, the case for reparations for black people is very strong. But it will not happen without *a lot* of hard and painful work.

As the Supreme Court justice William O. Douglas once wrote: "The true curse of slavery is not what it did to the black man, but what it has done to the white man. For the existence of the institution produced the notion that the white man was of superior character, intelligence, and morality."[243] In order to get to the other side of reparations, we must dismantle that notion. "Great nations don't ignore their most painful moments. They embrace them." Let's get to work.

PART III

RIGHTING WRONGS

We thought we was goin' to be
richer than the white folks.

—FELIX HAYWOOD, AGE 92, FORMERLY ENSLAVED[1]

On June 19, 1865, Union Army Major General Gordon Granger marched to Galveston, Texas, to issue General Order No. 3 and tell the people of the state of Texas that "all slaves are free." In addition, the formerly enslaved possessed "an absolute equality of personal rights and rights of property between former masters and slaves." One of those newly liberated men was a black Texan named Felix Haywood.

Around 1937, a ninety-two-year-old Haywood was interviewed as part of a government public works project. He described the events of that day as miraculous: "Just like that we was free."[2] He recalled how optimistic he'd been, how he'd suddenly believed all things were possible. "We thought we was goin' to get rich like the white folks. We thought we was goin' to be richer than the white folks, 'cause we was stronger and knowed how to work, and the whites didn't and they didn't have us to work for them anymore. But it didn't turn out that way. We soon found out that freedom could make folks proud but it didn't make 'em rich."[3]

Felix Haywood had every reason to think that once freedom came, the future for black people in America could be limitless. He was right about the power of black labor but wrong about its trajectory. Black Americans knew how to work, but the system was built to generate white wealth, and it would continue to do that, just using different forms of black financial exploitation. History reveals our addiction to reaping the benefits of black labor while simultaneously preventing black wealth creation, which also meant destroying what little wealth black people did manage to cobble together. It is time that we broke free from the habit.

In order to get reparations in my lifetime, white Americans and everyone else who wants to be allies must do more than read a book. They must begin by acknowledging that they have received and continue to receive benefits from a system designed to subjugate black Americans. Every time a white person drives down the road and doesn't fear being pulled over by the police on suspicion of possessing drugs, every time they don't have to wait in line to vote, every time they buy a home or are shown a home they want to buy, every time they hail a taxicab that stops for them, every time they are interviewed for a job where the hiring manager looks like them and makes the interview process a little less stressful, and every time their children leave home and they do not worry that they might never see that child alive again because their race puts a target on their back—they have benefited from their whiteness, silently and invisibly, compounding over generations. And they must support compensating the black community with reparations.

Let me see if I can guess what you're thinking. By now, you might be convinced that reparations are the right thing to do. You think it's unfair that other groups have been compensated for similar losses, yet black Americans have never received anything. You understand that the end of chattel slavery did not end government-sanctioned antiblack discrimination. But you still have a lot of questions about the practicalities. And even if I convince you, what about everyone else? You're worried about the greatest obstacle of all: public opposition. What exactly is my plan for that?

I'll begin by describing the extent of the opposition and my plan to build public support. Next, I'll provide the practical steps needed to get reparations for black Americans, followed by my responses to the most frequently heard objections, along with my legal argument for how reparations could be declared constitutional. I will tell you why the reelection of President

Trump makes me optimistic that reparations can happen sooner rather than later. I will conclude by addressing a question that is rarely asked: What happens after we get reparations for black Americans?

I concede the extent of public opposition.

The first national poll about reparations was done by ABC News in 1997.[4] Why 1997? Perhaps because in June of that year, President Bill Clinton launched his national conversation on race at the University of California at San Diego.[5] The question polled was "Do you think the federal government should or should not pay money to Black Americans whose ancestors were slaves as compensation for that slavery?"[6] Only 19 percent supported reparations, with 77 percent opposed and 4 percent without an opinion. The racial breakdown was only 10 percent of white respondents supported reparations and 88 percent opposed. For black Americans 65/28 percent was the support/opposition breakdown.[7] Since 2001, polling shows that "a substantial majority of Americans oppose reparations, regardless of the modality, provider, or the recipient."[8] Whether compensation takes the form of direct cash payments or in-kind benefits, whether they are paid for by the federal government or by private corporations, or whether they are limited to descendants of those enslaved or not, the majority of those surveyed oppose reparations for black Americans.

Now for a deeper dive into a 2021 Pew Research Center survey on reparations for slavery.[9] Of those opposed to reparations, the highest percentage remain among white Americans.[10] That is ironic given that it is white Americans whose ancestors benefited the most from post-chattel slavery (not to mention chattel slavery), who got GI Bill benefits and FHA-insured mortgages, who lived in sundown towns and amassed great wealth doing so, who were not lynched and did not lose their property, and who did not have their property taken away through eminent domain.

AMERICANS BY RACE AND ETHNICITY
ARE FAR APART ON REPARATIONS [11]

	Support	Oppose
Black	77%	17%
Hispanic	39%	58%
Asian	33%	65%
White	18%	80%
All US adults	30%	68%

[Table 8]

AMERICANS OPPOSE REPARATIONS REGARDLESS OF AGE [12]

	Support	Oppose
18–29	45%	52%
30–49	34%	63%
50–64	24%	74%
65+	18%	81%

[Table 9]

AMERICANS OF BOTH PARTIES OPPOSE REPARATIONS [13]

	Support	Oppose
Democrats/Democrat leaning	48%	49%
Republicans/Republican leaning	8%	91%

[Table 10]

AMERICANS OF ALL EDUCATION LEVELS OPPOSE REPARATIONS [14]

	Support	Oppose
High school or less	25%	71%
Some college	30%	68%
Bachelor's +	34%	64%

[Table 11]

REGARDLESS OF INCOME, AMERICANS OPPOSE REPARATIONS[15]

	Support	Oppose
Lower income	42%	54%
Middle income	24%	74%
Upper income	27%	72%

[Table 12]

A majority of black Americans support reparations, whether they are Republican or Democrat; regardless of age, education, or income level; and no matter where they live in the country.[16] Everyone else, regardless of how you slice the data, has a majority of its members opposed.[17]

My plan to build public support for reparations developed organically, after I finished writing my book *The Whiteness of Wealth* in 2020.[18] In that book, I demonstrated how our federal income tax system takes money out of black taxpayers' pockets every April 15 while subsidizing most white taxpayers. I knew that my next book would be about reparations, because by then I understood the magnitude of the problem. I realized just how much the system in America is skewed toward white Americans building wealth while depleting black wealth and that several systems—including the tax system—needed transforming. The most direct solution that I could come up with was reparations. So I started working on this book.

Meanwhile the success of *The Whiteness of Wealth* in the tax world brought me to the attention of the faculty at my alma mater, Georgetown Law. In the spring of 2021, they offered me an opportunity to visit that fall and to be considered for a permanent full-time position. I agreed and decided over the summer that my "job talk" that fall would be my book project on reparations. (A job talk is a formal presentation to the faculty of an applicant's recent research and is a requirement of the interview process.) I wanted the Georgetown Law faculty to be aware that I would be tackling the very controversial topic of reparations in my next book. If their response was no thank you and they chose not to hire me, I would understand, and I would be fine—I already had a job.

You might be thinking, what was I worried about? Law faculties, particularly elite ones, are all left-leaning, and Georgetown is considered to be on the far-left end of that liberal continuum.[19] My decades-long experience as a black woman law professor, however, has taught me that left-leaning is in the eye of the beholder, and most law school faculties remain majority white and are not at all *progressive* when it comes to matters of race. I was curious and a bit nervous about how my job talk would be received.

I was pleasantly surprised. The faculty was extremely supportive of the project, but I still faced a lot of skepticism and quite frankly very good questions for which, at the time, I did not have adequate responses. Since this was the beginning of my research, the unanswered questions gave me no real cause for concern. But if this group, which was generally supportive of reparations, was so skeptical, I wondered, how was I ever going to convince a majority of Americans to endorse compensation for black Americans?

Then I remembered.

My then–Emory colleague, the psychologist Drew Westen, author of *The Political Brain*,[20] taught me years before that when it comes to talking about race with white people, there are ways to do it successfully and ways that doom you to failure. I needed to learn how to talk differently about reparations if I wanted to change the hearts and minds of others. My job talk made it clear that I would need help with my messaging.

The only thing standing in my way was money. How was I going to pay for it? Luckily, I had a research fund at Emory University, but it would not transfer over to Georgetown if I left. And since I am after all a tax lawyer who believes in leaving no money behind, my plan to build public support for reparations found its frame. I needed to find someone who could help me figure out which narratives would help change public opinion from opposition to support. This was a radical act of faith because I honestly believed that with help, I could create such messaging.

Most polling asks for answers, not explanations. Pollsters do not learn why a person answered the way they did. I was charting new waters—I wanted to find out which arguments would work to convert opponents on this controversial topic. So let me take you behind the curtain and show you the focus group messaging that worked and turned a frame into the building blocks for *Getting to Reparations*.

Immediately after my job talk, I reached out to Drew to ask him to connect me with someone who could help me figure out how to talk about reparations in a way that might work to build support, including and especially among white Americans. He referred me to Amy Simon of Goodwin Simon Strategic Research, an independent public opinion research firm. Along with her team, Sara Knight and James Telesford, Amy and I agreed to

work together to conduct a focus group on the topic of reparations for black Americans starting in the fall of 2021. The goal
was to explore the audience mindset around reparations and to
develop and test different messaging strategies for talking about
it to determine what kind of messages could increase support.

Amy later explained to me why she took on the project:
"Learning how to make a persuasive case for reparations is just
the kind of challenging messaging work that we value because it
is both important and emotionally complex. We have seen that
developing effective, persuasive messaging about racism as systemic or structural—which may be required to build support for
policies to address the resulting harms—is particularly challenging because so many people perceive racism to be only the individual bad (racist) actions of individual bad (racist) people. So
having the opportunity to dig into how to effectively communi-
cate about systemic and structural racism and appropriate policy
and legal responses—like reparations, for example—feels important on a broader level, too."

Goodwin Simon gathered a group of twenty-nine people, sixteen women and thirteen men, ranging in age from twenty-one
to sixty. They all participated online for four days, from April 28
to May 6, 2022. The group represented a mix of education levels
as well as geographical regions, accounting for the Northeast,
Midwest, South, and West. (As I outlined in Part II, the badge of
slavery followed black people no matter which of these regions
they lived in.) Their racial makeup included nine white, eight
black, eight Hispanic, three Asian–Pacific Islanders, and one Native American. Their political affiliations spanned from very liberal and somewhat liberal to moderate, including Democrats,
Independents, and one Republican. The focus group excluded
those who identify as conservative and those who strongly dis-

agree that structural racism and race-based discrimination need to be addressed in the United States, because we determined that their minds could not be changed over a few short days.

As part of their preparation, the team began by doing what I call "opposition research," or taking an inventory of the most common arguments opposing the very idea of reparations. These arguments include some versions of: *I'm not responsible for what happened with slavery hundreds of years ago. It's too hard to figure out who should get payment. It will cost too much. Black Americans will make bad choices on how to spend the money or, worse, get swindled. I didn't own slaves and neither did my ancestors, so why should I have to pay? If we pay black prisoners, their victims may wind up paying them, and that would be awful. There have already been reparations: affirmative action, civil rights bills, etc.*

Together Goodwin Simon's team and I gathered facts and historical research that might be effective at addressing and debunking these recurring arguments, such as: *The end of chattel slavery was not the end of racial discrimination. Being white in America means that you have access to government programs that black Americans do not. Racial segregation was created through government policies and practices. Reparations could consist of more than just cash payments.* Once we assembled that research, we were ready to incorporate it into draft messages to test in our focus group.

When most people hear the word *reparations,* they think of individual cash payments. That was the form of reparations in the four cases in Part I. However, I argued to the focus group that reparations should include investments in the black community in addition to individual cash payments. After all, the harm done was and is community based, even if devastating to each victim. Reparations should fund community-based and systemic-focused solutions. Our current system for building wealth is designed for stripping black wealth, so a cash infusion to individual black Americans without transforming that system would not end well for black wealth building. The multiple systems for white wealth building described in Part II need to be dismantled, so that all Americans, including black Americans, have an equal opportunity to excel. Examples that I provided to the focus group included increased federal funding for K–12 education, investments in neighborhoods previously destroyed by government discrimination, and criminal justice reforms. Today, as discussed below, I would add tax reform to the list.

The other point that we made clear to the participants was that antiblack discrimination was still legal after the Thirteenth Amendment ended chattel slavery. They were told about government-sponsored FHA redlining, which enabled white families to buy homes and build wealth but denied those opportunities to black Americans. They were made aware of racially restrictive covenants that excluded black Americans from buying homes in certain neighborhoods and subdivisions until the 1968 Fair Housing Act became law.

At the beginning of the focus group process, we asked participants to rank their attitude toward reparations on a scale from 0 to 10, with 0 being fully in support and 10 being completely opposed. We asked them to rank their attitude again at the end of the four-day process. Initially the participants' attitudes were spread throughout the scale, but after engaging in the various discussions, exercises, and readings, they all shifted to neutral or in favor of reparations.

For example, on the first day, a participant (Hispanic female, somewhat liberal Democrat, 53, noncollege, South) who ranked herself at 10 explained, "I don't think taxpayers should have to pay for what happened with slavery. It was so long ago and just doesn't seem fair to make today's citizens pay for what yesteryear citizens did." Over the four days, she learned how black Americans had been excluded from accessing FHA-insured mortgages and denied the business loans that had helped build today's white middle class. She learned that black Americans paid taxes into a system that intentionally denied access to black people. By day four she had changed her mind and ranked herself at 0: "My thoughts have definitely shifted. I had no idea of some of the things I learned about in this study. Like about the laws that were enacted to further keep Black Americans from having what all other Americans had after they were freed as slaves."

Another participant (black female, somewhat liberal independent, 57, noncollege, Midwest) who initially ranked herself at 10 challenged the notion that black Americans should receive reparations: "What about the Holocaust? What about the Chinese people? There's been so many slaves in the history of this world, not just Black slaves, there's been all types of slaves. There has been all types of persecution including what is going on even now as we speak about the Russian war. You can't make innocent people that weren't even born at that time pay for this with their tax money. They're having a hard enough time paying back student loans and credit card bills. It's not fair to them and it wouldn't make any sense."

Yet on day four, she too moved to 0, as her opinion had changed after learning about all the ways in which black Americans have been systematically persecuted and discriminated against by the government *since* the abolition of slavery. "I didn't know they abused Black people in such a way and [they] knew about it all along and made it legal to do so and made it legal to make money off the backs of slaves and their descendants. How shameful."

Many of the participants brought up seemingly valid arguments against reparations. One participant (white female, somewhat liberal Democrat, 33, noncollege, South) who initially ranked herself at 8 commented: "Look around: Our country is failing, and if we were to give reparations to a specific group of people I fear that it would just further divide our people. While the idea of reparations is nice and at heart may be a morally good answer, I don't think it is an answer that currently fits within our financial and political landscape." In spite of her initial concerns about causing further political and social strife, she was eventually convinced that reparations were the right thing to do and shifted to a 0. "Yes, when I first heard the term *reparations* I immediately jumped to direct payments and how logistically and politically troublesome that would be in the end. After I realized reparations could be numerous different things, I realized that I already agreed that a lot of them should be happening."

Another focus group member (white male, moderate independent, 26, college, Northeast), who initially ranked himself at 7, returned to that old argument that says reparations are unfair to taxpayers. "I think the people of today should not pay for past mistakes, but I think policies should be passed to help support black Americans," he said. By the end he had moved to a 2, once he understood that reparations can mean many things. "I thought reparations only included monetary awards, and I was clearly wrong. There are many different ways reparations can be used to help out black Americans."

The concern that reparations might lead to retaliation against black Americans also came up. As one participant (white female, somewhat liberal Democrat, 35, noncollege, South) who started out at a 7 stated: "I am conflicted on what exactly this would look like for taxpayers. I also fear the negative effect this could have on the black community, like would this divide our nation more? Would hate crimes spike? Would people find ways to take advantage of this? Many pros and cons to weigh out on this topic." However, strategic messaging about the many forms reparations could take finally broke through her resistance and shifted her outlook to a 2: "Yes, I was skeptical of what the reality of reparations would be exactly. But after reading more and more, I feel far more confident that reparations would be a great thing for our country, especially for our black neighborhoods/families. It would help everyone though, not just black Americans. I am hoping this would bridge the gap that is often forced between us. It would be so beautiful to see the same love and support white communities get, to be poured into our black communities as well."

The results of the focus group proved to me what I had already suspected based on my conversations with Drew over the years: that people could be persuaded of the necessity and feasibility of reparations when the information was conveyed in the right context; and that the value of equality of opportunity and fairness could cross partisan boundaries and be helpful for garnering support. One aspect of our messaging that was especially effective was that we drew a historical throughline from the Thirteenth Amendment and the end of chattel slavery to today and demonstrated all the ways in which slavery had shape-shifted so that the government could continue to discriminate against black Americans. Another important aspect was explaining how the government had successfully paid compensation to other groups in the past, including white enslavers. Once participants understood the true cost of the harms imposed, and that the payments were not limited to individual black Americans but included systemic changes, and saw that reparations were an attainable solution for compensating those harms, their attitudes dramatically shifted in favor of reparations.

Our focus group testing provides a powerful lesson in the importance of teaching the history of racism in our country, particularly when it comes to changing public opinion, and it perhaps explains why Republicans are waging a political campaign to take race history out of our public schools.[21] Consider President Donald Trump's Executive Order 13950, issued on September 20, 2020, which forbids training or teaching government employees (and federal contractors) about "divisive concepts."[22] That includes those where "any individual should feel discomfort, guilt, anguish, or any other form of psychological distress on account of his or her race or sex." In other words, this campaign is attempting to ban empathy through banning books. Can you read Part II as a white person (or as a member of any other race or ethnicity) and not feel *some* discomfort? I barely survived writing it.

As my Georgetown Law colleague Janel George has observed, "Since January 2021, forty-four states have introduced gag laws or taken other steps that would restrict how teachers can discuss race or how curricula can address race, racism, and sexism."[23] She too sees a connection between Trump's executive order and those state laws, noting that they "replicate the language of Executive Order 13950."[24] Teaching the complete story of American history is going to be harder than ever.

For all that the focus group revealed, the reparations scenario is still hypothetical, and research suggests that support may wane over time.[25] Would those who changed their minds during the focus group process still favorably view reparations two years later? I am currently working with Goodwin Simon on a significantly expanded messaging research project with multiple rounds of focus groups and surveys to address those concerns and to delve even more deeply into ways to expand and deepen support for reparations.[26]

Our early focus groups excluded those who identified as very conservative, who strongly agree that "structural racism is not a major problem in the United States," and who express other strong beliefs about race, including that racism happens at an individual level and there is no current need to address it. I believe there is a winning message that will resonate with some conservatives: Without the governmental discrimination faced by black Americans, they would not need monetary assistance. Felix Haywood's vision would have become a reality. Recall that reparation payments to Japanese Americans garnered significant conservative support, as did the Indian Claims Commission. To provide reparations now would serve as a monument against intrusive big government that told an entire race of people where they could live, who they could marry, which homes they were allowed to buy, and which colleges they might attend. The government must be held accountable.

Getting to Reparations argues primarily two things: The United States has a history of paying reparations; and black Americans are deserving of reparations for what we experienced after the Thirteenth Amendment legally ended chattel slavery. The focus group testing demonstrates that those arguments can be persuasive.

The political scientist Tatishe M. Nteta, Provost Professor of Political Science at the University of Massachusetts Amherst, has also conducted polling around reparations and observes,

"When we ask people why they oppose, it's not about the cost. It's not about logistics. It's not about the impossibility to place a monetary value on the impact of slavery. It is consistently this notion that the descendants of slaves do not deserve these types of reparations."[27]

I believe that demonstrating the precedent for paying reparations to groups other than black Americans, along with spelling out the history of discrimination against black Americans post-slavery, could build support for reparations among a majority of Americans. And here is where the 2024 election of Donald Trump as president can help us get there faster. I believe that white racial identity politics was a driving factor in his election, and with all three branches of government under Republican control, we will see more pandering to those voters. His actions while president will make it difficult, if not impossible, for people of goodwill to believe that we are post-racial or have transcended race. They will be one step closer to seeing America clearly and how far we have yet to go to be an inclusive democratic society. Yes, chattel slavery has ended, but discrimination against black Americans continues.

Because the legacy of slavery is pervasive and is found in every nook and cranny of American life, piecemeal solutions will be insufficient. We need a big plan, one with systemic tentacles that would reach every aspect of society. Therefore I am calling for the creation of a commission to study the problem and make bold recommendations. And I need allies to support that process as well as their recommendations. We need to dare to imagine what it would take to build a future where black success (financial, social, and/or political) is no longer newsworthy but the expected norm.

The "go big or go home" approach to reparations was a sticking point for President Obama. When he was interviewed by Ta-Nehisi Coates, the president stated:

> Theoretically, you can make, obviously, a powerful argument that centuries of slavery, Jim Crow, discrimination are the primary cause for all those gaps. That those were wrongs done to the black community as a whole, and black families specifically, and that in order to close that gap, a society has a moral obligation to make a large, aggressive investment, even if it's not in the form of individual reparations checks, but in the form of a Marshall Plan, in order to close those gaps. It is easy to make that theoretical argument. But as a practical matter, it is hard to think of any society in human history in which a majority population has said that as a consequence of historic wrongs, we are now going to take a big chunk of the nation's resources over a long period of time to make that right.[28]

I believe that if a commission were to study the issue and make such a recommendation, we would be able to build that kind of society—together.

The establishment of a commission to study reparations is not a new idea. The CWRIC, which led to Japanese Americans receiving compensation under the Civil Liberties Act of 1988, was created by congressional action. The next year, taking inspiration from the 1988 act, Rep. John Conyers, Jr. (D-MI), introduced H.R. 40, a bill to create a commission to study reparations.[29] He reintroduced the same bill every year for almost thirty years, until he retired in 2017.[30] Rep. Sheila Jackson Lee (D-TX) then picked up the baton, subsequently reintroducing H.R. 40.[31] In

2019 it had twenty co-sponsors, including Sen. Kamala Harris (D-CA).[32] That led to two congressional hearings in 2019 and 2021, but it did not lead to a congressionally approved commission.[33] My plan for a commission is different. I propose that a presidential executive order, not Congress, create the commission.

The Post-Slavery Discrimination Commission (PtSD Commission) could be created with the stroke of a pen. (I am intentionally calling it the PtSD Commission to draw attention to the generations of trauma the government inflicted upon black Americans.) Because the commission can be created unilaterally by the president, I have to convince only one person—not a majority of the 535 members of Congress.

President Biden, for example, expressed his support for "a study of reparations" for descendants of enslaved people.[34] But his support was limited to congressional action.[35] Vice President Harris also expressed her support for studying reparations, commenting that "America needs a history lesson, to be honest about it, and we need to study it in a way that we are having a very comprehensive and fact-based conversation about policies and the connection between those policies and harm if we're going to have a productive conversation."[36] The 2024 Democratic Party Platform called for a congressionally supported commission to study reparations.[37] But H.R. 40 has never made it out of committee or even received a committee vote. Expecting Congress to act is the very definition of insanity. I take a more practical approach.

The next elected Democratic president could issue an executive order creating a commission tasked with the following objectives: to establish a commission to study and consider proposals for reparations regarding the post–Thirteenth Amendment discrimination faced by black Americans in all facets of life as well as analyze the roots of white wealth in America; to study the government's role that, directly and indirectly, prevented black Americans from having equal opportunities, including the complicity of the judicial branch in subordinating black Americans; to quantify the wealth and economic loss stripped from black Americans due to continuing racism and to analyze the white wealth building that occurred simultaneously; to examine the link between that governmental failure and the loss of untold intergenerational black wealth that could not be created as a result; and to recommend appropriate remedies to Congress. (See the Appendix for an example of what such an executive order could look like.)

Such an executive order is unlikely to be issued during a Republican presidency—and certainly not during the second term of Donald Trump. When he was previously president, for example, and was asked about reparations for black Americans, he said he didn't "see it happening."[38] He did suggest, however, that China owed the world $60 trillion in reparations for Covid-19.[39] The Republican Party has come a long way since President Reagan signed into law the Civil Liberties Act of 1988.

The PtSD Commission could tackle all the questions, seek out a wide range of expertise, and make recommendations. The CWRIC's report was almost five hundred pages long, for an incarceration that lasted less than five years. The PtSD Commission's report could number hundreds of thousands of pages, given the time frame and the extent of the harm that I have only touched upon in Part II. The commission should include subcommittee working groups focused on discrete topics including: (i) Criminal Justice Reform; (ii) Economic and Financial Well-Being; (iii) Education; (iv) Eligibility; (v) Environmental Justice;

(vi) Funding Alternatives; (vii) Housing and Homeownership; (viii) Physical Health and Mental Well-Being; (ix) Technology and Intellectual Property; and (x) Voting.

Membership of the commission should include an over-whelming majority of black Americans. It should feature seven to nine members who do not serve on any subcommittees but instead serve as co-chairs. Each subcommittee should include five commissioners. That may place the PtSD Commission at more than fifty members. The work, however, would mainly be completed by the subcommittees, guided by the seven to nine co-chairs. The subcommittees would make reports and recommendations to the full commission. The full commission would meet and ultimately vote on those reports and recommendations, but the co-chairs would be responsible for gathering the subcommittee reports and compiling all recommendations.[40] The co-chairs' priority would be to steer the process in ways that increase public support for reparations.

Funding would be needed to pay for the PtSD Commission, and that could happen through a variety of means. The Supreme Court Commission, for example, was funded through the executive office of the president.[41] While H.R. 40 called for a $12 million appropriation, an appropriation rider could be included in the budget. Alternatively, you could place the commission inside a government agency and repurpose funds allocated to that agency. We are not talking about significant amounts of money relatively speaking, making it easier to accomplish. Getting the commission staffed and up and running, however, would take some care.

The CWRIC can still provide a ready model for how the PtSD Commission could be designed. The CWRIC included a lot of politicians as well as people who were politically connected. Its charge required recommendations, which members ultimately made after many months of public hearings. It was set up for success. But the PtSD Commission has a burden that the CWRIC did not—it has to be a vessel for building public support. Most Americans oppose reparations for black Americans. Without significant public support, Congress is unlikely to ever take up a debate on reparations legislation, regardless of what recommendations the commission makes. The PtSD Commission needs to change opposition into support and create advocates for their recommendations.

Although there were opponents to the DC Emancipation Compensation Act, Congress still enacted the legislation. I know of no national polling regarding public support or opposition for the Indian Claims Commission or the Civil Liberties Act of 1988. There were conflicting reports at the time regarding public support for Japanese American reparations.[42] Having to convince the public to support compensation for black Americans is unique, highly problematic, and yet another example of America's addiction to treating black Americans differently from their nonblack peers, something I refer to as black exceptionalism.

For starters, the PtSD Commission would have to attract both national and local media. That makes the commission's composition critical. My ideal co-chairs would include: a former legislator or former member of Congress; a Japanese American who was previously involved with the CWRIC in some way; someone with gravitas and legal expertise, like a former Supreme Court justice; Republican and/or bipartisan appointees; a clergy member; current or former state legislators; business leaders; maybe a single academic or journalist; and a media-savvy and smart public figure or two (understanding the baggage that public figures bring). (Plenty of academics would testify at the hearings. Their expertise would be an important part of the process.) Allowance should be made to compensate some commissioners. Generally these positions are nonpaying, but that means you are limiting the pool to those who can afford to do the work without pay; if the work is minimal, no pay is warranted. In this instance you would want to attract people who are not necessarily wealthy, and service on this commission would be a *lot* of work.

Some who support reparations may nevertheless oppose creating a PtSD Commission because they argue that commissions are places where good ideas go to die. They provide elected leaders with plausible deniability. Biden's Presidential Commission on the Supreme Court of the United States, which he created in April 2021 via executive order, is the perfect example. Commissions can definitely be useful stalling tactics. But the CWRIC was not, and a PtSD Commission could similarly be designed to succeed. You can tell which commissions will be productive from those that will not by two important metrics: their charge and their composition. President Biden's Supreme Court Commission was doomed by both. Its charge did not allow for it to make recommendations, as its sole function was to produce a report.[43] Second, it was composed of too many academics.[44] (In my opinion, academics are good at informing and deliberating but are not so good at politics and getting things done, even if recommendations had been allowed.)

The PtSD Commission should have at least a three-year term. (The CWRIC was created in 1980 and issued its report with recommendations in December 1982.) The first year would include the critical work of staffing and appointing the commissioners, and getting the commission up and running. The subcommittees would hold hearings and get their work done during the second year, with the understanding that this phase might take more time. The final year's work would be drafting the report and making recommendations to be voted upon by the full commission. That vote would be followed as soon as possible by the introduction of congressional legislation and subsequent passage, then the president's signature. This process should be accomplished within a single term of the president. But if not, the public support generated by this time should help a Democratic president's reelection. If the PtSD Commission has done the job properly, then public support for reparations will demand congressional action. And if instead, public opposition has increased, then we will be better equipped for the next political battle. As Sun Tzu stated in *The Art of War*: "If you know the enemy and know yourself, you need not fear the result of a hundred battles. If you know yourself but not the enemy, for every victory gained you will also suffer a defeat."[45]

Some hearings would be curated and televised in order to educate the public and build a broad consensus of support. They would have to be more impactful than the January 6 Commission hearings, which most agree did very little to change public opinion.[46] Less than 10 percent of the public acknowledged watching the hearings "very closely."[47] The hearings must grab the attention of ordinary people in order to build support for reparations, which is why the public figure appointments would be crucial. The PtSD Commission would need buzz to capture the public's attention in a world full of distractions. The task ahead of the commission would not be for the faint of heart.

And while the PtSD Commission would have to tackle all questions, I will briefly offer my views on a few. I think it is important that a large cross-section of black people other than me get together and decide the ultimate answers. I have lived a relatively privileged life—my parents were the beneficiaries of my father's white male boss's generosity, which is why they owned a home that helped build their wealth.[48] My parents have given me money, and unlike most black college graduates, I have not sent money home to them.

Community organizations that have worked on this issue for a very long time should be consulted. People who have been wrongly imprisoned, targeted by the war on drugs, victimized by racial health disparities, or forced to live in substandard public housing, and the families of those wrongfully executed, among others, ought to have their opinions listened to far more than mine. That is what would happen during the commission hearings. My scholarly expertise gives me unique insights, which is why my analysis is relevant, but I want you to be mindful that my voice cannot be the only one deserving of respect.

I do not plan to give detailed legislative solutions here. That is what the PtSD Commission would be designed to do. The devil would be in the details and would simply give fodder for opponents. Besides, too many experts have thought about these issues far longer than I, and their expertise should be included in the commission process.

I begin with the generalized objection that somehow reparations would be divisive. Do you know what else is divisive? Taking black Americans' property, lynching, preventing black Americans from living and working where they want, and targeting them with police violence. If ending our country's history of treating black Americans as second-class citizens is viewed by some as divisive, they need a history lesson. If their views remain unchanged after that, they cannot hold the rest of us hostage. We must keep moving our country forward.

Another argument against reparations is that it will not solve the real problem: It won't change the personal views and stereotypes individuals hold against black Americans. I don't identify that as the real problem. I see white supremacy and the systems of exclusion created thereby as the problem. I could not care less what people think about me as long as they are not in a position to do me harm. I want to see wealth-building systems created that work to help black Americans, no matter which racist beliefs individuals might continue to hold about black people. But if you are interested in changing negative perceptions about black Americans, then the history described in Part II is a good place to start.

Next, I turn to more specific "how would reparations actually work" questions. First up: eligibility. Should reparations be limited to descendants of enslaved people or should they be awarded to all black people in America? What about biracial Americans? What about black people who passed for white? How can we prevent fraudsters and other people who are not eligible from receiving reparations? Should we require DNA testing for qualification purposes? Why should black people trust the government to keep DNA test results and not to use the samples in a way that would harm black people in other contexts?

Eligibility raises very complicated questions and deserves a separate subcommittee, as I have recommended. But I do not want to gloss over the role that white supremacy plays in making the question of eligibility so challenging. As law professors Perea, Delgado, Harris, and Wildman provide in their casebook, *Race and Races: Cases and Resources for a Diverse America,* "Historically, racial classification in America arises out of what is apparently a uniquely American institution known informally as 'the one-drop rule,' which defines as black a person with as little as a single drop of 'black blood.' "[49] In other words, laws created the rules around race and how people across racial lines were supposed to interact.

The one-drop rule was created to keep anyone *remotely* black out of sharing the privilege of whiteness. That's why Homer Plessy was determined to be "black" under the law even though neither his parents nor his grandparents were black, only a single great-grandparent.[50] Having one African ancestor denied him the benefit of riding in the whites-only section of the train. That also explains how the Sicilians in Louisiana were "raced" other than white. That is what makes eligibility issues so difficult: The law constructed arbitrary rules around race that led to black Americans' stigma, discrimination, and exploitation.

Given that context, my response is relatively straightforward: All self-identifying black people in America should be eligible. In other words, anyone who identifies as black qualifies. In terms of proving eligibility, I would follow the approach taken when Japanese Americans received reparations. In that instance, the Department of Justice, as part of the executive branch, provided a list of all those imprisoned during World War II. The federal government had the responsibility of qualifying those who were eligible. They locked each and every one of them up, so they were responsible for making the list of who their actions harmed. Of the total of 82,219 people eligible for payments, fewer than fifteen hundred were not found.[51] The same could be true here.

The executive branch, including the Census Bureau, would bear the burden of providing a list of all black people in America. Homelessness, for example, would provide some difficulties, given the large share of black Americans who are homeless,[52] and they would need a work-around. State and local government agencies and not-for-profit organizations assisting the homeless may have useful information that they can provide to the government. (Community groups also assisted in locating Japanese Americans who were owed payments.)[53]

No proof on the part of black people will be required. Why? Because the government failed black people—and failed to keep adequate records. The burden should be placed on the government to make amends. In some cases, private white citizens burned down courthouses with the intention of destroying property titles and other records, as we saw in Part II; they would do anything to make it easier to usurp black Americans' wealth.

Any black person who is not on the list but thinks they were wrongfully excluded could come forward with evidence that they identify as black. No good explanation would be ignored. Those who passed as white would have a complicated case to make, yet it was racism that caused them to make the choice, and they too deserve an opportunity to be heard by the commission. The approach of the DC Compensated Emancipation Act was to generously interpret benefits, which should govern here as well.

For added protection, the government could also approach the claims process as it did the DC Compensated Emancipation Act, but instead of printing every claimant's name in the newspaper, they could provide a searchable database of all Americans who identify as black. If a nonblack person claims to be black, someone can challenge them. Pretending to be black would come with penalties, which could be civil and/or criminal. Penalties would also apply if someone falsely challenges a black person on the list. The approach that recent book bans have taken across the country, where a few people are responsible for requesting the majority of book bans from local libraries and schools, cannot be allowed if this process is to be successful.[54] We cannot have one person striking down every black person's claim.

Should reparations be limited to American residents and citizens? I hesitate to answer yes, given that our immigration laws have an antiblack bias.[55] The Center for Migration Studies of New York estimates that between 5 percent and 6 percent of black people living in America are undocumented. To include them would be the symbolically right answer, but to exclude them might be the practical one.

Also, any eligible black person who did not want to accept reparations could opt out, as was the case in the Civil Liberties Act of 1988; twenty-eight people refused payment.[56] Whether because they don't agree with the idea, or the approach, or anything else, they should not be forced to accept reparations if they do not want to.

What about the objection that reparations should be limited to descendants of those formerly enslaved? In reality, the majority of black people in America are descendants of the enslaved, but because *blackness* is what has been targeted post-slavery, then blackness alone should be the test. If you are black and live in America, then you are eligible for reparations. The hypothetical I always give to explain my position on this question is this: When a taxicab driver in New York City passes over a black person and instead picks up a white person—something I have personally experienced—they do not think *I am passing you over because you look like a descendant of an enslaved person and not a black immigrant.* They do not stop because they do not stop for anyone who looks black.

My position is going to anger some natural allies who are supporters of reparations but seek them only for descendants of the enslaved, often referred to as American Descendants of Slavery. I realize this. However, my theory of the case is that this country owes reparations for what it did to black Americans after slavery ended, and for how our federal government allowed slavery to shape-shift into new systems of oppression that not only targeted black descendants of slaves but black immigrants as well. I understand what their argument is—slavery was unlike anything else and that deserves special treatment; the descendants alone deserve reparations. I get it, but I come out differently.

Immigrants and native-born black Americans would be treated alike, because black immigrants are not treated like white Americans.[57] They have been subjected to white supremacy just like black Americans who descended from enslaved Africans. Just ask the surviving family members of the late Amadou Diallo, a Guinean immigrant. On February 4, 1999, he was "mowed down in a hail of NYPD bullets" outside his apartment building.[58] As a result, I argue that black immigrants deserve reparations because they've been tagged with the badges and incidents of slavery. They live here and experience what it means to be black in America.

Another common question is: Why should reparations be limited to black Americans? Aren't other groups equally deserving? Short answer: The history described in Part II is sui generis. No other group has experienced that level of sustained persecution because of their race as black people have—except perhaps for Tribal Nations, which have received some form of reparations. Insufficient yes, but at least something. The longer answer is, if you are thinking that poor white people should receive reparations, recall that they have not been targeted for exclusion from any of these systems of oppression *because* they were white.

Should there be a poor people's movement like the kind Dr. King started and that Rev. William J. Barber II valiantly continues?

Of course. But that is a solution to a different problem, only some of it intertwined with race. Could reparations for black Americans make it more likely that poor white Americans could also receive reparations in the future? Perhaps. However, when we talk about the history of black people in this country, it is race-based harm, not class-based, and therefore the appropriate solution must be race-based. My uncle Billy the lawyer was targeted not because he was poor but because he was black and "forgot his place."

An additional collateral objection may be that once black Americans receive what they are owed, it would inevitably lead to demands for reparations for others. Perhaps we should be concerned about that before going down this slippery slope. If you find yourself in this rabbit hole, then you've fallen prey to the status quo that does everything to distract you from focusing on black loss and the perpetrators who caused the harm. Black people should be able to have a conversation focused solely on them without also having to address the concerns of everyone else. When racially subordinated groups are pitted against one another, there is only one winner: white supremacy. Of course those conversations are important to have, just not as part of a process designed to get redress for black injury.

One final eligibility concern: Should white people who were caught in the antiblack web be eligible for reparations? Take the white owners of land near Bruce's Beach who also lost property through the eminent domain process because the state was determined to take the Bruces' property. They were not targeted because they were white, but because of their proximity to blackness. They should reach out to the State of California and ask it to do the right thing. That does not mean they should be eligible for reparations that are owed to black Americans.

What about poor white Southerners in states with ties to lynching, where the white poverty rates are higher because of the state's vile historical ties to murdering the innocent? Research shows that white Americans often oppose safety net programs if they believe black people will benefit.[59] White victims of white supremacy, I argue, should not be eligible for reparations for black people. Instead, they should be at the forefront of the fight to dismantle white supremacy and support black reparations— not asking for a share. They could also stop opposing safety net programs that would financially benefit them. White victims of white supremacy are in the best position to understand the real harm of white supremacy and to fight to dismantle it.

What form should reparations take? As I mentioned earlier, I want the lion's share of reparations to benefit the black community and not consist of cash payments to individuals. But other groups that have been harmed by the government have received cash reparations; so should black Americans. It could be an amount based on the number of years a person has lived in this country, or it could be a fixed amount for each eligible claimant. When it came to the DC Compensated Emancipation Act and the Indian Claims Commission, claimants received different amounts. However, when it came to reparations to Italy and members of the Japanese American community, each person's loss was valued the same when payment was made. Again, these are issues for the PtSD Commission to ultimately sort out.

I am confident that you are expecting me to give you a number or a range of how much all this is going to cost. Sorry to disappoint you—I cannot in good conscience do that because we honestly do not know the full extent of the government's plunder of black wealth. The plunderer intentionally failed to keep good records of the property stolen from black Americans who were lynched, or were victimized by convict leasing or sharecropping, or were barred from getting USDA loans, or were falsely imprisoned. The theft of black wealth on the one hand, and the prevention of black wealth creation on the other, took place for more than one hundred years at the hands of many who deliberately did not keep records. Would you keep a detailed written account of stealing another person's property? What if you didn't think you were doing anything wrong? As a result, I have no idea what the right amount is. No one does. But we could get a lot closer to an accurate count if we were allowed to study the question.

The economic crimes committed against black Americans need to be unearthed by the PtSD Commission, whose members will have to do some detective work. The commissioners would have access to academics as well as the testimony of victims who could provide historical records along with oral histories that can document losses. Many of the subcommittees would document and quantify the harm inflicted on black Americans. All those numbers would have to be included. This is what support for a reparations commission looks like. It requires you to put aside your angst over a number in order to take this historic journey to do what no other generation has done.

We do, however, have estimates for certain things.

One study estimated the cost of labor market discrimination for the forty-year period between 1929 and 1969 at $1.6 trillion. A number of studies have suggested how much black workers lose annually from ongoing race discrimination and occupational segregation in the labor market. For just one year in the 1970s, the cost of continuing racial discrimination in employment has been estimated between $94 billion and $123 billion. The loss of black-owned farmland during the twentieth century was calculated at $326 billion.[60] Estimates of the Tulsa massacre alone are between $32 million and $47 million in 2020 dollars.[61] Focusing on the land that was never distributed to the newly freed, estimates place the loss at anywhere between $168 billion to $12.6 trillion.[62] As for the racial wealth gap, the price tag is almost $8 trillion.[63] (I have not advocated for compensating for the losses associated with chattel slavery, which comes in as high as $111.4 trillion.[64] Why? Because I believe focusing on chattel slavery alone is a red herring and gives the opposition the upper hand in arguing that it happened so long ago. It misses the reality that chattel slavery shape-shifted and never really ended.)

I also believe that reparations legislation would have to include fundamental tax reform designed to erase the current anti-black bias in our federal income tax system.[65] Why? Because of the significant role that tax policy plays in propping up white supremacy. As I demonstrated in *The Whiteness of Wealth*, Congress has created tax breaks for white Americans that are generally denied to black taxpayers, as well as loopholes for tainted wealth that are received overwhelmingly by white Americans. For black Americans, this could mean a reparations tax credit as compensation both for paying taxes for services from which they were excluded and for paying higher taxes in a system that doesn't recognize the harmful effects of Jim Crow. It could also mean a federal income tax holiday for a period of years for every black American. For white Americans, it would include increased taxes on the richest among us, not solely because they are disproportionately white, but because their income and wealth are tainted by the systems of oppression put into place after slavery—even if individuals' ancestors never enslaved anyone.[66]

I believe that for tax reform in this context to be successful, the Department of the Treasury should not be leading the implementation effort.[67] It is ill suited to efforts centering on racial equity. According to a recent Treasury report to Congress, less than one half of 1 percent of its economists are black men, and less than 2 percent are black women.[68] My negative views on the Treasury Department are informed by my experience serving on the twenty-five-member Treasury Advisory Committee on Racial Equity, established by Treasury secretary Janet Yellen from 2022 to 2024.[69] Perhaps part of any systemic reform of our tax laws should include a transformed and reorganized Treasury Department, with new personnel and a racial equity focus.

A key concern is how would we ever pay for it? That would be the work of the PtSD Commission's subcommittee on funding alternatives, once the total dollar amount has been calculated.

The four case studies of reparations teach us one final lesson: Whatever compensation is awarded will be much smaller than the actual loss sustained. Black Americans, when awarded reparations, are going to receive less than they deserve.

Who is going to pay for it is precisely the type of question that the PtSD Commission will determine and make recommendations about. We can increase the deficit (as we did with the 2017 Trump tax cuts, which were received primarily by those with the highest incomes, who happened to be disproportionately white Americans). We can issue debt. We can tax the wealthy. According to the Center on Wealth and Philanthropy at Boston College, for the period between 2007 and 2061, it is estimated that almost 94 million estates will transfer approximately $72 trillion (using 2024 dollar amounts). We are at a unique moment in history, and tax policy can be a critical lever in creating a more equitable tomorrow. Estate tax reform, an income tax on millionaires (or billionaires), and a wealth tax are all possible sources of revenue and are logical sources, given their likely historical taint, that can be used to fund reparations.[70] The payments and funding mechanism can be spread out over several years, as when paying Japanese Americans.

One often-raised objection is that today's taxpayers should not be made to pay for yesterday's sinners. A good articulation of this argument comes from former Senate majority leader Mitch McConnell (R-KY), who stated in 2019, "I don't think reparations for something that happened 150 years ago for whom none of us currently living are responsible is a good idea."[71]

Senator McConnell's suggestion that he had nothing to do with previous generations' sins is ironic given that his great-great-grandfathers enslaved fourteen people and benefited from their exploited labor.[72] Research shows that after the Civil War, white Southern enslavers were able to rebound financially more quickly than white Southerners who were not enslavers.[73]

Senator McConnell went to public schools in Athens, Alabama, during Jim Crow. He lived "on the white side of Athens, where black residents were only allowed to visit for work and were typically paid very low wages."[74] The wealth that slavery produced for his ancestors didn't die when slavery ended. During the 1918 flu epidemic, Senator McConnell's grandfather bought a funeral home that continued in the family until it was sold. (The business still uses the McConnell family name.)[75] The funeral home purchase was quite fortunate for the McConnell family finances, given that the 1918 pandemic took the lives of 675,000 Americans. That is greater than the number of American casualties in World Wars I and II, as well as the Korean and Vietnam wars combined.[76]

Whatever else Senator McConnell inherited, he inherited whiteness, which perfectly positioned him to enjoy the life he has today. In contrast, the first black person was elected to a statewide office in Kentucky in 2015.[77] As of 2019, "there is only one black-owned business in downtown Athens: The Sweetest Thing Tea Room."[78]

Another group that claims absolution from chattel slavery (and another reason why I do not argue that reparations should be paid for chattel slavery) are those descended from white immigrants who arrived in this country after slavery ended. The late justice Antonin Scalia explained it this way:

> My father came to this country when he was a teenager. Not only had he never profited from the sweat of any black man's brow, I don't think he had ever seen a black man. There are, of course, many white ethnic groups that came to this country in great numbers relatively late in its history—Italians, Jews, Irish, Poles—who not only took no part in, and derived no profit from, the major historic suppression of the currently acknowledged minority groups, but were, in fact, themselves the object of discrimination by the dominant Anglo-Saxon majority.[79]

What this argument misses is that even though chattel slavery legally ended with the Thirteenth Amendment, federal, state, and local governmental discrimination against black people, enabled by the judiciary, continued, as described in Part II of this book. The benefits that white immigrants and American citizens accrued from this discrimination were omnipresent. The Homestead Act of 1862 benefited white immigrants but not black Americans. Being able to live wherever they wanted, work wherever they wanted, and buy whatever they wanted (if they had the money) remained a unique privilege extended primarily to white Americans, including white immigrants when Justice Scalia's father came to America. Think back to the story of Paul Thornton, the editor for the *Los Angeles Times,* who descended from Norwegian immigrants, and the wealth his family was able to build. They arrived in Glendale, California, a sundown town, in 1954 and became homeowners at a time when black Americans couldn't even live there, much less buy there. The immigrants to whom the late Justice Scalia refers were ultimately considered *white* in America, which afforded them access to wealth-building opportunities that were denied to most black Americans, born in America, solely because they were black.

After reading Part II, what white American could generally say they are truly innocent and have no tainted wealth? Your ancestors were not enslavers, but they could own property and begin to build wealth because they were white. They were not enslavers, yet they benefited from living in sundown towns across the country. Unless you are a Native American, your grandparent was an immigrant—and benefited from a system that at the time allowed legal discrimination against black people. As the PtSD Commission's subcommittee considers payment options, reparations should not be paid for by black Americans. Nevertheless, anyone claiming to be exempt from contributing to a reparations fund should be able to make their case to the subcommittee.

A logical objection to any price tag is, haven't we already paid black people some form of reparations? Senator McConnell has suggested, "We've tried to deal with our original sin of slavery by fighting a civil war, by passing landmark civil rights legislation. We've elected an African American president." Others will argue that affirmative action has been a form of reparations for black Americans and that it has already dealt with slavery and its lingering consequences. Such "offset" arguments are to be expected, given that, as we saw, they were used to try to defeat the plan to pay reparations for Japanese Americans. Some claimed that whatever losses Japanese Americans incurred as a result of incarceration had already been addressed by the Evacuation Claims Act of 1948, even though that was patently false.

That argument should not work here either because neither civil rights legislation nor affirmative action was ever limited to black Americans, the way post-slavery discrimination has generally been. Civil rights legislation has never been available solely for black plaintiffs. Making Juneteenth a national holiday gives the day off to everyone, not just black people. Affirmative action is also not an offset to any future reparations payments.

If affirmative action had permitted quotas and remedies for past discrimination that were available only for black Americans, I might have considered it a valid offset. But it didn't, so it isn't. (Also, if affirmative action were a blacks-only program, we might be closer to where Felix Haywood predicted we would be today.) As Justice Lewis Powell made clear in *California v. Bakke,* "Ethnic diversity . . . is only one element in a range of factors a university properly may consider in attaining the goal of a heterogeneous student body."[80] In other words, admitting black applicants solely because of race was unconstitutional under the Fourteenth Amendment's equal protection clause. And thanks to a 2023 Supreme Court decision, race can no longer be considered as even "one element" in college admissions.[81] Affirmative action has never been blacks-only, so it cannot be considered an offset for blacks-only reparations. Finally, the primary beneficiaries of affirmative action have been white women.[82]

What about the $2.2 billion payout to black "and other minority" farmers that the Biden administration made in 2024?[83] Shouldn't that be considered an offset to the estimated $326 billion in black farmland lost "due to discriminatory lending practices from the USDA and the forced sale" of their land? Of course, but only that part of the $2.2 billion that was paid to black farmers. Neither do all the anti-poverty programs that benefited more white people than black count as reparations. Anti-poverty programs can disproportionately benefit black people, but one reason we need them for black people is that white supremacy kept taking black people's property, increasing the likelihood of their living in poverty.

Last, will reparations to black Americans be upheld as constitutional against anticipated legal challenges? If, through a series of miracles, the PtSD Commission were to build majority public support, and its recommendations resulted in legislation passed by Congress and signed by the president, it would certainly face a legal challenge, just as the compensation made to Japanese Americans for their mass incarceration did. And while the equal protection clause of the Fourteenth Amendment was used as a shield of protection in that case, the same legal argument would act as a sword to pierce the hope of compensation for black Americans.

There is no doubt in my mind that the Supreme Court today would find reparations unconstitutional under the Fourteenth Amendment and would consider such a program as governmental antiwhite discrimination. Existing Supreme Court precedent will continue to be a bar to upholding any legislation authorizing reparations as constitutional, but there is another path forward. I believe that Congress could implement reparations under its powers granted by the Thirteenth Amendment. On that basis Congress could enact reparations, designed to take black Americans "from under the yoke of bondage . . . to reap the fruit of [their] own labor," in the twenty-first century, and it would be upheld as constitutional.[84]

As I have described, for many decades, Supreme Court precedent fashioned blackness into a continuing badge of slavery and inferiority. It wasn't just Congress or the states that stood in the way of "equal benefit of all laws . . . as is enjoyed by white citizens," but also the judiciary's limiting interpretation of the Thirteenth Amendment.

The foundation for my argument can be found in the 1968 Supreme Court opinion in *Jones v. Alfred Mayer,* where the Court stated, "Surely Congress has the power under the Thirteenth Amendment rationally to determine what are the badges and the incidents of slavery, and the authority to translate that determination into effective legislation."[85] In that case, prospective black homeowners Joseph Lee Jones and his wife, Barbara, sued Alfred Mayer, the developer of a subdivision in St. Louis. They had wanted to purchase a lot and build a home in the development, but Mayer refused to sell to them because his policy was "not to sell houses and lots to Negroes." The Joneses alleged that they were denied the opportunity to buy a home in a private subdivision solely because they were black.

The statute at the center of this case, 42 USCA §1982 Property Rights of Citizens, provides: "All citizens of the United States shall have the same right, in every State and Territory, *as is enjoyed by white citizens* thereof to inherit, purchase, lease, sell, hold, and convey real and personal property" (emphasis added). For this reason, both private and public racial discrimination in the sale or rental of property was prohibited, and the Supreme Court ruled that the congressional statute was a proper constitutional exercise of congressional power under the Thirteenth Amendment:[86]

Negro citizens, North and South, who saw in the Thirteenth Amendment a promise of freedom—freedom to "go and come at pleasure" and to "buy and sell when they please"—would be left with "a mere paper guarantee" if Congress were powerless to assure that a dollar in the hands of a Negro will purchase the same thing as a dollar in the hands of a white man. At the very least, the freedom that Congress is empowered to secure under the Thirteenth Amendment includes the freedom to buy whatever a white man can buy, the right to live wherever a white man can live. If Congress cannot say that being a free man means at least this much, then the Thirteenth Amendment made a promise the Nation cannot keep.[87]

The Supreme Court justices who decided *Jones v. Alfred Mayer* defined freedom the same way Reverend Frazier and the twenty ministers and Justice Harlan did. They understood the reach of the Thirteenth Amendment the same way members of Congress who enacted the Amendment did. The legislation that finally brought forth emancipation was intended to be broad and sweeping in scope, designed to eliminate all badges and incidents of slavery.

"The true curse of slavery is not what it did to the black man, but what it has done to the white man," Justice William O. Douglas wrote in his concurring opinion. "For the existence of the institution produced the notion that the white man was of superior character, intelligence, and morality. The blacks were little more than livestock—to be fed and fattened for the economic benefits they could bestow through their labors, and to be subjected to authority, often with cruelty, to make clear who was master and who slave." Douglas went on to conclude, "Some badges of slavery remain today. While the institution has been outlawed, it has remained in the minds and hearts of many white men. Cases which have come to this Court depict a spectacle of slavery unwilling to die."[88]

What can white Americans and other allies get from supporting the fight for reparations for black Americans? They can get a clear conscience. Choosing to support a commission that will lead to meaningful reparations means no longer having to engage in willful ignorance of our history or self-delusion and denial about the unearned benefits that white Americans have received. It means no longer expending energy victim blaming, which takes a lot of psychological energy to sustain. It means white Americans and other allies will have earned absolution by working to destroy a system that unfairly benefited them and that devastated the black community and hindered their economic achievement and ultimate advancement.

In 2019, at a congressional hearing on reparations, Katrina Browne, a white filmmaker, testified and "recounted her painful discovery that her Rhode Island ancestors had been 'the largest slave trading family in United States history,' and brought more than 12,000 Africans to the Americas in chains. Her message to the lawmakers: 'It is good for the soul of a person, a people and of a nation to set things right.'"[89]

But if you are interested in reparations having a more concrete benefit for white Americans, look no further than potential criminal justice reform. Eliminating the reality of police killing unarmed citizens would benefit white Americans as well as black Americans, because lots of white Americans are murdered by the police.[90]

I believe reparations can be found to be constitutional under the Thirteenth Amendment for one simple reason: De facto slavery did not end with its passage. Systemic racism against black people in the twenty-first century has its roots in the post-slavery period of the nineteenth century. When enslaved people were freed, they could not escape their blackness and were forced to carry it around wherever they went. Slavery shape-shifted into different forms of control over black Americans, whether it was through economic exploitation, mass incarceration, or racial violence—all of which have continued into the twenty-first century. Reparations are a necessary step in the attainment of true freedom, designed to eliminate badges and incidents of slavery once and for all. Congress has the clear right to remedy these vestiges of slavery under Section 2 of the Thirteenth Amendment.

The newly freed were vulnerable to financial exploitation when the federal government reneged on the promise of Field Order No. 15. As Reverend Frazier noted, the best way for black people to take care of themselves was "to have land, and turn it and till it by our labor . . . and we can soon maintain ourselves and have something to spare." They received no land in the end. Even those who were initially awarded land saw it taken from them and given back to their former white enslavers. They were left with the choice of starving or accepting onerous, exploitative sharecropping contracts that required them to work for their former enslavers without the bargaining power to negotiate a fair price for their labor.

Those who refused to sign sharecropping agreements could be arrested for vagrancy and, like Green Cottenham, sent to prison, where their forced labor enriched the state and companies like U.S. Steel in the convict leasing system. If they were lucky, free blacks might open their own business, as Tommie

Moss did, and become successful, but that increased the likelihood of facing mob violence egged on by a threatened white competitor. Black people could not escape their blackness. There was nowhere a black person could go, even though slavery was ended, to be free and experience the type of freedom known to white men.

The law sanctioned all of it. Legal antiblack discrimination continued for nearly a century after the end of slavery. The Federal Housing Administration, for example, legally engaged in redlining, whereby they refused to insure home loans in neighborhoods where black Americans lived. At the same time, black taxpayers funded FHA insurance and enabled the white middle class to build wealth through homeownership.[91]

Legal segregation in education was found unconstitutional in 1954, when *Brown v. Board of Education* was decided.[92] Even so, de facto antiblack discrimination continued thereafter. Further congressional action—such as the passage of the Civil Rights Act of 1964, the Voting Rights Act of 1965, and the Fair Housing Act of 1968—was needed to right that wrong. And while some progress was made, the judiciary has lessened the positive impact that could have been activated through the civil rights acts of the 1960s.

The trifecta of economic exploitation, mass incarceration, and racial violence has followed black Americans well into the twenty-first century. Although the Fair Housing Act of 1968 made redlining illegal, recall the City National Bank settlement. Subprime mortgages target black Americans with higher interest rates even though they qualify for lower interest rates.[93] Appraisals of black homes are less than those for white homes.[94] The economic exploitation of black Americans based solely upon their blackness has never stopped.

The crack/powder cocaine sentencing disparity led to the mass incarceration of black men at alarming rates and is just the latest version of the criminalization of blackness.[95] Racial violence, whether inflicted by private citizens or official actors of the state, has also never ceased. Ahmaud Arbery's lynching at the hands of white men in Georgia and George Floyd's murder by police officer Derek Chauvin in Minnesota, both incidents from 2020, demonstrate that racial violence occurs whenever black people are viewed as "not belonging" or "not behaving."

Congressional legislation to provide reparations could remove the "true curse of slavery." Congress granted itself both the power to end chattel slavery and the power to ensure that black Americans enjoyed equal benefits of the laws as white Americans. The first was accomplished, but the latter can be achieved only through reparations.

But why would I expect the Supreme Court, particularly today's Court, to find any such legislation constitutional, when they could still choose to apply the Fourteenth Amendment and strike the legislation as unconstitutional? First, if the Supreme Court were to find reparations legislation unconstitutional, it would add to the already low regard that a majority of Americans have for the judicial branch of our government.[96] Almost 60 percent of Americans disapprove of the job the Supreme Court is currently doing.[97] In other words, such a move would only serve to point out the continued victimization of black Americans at the hands of the judiciary. It could even encourage activists to pursue different pathways to action that might include more state and locally based reparations efforts.[98]

Our current Supreme Court includes a number of justices who support the original meaning and intent of the Constitution. They used it as the basis to overturn *Roe v. Wade* and the right to an abortion. My legal argument that reparations is constitutional under the Thirteenth Amendment is based on the original meaning of the amendment, as it was understood by those who were both for and against it. If the Court were to receive a legal challenge to any reparations statute and ignore the originalist arguments bolstering it under the Thirteenth Amendment or apply it in a way that made it largely unrecognizable, their racist biases would be exposed in an obvious way for all to see. And that could lead to a very different type of reform, of the Supreme Court itself, which could provide an alternate path to reparations legislation being upheld as constitutional.

The words Justice Douglas wrote in his 1968 decision are unfortunately still relevant: "Some badges of slavery remain today."[99] Progress toward reparations would signal the death knell for the "badges and incidents" of slavery that remain and would mark a first step in overcoming the national addiction to white supremacy. In sum, reparations are doable. There are virtually no questions that the PtSD Commission structure cannot figure out.

We have also seen how the end of chattel slavery did not end the reality of black American subordination. We should not expect reparations to be the end of the chapter on racism. (The Indian Claims Commission did not end the government's taking of land from Tribal Nations.)[100] We should expect a backlash to reparations, but the process would train many more watchful eyes to make sure that we don't slip back into familiar patterns of white supremacy. This time could be different. We can fight back armed with better information and the political will to change. Also, because most of the reparations funding would not be individual cash payments, the fear expressed by some, that black people would be vulnerable to fraud and subject to being swindled, can be eliminated.

The road ahead will be hard, but I remain optimistic. While reparations at the national level have not moved forward yet, state and local reparations efforts are now underway across the country.[101] The State of California's worker's compensation payments to Japanese Americans who were fired for being ethnically Japanese was a tailwind for the federal payments that came later.

The recent example of Bruce's Beach in the movement for acknowledging black loss and taking action also hails from California. Although most black Americans have never been compensated for the discriminatory and racist policies that allowed their property to be stolen from them, the descendants of at least one family have. It took one hundred years before the State of California righted the wrong done to the Bruces—a state where only 6.5 percent of the population is black. Bruce's Beach demonstrates how the law was used to exclude black Americans from Manhattan Beach, California—a legacy that remains today with the city's less-than-one-percent black population. California also created a Reparations Task Force and issued a one-thousand-page-plus report with recommendations.[102]

California is not alone in its recent reparations efforts—it has been joined by several other states and local governments. In 2021 the city of Evanston, Illinois, awarded up to $25,000 per person for race-based discrimination in housing experienced by black Americans between 1919 and 1969.[103] In 2022 the town council of Amherst, Massachusetts, approved funding to pay out $2 million in reparations over a decade for black residents on youth programs, affordable housing, and grants for businesses.[104] In 2023 the Maryland General Assembly held a hearing to decide whether to create a committee to examine the issue of compensating descendants of the enslaved;[105] New York governor Kathy Hochul signed legislation creating a commission to study reparations for slavery in that state;[106] Oregon state senator Lew Frederick sponsored S.B. 619, which would establish a program to pay reparations to "Black Oregonians who can demonstrate heritage in slavery";[107] and the city council of Burlington, Vermont, established a task force to study reparations for descendants of enslaved people.[108]

While these are all positive developments, there have also been setbacks. For example, a lawsuit was filed against Evanston claiming an equal protection clause violation because the benefits were limited to black Americans.[109] State and local actions are not enough, underscoring the fact that elected officials, city councils, and state legislatures cannot be depended on to completely fund the reparations debt owed to black people. Bruce's Beach was the rare instance where elected officials accepted responsibility for harm done by previous legislators who bore no relation to them. Another reason we don't see more stories about property being returned is that records are often not available.

All black Americans bear some burden simply for living in the United States, regardless of the level of success they manage to achieve in a system not designed for them. And all white Americans benefit from that system. Household median wealth for a white family headed by a high school dropout is higher than that of a black family headed by a college graduate.[110] College-educated black Americans are more likely to send money home to their parents, at least in part due to their parents being the victims of Jim Crow policies, while college-educated white Americans are more likely to receive money from their parents.[111] High-income black Americans are less likely to own stock than their white peers.[112] Children in middle-class black families are "more likely to fall out of the middle class than . . . remain there."[113] Being black in America means you are owed reparations for the years of receiving the "[un]equal benefit of all laws . . . as is enjoyed by white citizens."[114]

As Toni Morrison has said, "The very serious function of racism . . . is distraction. It keeps you from doing your work. It keeps you explaining, over and over again, your reason for being. Somebody says you have no language and so you spend 20 years proving that you do. Somebody says your head isn't shaped properly so you have scientists working on the fact that it is. Somebody says that you have no art so you dredge that up. Somebody says that you have no kingdoms and so you dredge that up. None of that is necessary."[115]

The point of getting to the other side of reparations is to finally enable black Americans to stop explaining. Stop explaining why there are racial disparities, why we are disproportionately poor, why we aren't prone to criminal acts, why we aren't further along economically. What's more, it would bring about the long-overdue economic, political, and social inclusion of a people who never asked to come here but whose ancestors were forced here in chains and who (along with black immigrants) have been targeted for their blackness ever since. Instead of black Americans feeling like outsiders in our own country, reparations would invite us in, because getting reparations includes transforming policies and practices so that they no longer subordinate black people.

The process of getting reparations would mean that we learn about *all* our history and make sure our children are taught the truth about our country. We should teach the history of race and racism the same way we teach math and chemistry—as accurately as we can.[116]

Directly confronting racism targeting black Americans, acknowledging it, and making repair for it will make us stronger as a country. Failing to deal with our racist past makes us weaker, and that vulnerability will continue to be exploited.[117]

As I described previously, President Biden told us: "Great nations don't ignore their most painful moments. They embrace them." But we often would rather quickly move on and forget that part of our history, which is difficult to accept. As Justice Harlan predicted more than a century ago, establishing a system of Jim Crow would "render permanent peace impossible and . . . keep alive a conflict . . . which must do harm to all concerned." That part of our history has been too easily forgotten and erased. And while that is who we were, that is not what we can become . . . together. Getting to reparations means finally coming to grips with our past and the reality that "the true curse of slavery is not what it did to the black man, but what it has done to the white man."

On the other side of reparations, many more would see what had previously been invisible. Getting reparations for black Americans would forever open the eyes and minds of those willing to see, understand, and take action. It would enable us to move beyond our current and familiar stalemate.

Reverend Frazier and the other black ministers who met with General Sherman in 1865 at the end of the Civil War did not get their wish "to be placed on land until we are able to buy it and make it our own" or "to live by ourselves, for there is a prejudice against us in the South that will take years to get over." They had no way of knowing that 150 years later, prejudice would remain and would not be limited to the South but would stalk black people across the country.

Reparations are not only the right thing to do, but as I have shown, they are also the practical thing to do. We can secure reparations now because we have done it before. I started this project as a skeptic, but I am now a believer.

Facing the rising sun of our new day begun
Let us march on till victory is won.[118]

ACKNOWLEDGMENTS

This book is the result of a collaborative process, and I have so many wonderful people to thank. I begin with my insightful and fearless agent, Alia Hanna Habib, who pushed me to write a second book before I realized that I was ready. Katie Gee Salisbury, whose piercing questions and collaboration always led to deeper truths and helped make me a better writer. Madhulika Sikka, my Crown editor, whose support, encouragement, and keen eye transformed this book into the best version of itself. And to my dear friend Melissa Waters, a world-class storyteller, and the doula who helped me bring this book into the world. Words are inadequate to express my gratitude for always being there even though you have a full life of your own.

To my Crown family and the Gernert Company team. You make all of this so much easier.

I would like to thank my Georgetown law colleagues who read and commented on draft chapters: Lelaine Bigelow, Sheryl

Cashin, Josh Chafetz, Nakita Cuttino, Michele Goodwin, Eun Hee Han, Tiffany Jeffers, Sherri Keene, Betsy Kuhn, Christy Lopez, Victoria Nourse, Eloise Pasachoff, Gregory Shaffer, Shamaal Sheppard, Cliff Sloan, Brad Snyder, and Don Wallace.

I wish to thank the numerous Georgetown Law research assistants who have each made contributions to the book: Himaya Seidu Agwedicham, Morgan Flitt, Ceallach Gibbons, Fiona Higgins, Christie Lai, Arianna Mackey, Manny Nimarko, Jordyn Perry, and David Zucker. A special thanks to Tianna Mobley for her invaluable research assistance.

I owe a debt of gratitude to everyone else who provided helpful comments and feedback on earlier drafts, including Temi F. Bennett, Montré Carodine, Robert Chang, Marcia Chatelain, Darrick Hamilton, Sara Knight, Everett Long, Joseph P. Reidy, Ezra Rosser, Charles Seguin, Amy Simon, Fred Smith, and James Telesford.

This work stands on the shoulders of so many academics and researchers, too numerous to list, but I'm going to try by acknowledging a few: S. Megan Berthold, Carlton Fletcher, Arthur A. Hanses, Harry H. L. Kitano, Mitchell T. Maki, Dorothy S. Provine, Russell K. Shoho, Kevin J. Winkle, and a special shoutout to William A. ("Sandy") Darity, Jr., Samuel DuBois Cooke Distinguished Professor of Public Policy at Duke University, for his years of reparations research.

The unsung heroes and heroines award goes to the Georgetown Law Library, especially Daniel Donahue, Suzanne Miller, and Thanh H. Nguyen. I want to especially thank Rhonda Carter, Sumter County Register of Deeds Director, and Abby Cole and the South Caroliniana Library at the University of South Carolina.

I would like to thank Emory University and Georgetown Law for their financial support.

I want to acknowledge the Rockefeller Foundation for my Bellagio residency in the fall of 2022 and the support of Danielle Goonan. I would also like to thank the Robert Wood Johnson Foundation for their support and encouragement.

And finally, my gratitude to the world's greatest cheerleaders, my mother, Dorothy Brown, and my nephew, Jamaal Williams, for always having my back.

APPENDIX

Model Executive Order on the Establishment of the Presidential Commission on Post-Slavery Governmental Discrimination Against Black Americans[1]

By the authority vested in me as President by the Constitution and the laws of the United States of America, it is hereby ordered as follows:

Section 1. Establishment.

There is established the Presidential Commission on Post-Slavery Governmental Discrimination Against Black Americans (PtSD Commission) and the creation of the following ten sub-committees to study and consider proposals for reparations: (i) Criminal Justice Reform; (ii) Economic and Financial Well-Being; (iii) Education; (iv) Eligibility; (v) Environmental Justice; (vi) Funding Alternatives; (vii) Housing and Homeownership;

(viii) Physical Health and Mental Well-Being; (ix) Technology and Intellectual Property; and (x) Voting.

Section 2. Membership.

(a) The PtSD Commission shall be composed of not more than 55 members appointed by the President.

(b) Members of the PtSD Commission will have a demonstrated commitment to improving race relations in America. They will agree that structural racism and race-based discrimination need to be addressed in the United States. They will be in a position to devote substantial time and attention to the work of the PtSD Commission. They can be compensated in recognition of the significant work required to serve on the Commission.

(c) The President shall designate up to nine members of the PtSD Commission to serve as Co-Chairs and a Vice Chair to be selected from the remaining Commissioners.

Section 3. Powers.[2]

(a) For the purpose of carrying out this Executive Order, the PtSD Commission may do all of the following:

(1) Hold hearings and sit and act at any time and location.

(2) Request the attendance and testimony of witnesses.

(3) Request the production of books, records, correspondence, memoranda, papers, and documents.

(4) Seek an order from an appropriate Court compelling testimony or compliance with a subpoena, through assistance from the Department of Justice.

Section 4. Functions.

(a) The PtSD Commission shall produce a report for the President that includes the following:

(i)   a study of the post–Thirteenth Amendment discrimination faced by black Americans once chattel slavery ended across the country, in all facets of life, as well as an analysis of the roots of white wealth in America;

(ii) a study of the government's role that directly and indirectly prevented black Americans from having equal opportunity, including an examination of the complicity of the federal and state judicial branches in subordinating black Americans after the Thirteenth Amendment became law;

(iii) a quantification of the wealth and economic loss stripped from black Americans due to continuing racism after the Thirteenth Amendment; documentation of the complicity and neglect of state and federal law enforcement; and documentation of the wealth building that occurred in the white community simultaneously;

(iv) an examination of the link between that governmental failure and the resulting untold loss of intergenerational black wealth that could not be created as a result; and

(v)   recommendations for appropriate remedies to Congress based upon the findings in (i) to (iv) above.

(b) The PtSD Commission shall be organized into the previously mentioned ten subcommittee working groups. The working groups will regularly meet, solicit public comment where appropriate, include expert views, and ensure that their work is informed by a broad spectrum of relevant ideas. The working groups will make reports and recommendations to the full Commission. Only votes by the full Commission can be binding on the Commission.

(c) The PtSD Commission Co-Chairs shall solicit public comment from across the country, including other expert views, to ensure that its work is informed by a broad spectrum of relevant ideas.

(d) The PtSD Commission shall hold public hearings across the country that will be livestreamed and recorded. Subcommittee working group meetings are not required to be open to the public.

(e) The PtSD Commission shall accept comments through a variety of mechanisms including in-person hearings, email, text, and telephone. Hybrid participation (in person and online) shall be allowed.

(f) The PtSD Commission Co-Chairs shall periodically update the American people through televised programming.

(g) The PtSD Commission shall create a website that will be kept up-to-date.

(h) The PtSD Commission shall submit its report to the President within three years of its first public meeting.

Section 5. Administration.

(a) The Office of Administration within the Executive Office of the President shall provide funding and administrative support for the Commission to the extent permitted by law and within existing appropriations. To the extent permitted by law, including the Economy Act (31 USC 1535), and subject to the availability of appropriations, the General Services Administration shall provide administrative services, including facilities, staff, equipment, and other support services as may be necessary to carry out the objectives of the Commission, including outreach assistance.

(b) Members of the PtSD Commission can be compensated for their work, and shall be allowed travel expenses, including per diem in lieu of subsistence, to the extent permitted by law for persons serving intermittently in the Government service (5 USC 5701–5707).

(c) Insofar as the Federal Advisory Committee Act, as amended (5 USC App.) (Act), may apply to the Commission, any functions of the President under the Act, except for those in Section 6 of the Act, shall be performed by the Administrator of General Services.

Section 6. Termination.

The PtSD Commission shall not terminate before one year after it submits its report to the President in order to allow the Commissioners to advocate for the approved recommendations.

Section 7. General Provisions.

(a) Nothing in this order shall be construed to impair or otherwise affect:

(i) the authority granted by law to an executive department or agency, or the head thereof; or

(ii) the functions of the Director of the Office of Management and Budget relating to budgetary, administrative, or legislative proposals.

(b) This order shall be implemented consistent with applicable law and subject to the availability of appropriations.

(c) This order is not intended to, and does not, create any right or benefit, substantive or procedural, enforceable at law or in equity by any party against the United States, its departments, agencies, or entities, its officers, employees, or agents, or any other person.

NOTES

Introduction

1. Garrison Frazier, "Colloquy with Colored Ministers," *Journal of Negro History* 16, no. 1 (1931): 88.
2. Nancy Alderman, "A Biography of Charles Green," *Savannah Biographies* 78 (1980): 16, https://digitalcommons.georgiasouthern.edu/sav-bios -lane/78.
3. Sarah McCammon, "The Story Behind '40 Acres and a Mule,'" *All Things Considered*, NPR, January 12, 2015.
4. Frazier, "Colloquy with Colored Ministers," 89.
5. Eric Foner, *Reconstruction: America's Unfinished Revolution, 1863–1877* (New York: HarperPerennial, 2014), 70–71.
6. Barton Myers, "Sherman's Field Order No. 15," *New Georgia Encyclopedia*, https://www.georgiaencyclopedia.org/articles/history-archaeology/ shermans-field-order-no-15.
7. General William T. Sherman, "Special Field Orders No. 15," January 16, 1865, https://www.loc.gov/item/mss83434256.
8. Foner, *Reconstruction*, 71.
9. Foner, *Reconstruction*, 71.
10. My mother, Dorothy Brown, gave me some of this information, and the Georgetown University Law Library provided additional research to fill out many of the details.
11. Information from my mother, Dorothy Brown.

12. Richard Boisvert, interview by Marvin Lare, February 23, 2006, in *Champions of Civil and Human Rights in South Carolina,* a digital exhibition by the Department of Oral History at the University of South Carolina, https://digital.library.sc.edu/exhibits/champions/volume-5-2/part-1/richard-boisvert.

13. Deed of sale between Hattie M. Pratt and William B. James and Lucille Collins James for $650 on March 18, 1950, copy in author's possession. I owe a huge debt of gratitude to Suzanne Miller, Georgetown Law research librarian, and to Rhonda Carter, Sumter County Register of Deeds director, for tracking this information down.

14. Boisvert interview.

15. "Activist William B. James Dies," *Item,* February 6, 1989.

16. Hannah Natanson, Lauren Tierney, and Clara Ence Morse, "Which States Are Restricting, or Requiring Lessons on Race, Sex, or Gender," *Washington Post,* April 4, 2024.

17. Stephanie Condon, "After 148 Years, Mississippi Finally Ratifies 13th Amendment, Which Banned Slavery," CBS News, February 18, 2013.

Part I: Our Hidden History

1. "The whole number of petitions presented during this time was nine hundred and sixty-six, and the number of 'persons held to service or labor' embraced in the petitions, for whom compensation was claimed, is three thousand one hundred." *Emancipation in the District of Columbia: Letter from the Secretary of the Treasury,* 38th Cong. 2 (February 17, 1864).

2. "In 1858, Attorney General Jeremiah S. Black issued an opinion on the patentability of a 'new and useful machine invented by a slave.' He needed only three sentences to explain that an invention by an enslaved inventor could not be patented. . . . This reasoning also placed free African Americans outside the bounds of patent law." Kara Swinson, "Race and Selective Legal Memory: Reflections on Invention of a Slave," *Columbia Law Review* 120, no. 4 (2020): 1077, 1078 (citations omitted).

3. Gail S. Cleere, *The House on Observatory Hill: Home of the Vice President of the United States* (Washington, DC: US Government Printing Office), 5–6.

4. Mary Mitchell, *Divided Town* (Barre, MA: Barre Publishers, 1968), 66.

5. Eighth Census of the United States 1860, Series M653, Record Group 29, National Archives, Washington, DC. I would like to thank Tianna Mobley for her help in tracking down these records.

6. Amounts were calculated by author from the Barber petition, with $72 added for Eliza Toyer, for a total amount of $1,512.

7. Carlton Fletcher, "Slaves of Margaret Barber," Glover Park History, n.d., https://gloverparkhistory.com/estates-and-farms/north-view/slaves-of-margaret-barber.

8. Page Milburn, "The Emancipation of the Slaves in the District of

Columbia," *Records of the Columbia Historical Society* 16 (1913): 96–119. "The two leading newspapers, *The National Intelligencer* and *The Evening Star,* were opposed to the pending bill. Their editors however had to be careful not to say too much, or to speak too vehemently, for every citizen of the capital was closely watched in those days, and any suspicion of disloyalty to the Government made it very embarrassing, and might lead to a temporary residence in the Old Capitol Prison." Milburn, "Emancipation of Slaves in the District of Columbia," 103–4.

9. *Washington Evening Star,* March 19, 21, 1862, cited in Kenneth J. Winkle, "Emancipation in the District of Columbia," in *Civil War Washington: History, Place, and Digital Scholarship,* ed. Susan C. Lawrence (Lincoln: University of Nebraska Press, 2015), 65.

10. Silvana R. Siddali, *From Property to Person: Slavery and the Confiscation Acts, 1861–1862* (Baton Rouge: Louisiana State University Press, 2005), 120.

11. On the process as "petitions for compensation," see *Emancipation in the District of Columbia: Letter from the Secretary of the Treasury,* 38th Cong. 2 (February 17, 1864).

12. "Sec. 11. And be it further enacted, That the sum of one hundred thousand dollars, out of any money in the Treasury not otherwise appropriated, is hereby appropriated, to be expended under the direction of the President of the United States, to aid in the colonization and settlement of such free persons of African descent now residing in said District, including those to be liberated by this act, as may desire to emigrate to the Republics of Hayti or Liberia, or such other country beyond the limits of the United States as the President may determine: Provided, The expenditure for this purpose shall not exceed one hundred dollars for each emigrant." *An Act for the Release of Certain Persons held to Service or Labor in the District of Columbia,* 37th Cong., Sess. 2 (April 16, 1862).

13. Milburn, "Emancipation of Slaves in the District of Columbia," 117.

14. Mitchell, *Divided Town,* 64–65.

15. Mitchell, *Divided Town,* 67.

16. Dorothy S. Provine, *Compensated Emancipation in the District of Columbia: Petitions under the Act of April 16, 1862* (Westminster, MD: Heritage Books, 2008), 94–95.

17. Provine, *Compensated Emancipation in the District,* 94–95.

18. Mary Mitchell, "'I Held George Washington's Horse': Compensated Emancipation in the District of Columbia," *Records of the Columbia Historical Society,* no. 63/65 (1963/1965): 224.

19. Stephanie E. Jones-Rogers, *They Were Her Property: White Women as Slave Owners in the American South* (New Haven, CT: Yale University Press, 2019), 165.

20. Mitchell, "'I Held Washington's Horse,'" 228.

21. *Emancipation in the District of Columbia: Letter from the Secretary of the Treasury,* 38th Cong., 37–38 (February 17, 1864).

22. All eight petitions include the descriptor *colored* after the person's name. They are: Josiah Burgess, Gabriel Coakley, Robert Gunnell, Mary Hasson, Henry Hatton, Betty Roberson, Jacob Ross, and Amelia Tilghman. Provine, *Compensated Emancipation in the District,* 223–24, 85, 114, 136, 14, 118, 120, 151–52. George White, whose petition was filed late, was recommended to receive payment of $613.20. *Emancipation in the District of Columbia: Letter from the Secretary of the Treasury,* 38th Cong. 2 (February 17, 1864), 74. For in-depth reporting on Gabriel Coakley's subsequent history, listen to "Let's Get Free," episode 1 of Trymaine Lee's podcast *Uncounted Millions: The Power of Reparations,* February 15, 2024, https://www.msnbc.com/msnbc-podcast/uncounted-millions-get-free -rcna138686.

23. Winkle, "Emancipation in the District," 71.

24. Winkle, "Emancipation in the District," 71.

25. Mitchell, "'I Held Washington's Horse,'" 226–27.

26. Milburn, "Emancipation of Slaves in the District of Columbia," 118.

27. Kenneth J. Winkle, "Emancipation Petitions: Historical Contexts," in *Civil War Washington: History, Place, and Digital Scholarship,* ed. Susan C. Lawrence et al. (Lincoln: University of Nebraska Press, 2015).

28. Kenneth J. Winkle, "Mining the Compensated Emancipation Petitions," in Lawrence et al., *Civil War Washington,* 95.

29. Joseph P. Reidy, *Illusions of Emancipation: The Pursuit of Freedom and Equality in the Twilight of Slavery* (Chapel Hill: University of North Carolina Press, 2019), 185–86.

30. Reidy, *Illusions of Emancipation,* 186.

31. *Evidence Relating to the Petition of Charlotte Beckett and Children,* October 1, 1862, in Records of the Accounting Officers of the Department of the Treasury, 1775–1978, Record Group 217.6.5, National Archives, Washington, DC. Within the National Archives' Archival Description Catalog, see ARC Identifier 4644616 / MLR no. A1 347. A microfilm reproduction of the original document is held in Microcopy 520, Reel 6, NARA.

32. Reidy, *Illusions of Emancipation,* 186.

33. Winkle, "Mining the Compensated Emancipation Petitions," 96.

34. Mitchell, "'I Held Washington's Horse,'" 227.

35. Reidy, *Illusions of Emancipation,* 190.

36. Mitchell, "'I Held Washington's Horse,'" 229.

37. Carlton Fletcher, "Glover Park History: Historical Sketches of Glover Park, Upper Georgetown, and Georgetown Heights," https://gloverparkhistory .com/estates-and-farms/north-view/slaves-of-margaret-barber.

38. Alan G. Gauthreaux, *Italian Louisiana: History, Heritage and Tradition* (Charleston, SC: History Press, 2014), 14.

39. Charles Webb, "The Lynching of Sicilian Immigrants in the American South, 1886–1910," *American Nineteenth Century History* 3, no.1 (2002): 45, 55.

40. Webb, "Lynching of Sicilian Immigrants," 57.
41. Webb, "Lynching of Sicilian Immigrants," 57.
42. Webb, "Lynching of Sicilian Immigrants," 59.
43. Gauthreaux, *Italian Louisiana,* 23.
44. Webb, "Lynching of Sicilian Immigrants," 57.
45. Christine DeLucia, "Getting the Story Straight: Press Coverage of Italian-American Lynchings from 1856–1910," *Italian Americana* 21, no. 2 (2003): 213.
46. John Smith Kendall, *History of New Orleans* (Chicago: Lewis Publishing Co., 1922), 1:481. The concept of "reparation" is defined in the International Law Commission's Articles of State Responsibility as follows: "Full reparation for the injury caused by the internationally wrongful act shall take the form of restitution, compensation and satisfaction, either singly or in combination, in accordance with the provisions of this chapter" (Article 34). *Responsibility of States for Internationally Wrongful Acts,* United Nations, 2005, https://legal.un.org/ilc/texts/instruments/english/draft_articles/9_6_2001.pdf.
47. Alan G. Gauthreaux, "An Inhospitable Land: Anti-Italian Sentiment and Violence in Louisiana, 1891–1924," *Journal of the Louisiana Historical Association* 51, no. 1 (2010): 50–51. On March 15, 1891, the US secretary of state, James G. Blaine, repeatedly told Italian ambassador Fava that "the federal government would eventually approve a request of indemnity." Charles Seguin and Sabrina Nardin, "The Lynching of Italians and the Rise of Antilynching Politics in the United States," *Social Science History* 46 (2022): 76.
48. "Secretary of State Blaine wrote to the Marquis Imperiali stating, 'The President, . . . instructs me to tender you 125,000 francs,' the total amount to be distributed among the victims' families." Gauthreaux, *Italian Louisiana,* 77.
49. Gauthreaux, *Italian Louisiana,* 9.1.
50. Some of their names were reported in the newspaper incorrectly. Lorenzo Saladino was reported correctly, but Decino Sorcoro should have been reported as Salvatore Arena, and Angelo Mancuso should have been reported as Giuseppe Vontorelli.
51. Anna Thibodeaux, "St. Charles Parish Had Its Own Italian Lynchings in 1896," *St. Charles Herald Guide* (Louisiana), April 29, 2019, https://www.heraldguide.com/news/st-charles-parish-had-its-own-italian-lynchings-in-1896.
52. Gauthreaux, *Italian Louisiana,* 90.
53. Gauthreaux, *Italian Louisiana,* 90–91.
54. Thibodeaux, "St. Charles Parish Lynchings."
55. Thibodeaux, "St. Charles Parish Lynchings."
56. Thibodeaux, "St. Charles Parish Lynchings."
57. Gauthreaux, *Italian Louisiana,* 92.
58. Gauthreaux, *Italian Louisiana,* 92.

59. Gauthreaux, *Italian Louisiana*, 93.

60. Gauthreaux, "Inhospitable Land," 57–59.

61. Jessica Barbata Jackson, *Dixie's Italians: Sicilians, Race, and Citizenship in the Jim Crow Gulf South* (Baton Rouge: Louisiana State University Press, 2020), 59.

62. Jackson, *Dixie's Italians*, 60.

63. Jackson, *Dixie's Italians*, 60.

64. Jackson, *Dixie's Italians*, 60.

65. Jackson, *Dixie's Italians*, 60.

66. Gauthreaux, "Inhospitable Land," 61.

67. Jackson, *Dixie's Italians*, 61.

68. Jackson, *Dixie's Italians*, 61.

69. Jackson, *Dixie's Italians*, 62–63.

70. Jackson, *Dixie's Italians*, 63.

71. Patrizia Fama Stahle, "Protection of Italian Laborers on U.S. Soil: Proposals of a Federal Anti-Lynching Law and Relations Between Italy and the United States," *Italian Americana* 35, no. 1 (2017): 16.

72. Stahle, "Protection of Italian Laborers," 16.

73. Stahle, "Protection of Italian Laborers," 16.

74. In addition to compensation on behalf of Italian citizens, the United States also made payments on behalf of other countries' citizens, including China and Mexico. William D. Carrigan and Clive Webb, "African Americans and the Lynching of Foreign Nationals in the United States," *Journal of World History* 33, no. 4 (2022): 669–702. Congress approved "payment of $147,000 in indemnities" to China (677). "On January 18, 1898, President McKinley requested that Congress authorize a $2000 indemnity to [the family of a Mexican lynched in California]" (680).

75. Joseph William Singer, "Indian Title: Unraveling the Racial Context of Property Rights, or How to Stop Engaging in Conquest," *Albany Government Law Review* 10 (2017): 9 (emphasis in the original).

76. See *Johnson v. McIntosh*, 21 U.S. (8 Wheat.) 543 (1823). Here the Supreme Court held that American Indians had no right to sell land, just the right of occupancy.

77. David E. Wilkins, *Hollow Justice: A History of Indigenous Claims in the United States* (New Haven, CT: Yale University Press, 2013), 6.

78. *Johnson v. McIntosh*, 21 U.S. at 543. See also Jessica A. Shoemaker, "An Introduction to American Indian Land Tenure: Mapping the Legal Landscape," *Journal of Law, Property, and Society* 5 (2020): 1–100.

79. *Cherokee Nation v. Georgia*, 30 U.S. 1 (1831).

80. US Indian Claims Commission, "Final Report," August 13, 1946–September 30, 1978, 1.

81. Indian Claims Commission, "Final Report," 5.

82. *Johnson v. McIntosh*, 21 U.S. at 590. See also Robert A. Williams, Jr., *The American Indian in Western Legal Thought: The Discourses of Conquest*

(New York: Oxford University Press, 1990), tracing the racist origins and racist reasoning of the Court's treatment of American Indians.

83. Wilkins, *Hollow Justice*, 68.

84. Wilkins, *Hollow Justice*, 67.

85. *An Act to Create an Indian Claims Commission, to Provide for the Powers, Duties, and Functions Thereof, and for Other Purposes*, 79th Cong., 2nd Sess., August 13, 1946 (Section 23), 60 Stat. 1055, https://maint.loc.gov/law/help/statutes-at-large/79th-congress/session-2/c79s2ch959.pdf.

86. Nothing in the statute explicitly forbids returning land to the Tribes. However, the commission awarded only monetary damages. The Sioux Tribe has never taken any of its award because it believes the return of land is what is required. See Edward Lazarus, *Black Hills/White Justice: The Sioux Nation Versus the United States, 1775 to the Present* (New York: HarperCollins, 1991). The money sits in a government account. Henry Gass, "When $1 Billion Isn't Enough. Why the Sioux Won't Put a Price on Land," *Christian Science Monitor*, July 24, 2023.

87. Wilkins, *Hollow Justice*, 68.

88. Wilkins, *Hollow Justice*, 69.

89. Wilkins, *Hollow Justice*, 71.

90. *Act to Create an Indian Claims Commission*, 60 Stat 1052 (Section 13a). Notification was also to be sent to the superintendents of all Indian agencies who were to provide detailed explanations to the Native communities within their region.

91. *Act to Create an Indian Claims Commission*, 60 Stat 1052 (Sections 10, 12).

92. Wilkins, *Hollow Justice*, 75.

93. Indian Claims Commission, "Final Report," 15.

94. *Citizen Band of Potawatomi Indians of Oklahoma, and Potawatomi Nation Represented by Citizen Band of Potawatomi Indians of Oklahoma et al., the Potawatomie Nation of Indians, the Prairie Band of the Potawatomie Nation of Indians et al., v. The United States*, 11 Ind. Cl. Comm. 641 (1962).

95. *Citizen Band of Potawatomi Indians of Oklahoma, et al. v. United States*, 15 Ind. Cl. Comm. 234 (1965).

96. *Citizen Band of Potawatomi Indians of Oklahoma, et al. v. United States*, 30 Ind. Cl. Comm. 144 (1973).

97. Michael Lieder and Jake Page, *Wild Justice: The People of Geronimo vs. the United States* (Norman: University of Oklahoma Press, 1999), 90.

98. Wilkins, *Hollow Justice*, 122–23.

99. *United States v. Pueblo of San Ildefonso*, 513 F.2d 1383 (Fed. Cir. 1975).

100. Lieder and Page, *Wild Justice*, 257; and Wilkins, *Hollow Justice*, 103.

101. David Reyes, "Night Visitors Brought Halt to Family's Hopes: Relocation: Odyssey of O.C.'s Masudas Mirrored Fates of Thousands Along the West Coast," *Los Angeles Times*, February 17, 1992.

102. Arthur A. Hansen, "Nikkei Agriculture in Orange County, California, the Masuda Farm Family, and the American Way of Redressing Racism—

Part 2 of 6," *Discover Nikkei,* November 30, 2012, https://discovernikkei
.org/en/journal/2012/11/30/masuda-family-2.

103. Tom Berg, "Family's Love of Country Overcame Injustices," *Orange County Register,* May 27, 2014.

104. Berg, "Family's Love of Country."

105. Hansen, "Nikkei Agriculture in Orange County . . . —Part 3 of 6," *Discover Nikkei,* December 7, 2012, https://discovernikkei.org/en/journal/2012/12/7/masuda-family-3/; Russell K. Shoho, *From the Battlefields to the Home Front: The Kazuo Masuda Legacy* (California: Nikkei Writers Guild, 2009), 3.

106. Commission on Wartime Relocation and Internment of Civilians [CWRIC], *Personal Justice Denied* (Seattle: University of Washington Press, 1997), 47.

107. Hansen, "Nikkei Agriculture—Part 3 of 6."

108. Hansen, "Nikkei Agriculture—Part 3 of 6."

109. Shoho, *Battlefields to the Home Front,* 3.

110. Mitchell T. Maki, Harry H. L. Kitano, and S. Megan Berthold, *Achieving the Impossible Dream: How Japanese Americans Obtained Redress* (Urbana: University of Illinois Press, 1999), 117.

111. Maki, Kitano, and Berthold, *Achieving the Impossible Dream,* 117–18.

112. "By October 1942, the government was holding over 100,000 evacuees in relocation centers." CWRIC, *Personal Justice Denied,* 185.

113. In 1913 Congress passed the Alien Land Act, which prevented noncitizens from purchasing or leasing land, specifically targeting Japanese immigrants. However "one observer reported in 1934 that the law was virtually a dead letter in many if not all parts of the state. This condition continued until shortly after the outbreak of war with Japan in December, 1941." Edwin E. Ferguson, "The California Alien Land Law and the Fourteenth Amendment," *California Law Review* 35, no. 1 (1947): 72. This could help explain how this purchase occurred. See also CWRIC, *Personal Justice Denied,* 457.

114. *Korematsu v. United States,* 323 U.S. 214 (1944). And a year before *Korematsu,* the Supreme Court upheld the criminal curfews targeted at Japanese American citizens. In *Hirabayashi,* the Court acknowledged that "distinctions between citizens solely because of their ancestry are by their very nature odious to a free people whose institutions are founded upon the doctrine of equality." But it went on to conclude that in this instance, the government could permissibly determine that "a group of one national extraction may menace [public] safety more than others." *Hirabayashi v. United States,* 320 U.S. 81 (1943) at 120–21.

115. Hansen, "Nikkei Agriculture in Orange County . . . —Part 4 of 6," *Discover Nikkei,* December 14, 2012, https://discovernikkei.org/en/journal/2012/12/14/masuda-family-4.

116. Hansen, "Nikkei Agriculture in Orange County—Part 4 of 6."

117. Shoho, *Battlefields to the Home Front*, 9.
118. Masato Uyeda, testimony, September 10, 1981, in *Commission on Wartime Relocation and Internment of Civilians: Hearings Held in Seattle, Washington*, 48. These records are not available for online search. https://catalog.archives.gov/id/734681.
119. Grace Watanabe Kimura, testimony, September 22, 1981, in *Commission on Wartime Relocation and Internment of Civilians: Hearings Held in Chicago, Illinois*, 148. https://collections.carli.illinois.edu/digital/collection/nei_japan/id/1638 (Japanese American Redress Collection, Northeastern Illinois University).
120. Shuzo Chris Kato, testimony, September 9, 1981, in *Commission on Wartime Relocation and Internment of Civilians: Hearings Held in Seattle, Washington*, 265.
121. Shoho, *Battlefields to the Home Front*, 37.
122. Berg, "Family's Love of Country."
123. Hansen, "Nikkei Agriculture in Orange County, . . . Part 5 of 6," *Discover Nikkei*, December 21, 2012, https://discovernikkei.org/en/journal/2012/12/21/masuda-family-5. And in a story full of twists and turns, yet another occurred when the government adopted the policy a day before the Supreme Court decision, apparently because they were tipped off. Cliff Sloan, *The Court at War: FDR, His Justices, and the World* (New York: PublicAffairs, 2023), 321–24.
124. Hansen, "Nikkei Agriculture in Orange County—Part 5 of 6"; "Threats Told by Japanese Girl," *Santa Ana Register*, May 15, 1945.
125. "Winchell Blasts Alleged Threats Against Japanese-American Girl Here," *Santa Ana Register*, May 28, 1945.
126. Neal Gabler, *Winchell: Gossip, Power and the Culture of Celebrity* (New York: Knopf, 1994), xi.
127. Berg, "Family's Love of Country."
128. Hansen, "Nikkei Agriculture in Orange County—Part 5 of 6."
129. "Very few could come back to their prewar holdings. Only about 25 percent of the prewar farm operators, for example, retained property." CWRIC, *Personal Justice Denied*, 241.
130. Hansen, "Nikkei Agriculture in Orange County—Part 5 of 6."
131. Hansen, "Nikkei Agriculture in Orange County—Part 5 of 6."
132. Hansen, "Nikkei Agriculture in Orange County—Part 5 of 6."
133. CWRIC, *Personal Justice Denied*, 461.
134. CWRIC, *Personal Justice Denied*, 461.
135. *Commission on Wartime Relocation and Internment of Civilians: Hearings Held in Chicago, Illinois*, September 22, 1981 (testimony of Toaru Ishiyama, 260–63).
136. Maki, Kitano, and Berthold, *Achieving the Impossible Dream*, 64.
137. Maki, Kitano, and Berthold, *Achieving the Impossible Dream*, 64.
138. CWRIC, *Personal Justice Denied*, xvi.

139. Pub. L. No. 96-317, 94 Stat. 964 (1980); CWRIC, *Personal Justice Denied,* xvii.

140. Maki, Kitano, and Berthold, *Achieving the Impossible Dream,* 97.

141. Timothy P. Maga, "Ronald Reagan and Redress for Japanese Internment, 1983–1988," *Presidential Studies Quarterly* 28, no. 3 (1998): 608n8.

142. Pub. L. No. 97-3, 95 Stat. 5 (1981). The "law allowed the Speaker of the House and the President Pro Tempore of the Senate to select one additional commissioner each." The House selected Father Drinan and the Senate chose Father Gromoff. Maki, Kitano, and Berthold, *Achieving the Impossible Dream,* 97.

143. Maki, Kitano, and Berthold, *Achieving the Impossible Dream,* 97.

144. Maki, Kitano, and Berthold, *Achieving the Impossible Dream,* 119.

145. Maki, Kitano, and Berthold, *Achieving the Impossible Dream,* 120.

146. CWRIC, *Personal Justice Denied,* 18.

147. CWRIC, *Personal Justice Denied,* 457.

148. CWRIC, *Personal Justice Denied,* 456.

149. CWRIC, *Personal Justice Denied,* 457.

150. CWRIC, *Personal Justice Denied,* 241.

151. *Commission on Wartime Relocation and Internment of Civilians: Hearings Held in Seattle, Washington,* September 10, 1981 (testimony of Masato Uyeda, 47, 49).

152. *Commission on Wartime Relocation and Internment of Civilians: Hearings Held in Seattle, Washington,* September 9, 1981 (testimony of Shuzo Chris Kato, 261–62).

153. *Commission on Wartime Relocation and Internment of Civilians: Hearings Held in Chicago, Illinois,* September 22, 1981 (testimony of Masaru K. Yamasaki, 141–43). https://collections.carli.illinois.edu/digital/collection/nei_japan/id/2420 (Japanese American Redress Collection, Northeastern Illinois University).

154. CWRIC, *Personal Justice Denied,* 459.

155. CWRIC, *Personal Justice Denied,* 459.

156. CWRIC, *Personal Justice Denied,* 460–61.

157. CWRIC, *Personal Justice Denied,* 460–61.

158. CWRIC, *Personal Justice Denied,* 462–64.

159. Payments were also made to the Aleuts. "When the Japanese attacked and captured the two westernmost Aleutian islands, Kiska and Attu, the military evacuated the Aleuts. . . . The Commission found no persuasive showing that the evacuation of the Aleuts was motivated by racism or that it was undertaken for any reason but their safety. . . . [H]owever the approximately 900 evacuated Aleuts suffered at the hands of the government in two distinct ways. First, no plan had been developed to care for them by the civilian agencies in the Department of the Interior which had responsibility for Aleut interests. As a result, they were transported to southeast Alaska and housed in camps set up typically at abandoned gold mines or canneries. Conditions varied among camps, but

housing, sanitation and eating conditions in most were deplorable. Medical care was inadequate; illness and disease were widespread. While exact numbers are not available, it appears that approximately ten percent of the Aleut evacuees died during the two to three years they spent in the camps. . . . Second, on returning to their villages, the Aleuts found that many houses and churches had been vandalized by the U.S. military. Houses, churches, furniture, boats and fishing gear were missing, damaged or destroyed. They lost religious icons. . . . The losses were never remedied adequately. . . . The Commissioners, . . . recommend that Congress appropriate funds and direct a payment of $5,000 per capita to each of the few hundred surviving Aleuts who were evacuated." CWRIC, *Personal Justice Denied,* 464–66. The Aleuts are not discussed further in the book.

160. Martha Nakagawa, "National Council for Japanese American Redress," *Densho Encyclopedia,* August 9, 2024, https://encyclopedia.densho.org/National_Council_for_Japanese_American_Redress/#Impact_on_Redress_Bill_and_Dissolution.
161. Nakagawa, "National Council for Redress."
162. Nakagawa, "National Council for Redress."
163. Maki, Kitano, and Berthold, *Achieving the Impossible Dream,* 191. See also Ronald Reagan, "Statement of Administration Policy: H.R. 442—Civil Liberties Act of 1987," September 10, 1987, https://www.presidency.ucsb.edu/documents/statement-administration-policy-hr-442-civil-liberties-act-1987.
164. Maki, Kitano, and Berthold, *Achieving the Impossible Dream,* 191.
165. Maki, Kitano, and Berthold, *Achieving the Impossible Dream,* 191.
166. Thomas H. Kean, *The Politics of Inclusion* (New York: Free Press, 1988), 198.
167. Maki, Kitano, and Berthold, *Achieving the Impossible Dream,* 149n46.
168. Maki, Kitano, and Berthold, *Achieving the Impossible Dream,* 149n47.
169. Maki, Kitano, and Berthold, *Achieving the Impossible Dream,* 192.
170. Maki, Kitano, and Berthold, *Achieving the Impossible Dream,* 192.
171. Maki, Kitano, and Berthold, *Achieving the Impossible Dream,* 192.
172. Maki, Kitano, and Berthold, *Achieving the Impossible Dream,* 193.
173. Maki, Kitano, and Berthold, *Achieving the Impossible Dream,* 193–94.
174. Maki, Kitano, and Berthold, *Achieving the Impossible Dream,* 194.
175. Maki, Kitano, and Berthold, *Achieving the Impossible Dream,* 189.
176. Maki, Kitano, and Berthold, *Achieving the Impossible Dream,* 190.
177. Maki, Kitano, and Berthold, *Achieving the Impossible Dream,* 190.
178. Maki, Kitano, and Berthold, *Achieving the Impossible Dream,* 194.
179. Maki, Kitano, and Berthold, *Achieving the Impossible Dream,* 194–95.
180. Pub. L. No. 100-383, 102 Stat. 903 (1988), Section 1, https://www.govinfo.gov/content/pkg/STATUTE-102/pdf/STATUTE-102-Pg903.pdf.
181. Maki, Kitano, and Berthold, *Achieving the Impossible Dream,* 195.
182. Ronald Reagan, "Remarks on Signing the Bill Providing Restitution for the Wartime Internment of Japanese-American Civilians," August 10, 1988, Ronald Reagan Presidential Library, https://www.reaganlibrary.gov/

archives/speech/remarks-signing-bill-providing-restitution-wartime
-internment-japanese-american.
183. Reagan, "Remarks on Signing the Bill."
184. *Jacobs v. Barr,* 959 F.2d 313 (1992).
185. *Jacobs v. Barr,* 959 F.2d at 314.
186. The Supreme Court denied the writ of certiorari. *Jacobs v. Barr,* 506 U.S. 831 (1992). And once the Supreme Court acted, NCJAR disbanded. Nakagawa, "National Council for Redress."

Part II: Everything, Everywhere, All at Once

1. "The debates demonstrated that both supporters and opponents of the [Thirteenth] amendment expected the constitutional change to provide sweeping power to protect civil rights. Section 2, as the congressmen understood it and the Supreme Court later interpreted it, provided the authority to end all manner of subjugation, not only chattel slavery. In the course of a contentious debate, a consensus developed that the Thirteenth Amendment would empower Congress to end arbitrary practices connected to the incidents of involuntary servitude." Alexander Tsesis, "Introduction: The Thirteenth Amendment's Revolutionary Aims," in *The Promises of Liberty: The History and Contemporary Relevance of the Thirteenth Amendment,* ed. Alexander Tsesis (New York: Columbia University Press, 2010), 11.
2. Tsesis, "Introduction," 10.
3. Risa L. Goluboff, *The Lost Promise of Civil Rights* (Cambridge, MA: Harvard University Press, 2007), 18.
4. Tsesis, "Introduction," 11.
5. George A. Rutherglen, "The Badges and Incidents of Slavery and the Power of Congress to Enforce the Thirteenth Amendment," in Tsesis, *Promises of Liberty,* 169.
6. Cong. Globe, 38th Cong., 1st Sess. 1490 (1864) (statement of James McDougall).
7. Rutherglen, "Badges and Incidents of Slavery," 168.
8. Alexander Tsesis, *The Thirteenth Amendment and American Freedom: A Legal History* (New York: New York University Press, 2004), 40.
9. Rutherglen, "Badges and Incidents of Slavery," 168.
10. Tsesis, "Introduction," 11.
11. Carol Anderson, *White Rage: The Unspoken Truth of Our Racial Divide* (New York: Bloomsbury, 2016), 30.
12. Anderson, *White Rage,* 30.
13. Cong. Globe, 39th Cong., 1st Sess., 1833 (1866) (statement of Rep. William Lawrence).
14. Trina Williams Shanks, "The Homestead Act: A Major Asset-Building Policy in American History," in *Inclusion in the American Dream: Assets,*

Poverty, and Public Policy, ed. Michael Sherraden (New York: Oxford University Press, 2005), 23–25.

15. Shanks, "Homestead Act," 35. According to Shanks, "The reality is that few homesteads were granted to black claimants" (36).

16. "Beginning in 1843, when he was first elected to the U.S. Congress, and over the next nineteen years, Johnson had championed the Homestead Act, which would *give*, not lease, 160 acres in the West to citizens who were 'without money'—meaning poor whites." Johnson was supportive of the original Homestead Act. Anderson, *White Rage,* 16 (emphasis in the original).

17. W.E.B. Du Bois, *Black Reconstruction in America, 1860–1880* (1935; reprint New York: Free Press, 1998), 230. For a recent take on the Freedmen's Bureau, see Justene Hill Edwards, *Savings and Trust: The Rise and Betrayal of the Freedman's Bank* (New York: Norton, 2024).

18. Du Bois, *Black Reconstruction in America,* 230.

19. Vann R. Newkirk II, "The Great Land Robbery," *Atlantic,* September 29, 2019. For the original quote, see Du Bois, *Black Reconstruction in America,* 601.

20. Dania V. Francis et al., "Black Land Loss: 1920–1997," *AEA Papers and Proceedings* 112 (2022): 38.

21. Quoted in Dolores Barclay, Todd Lewan, and Allen G. Breed, "Lynched for Their Land: Violence Used to Separate Blacks from Their Acreage," *Seattle Times,* December 2, 2001.

22. Annette Gordon-Reed, *Andrew Johnson* (New York: Times Books, 2011), Kindle ed., loc. 116.

23. John Hope Franklin, "The Civil Rights Act of 1866 Revisited," *Hastings Law Journal* 41, no. 5 (1990): 1136n9 (discussing "In re Turner, 24 F. Cas. 337 [C.C.D. Md. 1867]").

24. Franklin, "Civil Rights Act Revisited," 1137n11 (discussing "Stevens v. Richmond, Fredericksburg, and Potomac R.R. Co., Judge John C. Underwood Papers, Scrapbook 193, 203, 205, 227, Library of Congress").

25. Heather A. O'Connell, "The Impact of Slavery on Racial Inequality in Poverty in the Contemporary U.S. South," *Social Forces* 90, no 3 (2012): 716.

26. Franklin, "Civil Rights Act Revisited," 1141n41. Report of the Joint Committee on Reconstruction, 39th Cong., 1st Sess., pt. ii at 123 (1866). See also *New York Times,* June 27, 1865, at 1, col. 2; *New York Times,* August 1, 1865, at 1, col. 1.

27. Christopher R. Adamson, "Punishment After Slavery: Southern State Penal Systems, 1865–1890," *Social Problems* 30, no. 5 (1983): 559.

28. "All available evidence points to the fact that blacks were not sent to prison in great numbers prior to the war." Randall G. Shelden, "From Slave to Caste Society: Penal Changes in Tennessee, 1830–1915," *Tennessee Historical Quarterly* 38, no. 4 (1979): 464.

29. Shelden, "From Slave to Caste Society," 463.

30. W.E.B. Du Bois, "The Spawn of Slavery: The Convict-Lease System in the South," *Missionary Review of the World* 14 (1901): 74, https://www .crisisopportunity.org/articles/PDFS/DuBois_1901_Spawn.pdf.

31. Eric Foner, *Reconstruction: America's Unfinished Revolution, 1863–1877* (New York: HarperPerennial, 2014), 205.

32. "It was once a crime where I stand to teach a slave to read, but not a crime to buy or sell that slave." Frank B. Sanborn, "Negro Crime," in *Some Notes on Negro Crime Particularly in Georgia*, ed. W.E.B. Du Bois (Atlanta: Atlanta University Press, 1904), 1.

33. Douglas A. Blackmon, *Slavery by Another Name: The Re-Enslavement of Black Americans from the Civil War to World War II* (New York: Anchor Books, 2008), 8. See also Robin Bernstein, *Freeman's Challenge: The Murder That Shook America's Original Prison for Profit* (Illinois: University of Chicago Press, 2024).

34. Foner, *Reconstruction*, 205.

35. Blackmon, *Slavery by Another Name*, 7–8.

36. Shelden, "From Slave to Caste Society," 466.

37. Blackmon, *Slavery by Another Name*, 1. See also Talitha L. LeFlouria, *Chained in Silence: Black Women and Convict Labor in the South* (Chapel Hill: University of North Carolina Press, 2015).

38. Shelden, "From Slave to Caste Society," 465.

39. Blackmon, *Slavery by Another Name*, 7.

40. James Gray Pope, "Mass Incarceration, Convict Leasing, and the Thirteenth Amendment: A Revisionist Account," *New York University Law Review* 94 (2019): 1505.

41. Blackmon, *Slavery by Another Name*, 1–2.

42. Michele Goodwin, "The Thirteenth Amendment: Modern Slavery, Capitalism, and Mass Incarceration," *Cornell Law Review* 104, no. 4 (2019): 943.

43. Blackmon, *Slavery by Another Name*, 375.

44. Blackmon, *Slavery by Another Name*, 377. There were also concerns about children, especially orphans, being exploited this way. "Without a network of institutions to ensure their protection, some African American children fell victim to exploitation." C. Spencer, "Negro Children Sold into Slavery," *Chicago Inter-Ocean*, May 1913, Folder 39-13 (39-13), Illinois Writers Project, Vivian C. Harsh Collection, Carter G. Woodson Regional Library, Chicago. See also Arthur Alden Guild, "Baby Farms in Chicago: An Investigation Made for the Juvenile Protective Association," Juvenile Protective Association, 1917. Marcia Chatelain provided me with this information from a draft of her forthcoming book.

45. Kidada E. Williams, *I Saw Death Coming: A History of Terror and Survival in the War Against Reconstruction* (New York: Bloomsbury, 2023), xvii.

46. Robert A. Gibson, "The Negro Holocaust: Lynching and Race Riots in the United States, 1880–1950," *Yale-New Haven Teachers Institute* (1979), https://teachersinstitute.yale.edu/curriculum/units/1979/2/79.02.04/2.

47. Philip Dray, "How a Lynching in New York 130 Years Ago Reverberates Today," *Time,* June 2, 2022.

48. Lorenzo J. Greene and Carter G. Woodson, *The Negro Wage Earner* (Washington, DC: Wildside Press, 1930), 37.

49. Greene and Woodson, *Negro Wage Earner,* 46.

50. US Bureau of the Census, *Official Register of the United States, Containing a List of the Officers and Employés in the Civil, Military, and Naval Service of the First of July, 1891; together with a List of Vessels Belonging to the United States,* vol. 2, *The Post-Office Department and the Postal Service* (Washington, DC: Government Printing Office, 1892), 1057.

51. Greene and Woodson, *Negro Wage Earner,* 193.

52. Paula Giddings, *Ida: A Sword Among Lions* (New York: Amistad, 2008), 175.

53. Giddings, *Ida,* 175.

54. Terence Finnegan, " 'Politics of Defiance': Uncovering the Causes and Consequences of Lynching and Communal Violence," *Journal of American History* 101, no. 3 (December 2014): 851. For more on how lynching results from "conflicts between black males and white males," see Terence Finnegan, *A Deed So Accursed: Lynching in Mississippi and South Carolina, 1881–1940* (Charlottesville: University of Virginia Press, 2013).

55. Giddings, *Ida,* 182.

56. Ida B. Wells, *Crusade for Justice: The Autobiography of Ida B. Wells* (Chicago: University of Chicago Press, 1970), 46.

57. Giddings, *Ida,* 210–14.

58. Shytierra Gaston, "Historical Racist Violence and Intergenerational Harms: Accounts from Descendants of Lynching Victims," *Annals of the American Academy of Political and Social Science* 694, no. 1 (2021): 87.

59. Barclay, Lewan, and Breed, "Lynched for Their Land."

60. W. Fitzhugh Brundage, *Lynching in the New South: Georgia and Virginia, 1880–1930* (Urbana: University of Illinois Press, 1993), Kindle ed., loc. 8.

61. Barclay, Lewan, and Breed, "Lynched for Their Land."

62. Gaston, "Historical Racist Violence," 87.

63. Gaston, "Historical Racist Violence," 88.

64. Gaston, "Historical Racist Violence," 87.

65. Barclay, Lewan, and Breed, "Lynched for Their Land."

66. Raymond A. Winbush, "And the Earth Moved: Stealing Black Land in the United States," in *Should America Pay?: Slavery and the Raging Debate on Reparations,* ed. Raymond A. Winbush (New York: HarperCollins, 2003), Kindle ed., loc. 71.

67. J. R. Grossman, *A Chance to Make Good: African Americans 1900–1929* (New York: Oxford University Press, 1997) Kindle ed., loc. 32.

68. Barclay, Lewan, and Breed, "Lynched for Their Land."

69. Todd Lewan and Dolores Barclay, "Torn from the Land: Black Americans' Farmland Taken Through Cheating, Intimidation, Even Murder," *Seattle Times,* December 2, 2001.

70. Barclay, Lewan, and Breed, "Lynched for Their Land."

71. Barclay, Lewan, and Breed, "Lynched for Their Land."
72. Anderson, *White Rage,* 58.
73. Anderson, *White Rage,* 58.
74. Barclay, Lewan, and Breed, "Lynched for Their Land."
75. Barclay, Lewan, and Breed, "Lynched for Their Land."
76. Lewan and Barclay, "Torn from the Land."
77. "In 1938, the court ruled the company [Masonite] had clear title to the land, which has since yielded millions of dollars in natural gas, timber and oil, according to state records. From the few property records that survived the fire, the AP was able to document that at least 204.5 of those acres had been acquired by Masonite after black owners were driven off by the Klan. At least 850,000 barrels of oil have been pumped from this property, according to state records. Today, the land is owned by International Paper, which acquired Masonite in 1988." Lewan and Barclay, "Torn from the Land."
78. Sherrilyn Ifill, *On the Courthouse Lawn: Confronting the Legacy of Lynching in the 21st Century* (Boston: Beacon Press, 2018).
79. Price Fishback et al., "New Evidence on Redlining by Federal Housing Programs in the 1930s," *Journal of Urban Economics* 141 (2024): 8.
80. Dorothy A. Brown, *The Whiteness of Wealth: How the Tax System Impoverishes Black Americans—And How We Can Fix It* (New York: Crown, 2021), 68.
81. Ira Katznelson, *When Affirmative Action Was White: An Untold History of Racial Inequality in Twentieth-Century America* (New York: Norton, 2005), 113.
82. Katznelson, *When Affirmative Action Was White,* 113.
83. Juan F. Perea, "Doctrines of Delusion: How the History of the G.I. Bill and Other Inconvenient Truths Undermine the Supreme Court's Affirmative Action Jurisprudence," *University of Pittsburgh Law Review* 75 (2014): 595.
84. Katznelson, *When Affirmative Action Was White,* 124.
85. Louis Lee Woods II, "Almost 'No Negro Veteran . . . Could Get a Loan': African Americans, the GI Bill, and the NAACP Campaign Against Residential Segregation, 1917–1960," *Journal of African American History* 98, no. 3 (2013): 392.
86. Woods, "Almost 'No Negro Veteran . . . Could Get a Loan,'" 392–93.
87. Shanks, "Homestead Act," 23.
88. *Dred Scott v. Sandford,* 60 U.S. 393, 407 (1857).
89. Shanks, "Homestead Act," 35.
90. "Either way, the reality is that few homesteads were granted to black claimants." Shanks, "Homestead Act," 36.
91. Shanks, "Homestead Act," 23.
92. Richard Edwards, "The Homestead Act and the Struggle for African American Rights," *Great Plains Quarterly* 41, no 3–4 (2021): 191.
93. Keri Leight Merritt, *Masterless Men: Poor Whites and Slavery in the Antebellum South* (Cambridge: Cambridge University Press, 2017), 38.

94. James Loewen, *Sundown Towns: A Hidden Dimension of American Racism* (New York: New Press, 2018), 4.
95. O'Connell, "Impact of Slavery on Racial Inequality in Poverty in U.S. South," 323.
96. Loewen, *Sundown Towns*, 4.
97. Loewen, *Sundown Towns*, 70.
98. Peggy Pascoe, *What Comes Naturally: Miscegenation Law and the Making of Race in America* (Oxford: Oxford University Press, 2009).
99. Loewen, *Sundown Towns*, 56.
100. "Historian Olen Cole Jr. tells how the Civilian Conservation Corps in the 1930s tried to locate a company of African American workers in a large park that bordered Burbank and Glendale. Both cities refused; the reason given was an 'old ordinance of the cities of Burbank and Glendale which prohibited Negroes from remaining inside municipal limits after sun down.'" Loewen, *Sundown Towns*, 100. See also Nicole Pasini, Bradley Calvert, and Christine B. Powers, *City of Glendale, California Report to the City Council* (September 15, 2020), https://justice.tougaloo.edu/wp-content/uploads/2020/09/GlendaleReport.pdf.
101. Pasini, Calvert, and Powers, *Glendale Report*, 4 https://justice.tougaloo.edu/wp-content/uploads/2020/09/GlendaleReport.pdf.
102. Loewen, *Sundown Towns*, 264–65.
103. Kali Holloway, "In California, a Case of Black Land Loss," *Nation*, June 1, 2021.
104. Holloway, "In California, a Case of Black Land Loss."
105. Resolution No. 23-0037, "A Resolution of the City Council of the City of Manhattan Beach Acknowledging and Apologizing for the City's Role in the Racially Motivated Condemnation of Properties in the Area Known as Bruce's Beach," https://www.manhattanbeach.gov/home/showpublisheddocument/52029.
106. Holloway, "In California, a Case of Black Land Loss."
107. Holloway, "In California, a Case of Black Land Loss."
108. Mindy Thompson Fullilove, *Eminent Domain and African Americans: What Is the Price of the Commons?* (Institute for Justice, n.d.), https://ij-org-re.s3.amazonaws.com/ijdevsitestage/wp-content/uploads/2015/03/Perspectives-Fullilove.pdf.
109. Pasini, Calvert, and Powers, *Glendale Report*, 3, https://justice.tougaloo.edu/wp-content/uploads/2020/09/GlendaleReport.pdf.
110. Pasini, Calvert, and Powers, *Glendale Report*, 3, https://justice.tougaloo.edu/wp-content/uploads/2020/09/GlendaleReport.pdf.
111. Pasini, Calvert, and Powers, *Glendale Report*, 4, https://justice.tougaloo.edu/wp-content/uploads/2020/09/GlendaleReport.pdf.
112. Paul Thornton, "Commentary: My Childhood Home in Glendale Cost $8,500 in 1954. What It's Worth Now Is Madness," *Los Angeles Times*, May 14, 2022.

113. Pasini, Calvert, and Powers, *Glendale Report,* 3, https://justice.tougaloo
.edu/wp-content/uploads/2020/09/GlendaleReport.pdf.

114. Woods, "Almost 'No Negro Veteran,'" 404.

115. Woods, "Almost 'No Negro Veteran,'" 403.

116. Woods, "Almost 'No Negro Veteran,'" 392.

117. "Justice Department Secures over $31 Million from City National Bank to
Address Lending Discrimination Allegations" (press release), January 12,
2023, https://www.justice.gov/opa/pr/justice-department-secures-over-31
-million-city-national-bank-address-lending-discrimination.

118. Heather O'Connell, "Historical Shadows: The Links Between Sundown
Towns and Contemporary Black-White Inequality," *Sociology of Race and
Ethnicity* 5, no. 3 (2019): 323.

119. Loewen, *Sundown Towns,* 58.

120. Loewen, *Sundown Towns,* 4.

121. Loewen, *Sundown Towns,* 56.

122. "There is reason to believe that more than half of all towns in Oregon,
Indiana, Ohio, the Cumberlands, the Ozarks, and diverse other areas were
also all-white on purpose." Loewen, *Sundown Towns,* 4–5.

123. Loewen, *Sundown Towns,* 75.

124. Loewen, *Sundown Towns,* 80.

125. Barclay, Lewan, and Breed, "Lynched for Their Land."

126. Loewen, *Sundown Towns,* 57.

127. Loewen, *Sundown Towns,* 56.

128. Loewen, *Sundown Towns,* 123.

129. "But that they purchased the said tract of land intending to defraud these
defendants by offering to sell lots in said 'Belmont' subdivision to negroes,
and attempting to compel these defendants into re-purchasing said
property at an advance and profit to said complainant." *Dumas v. Neill et
al.,* Circuit Court, Montgomery County (No. 2401) (1908).

130. Marc Fisher, "Chevy Chase, 1916: For Everyman, A New Lot in Life,"
Washington Post, February 14, 1999.

131. Fishback et al., "New Evidence on Redlining," 9.

132. Woods, "Almost 'No Negro Veteran,'" 393.

133. Woods, "Almost 'No Negro Veteran,'" 409.

134. Woods, "Almost 'No Negro Veteran,'" 409.

135. Woods, "Almost 'No Negro Veteran,'" 409.

136. F. John Devaney, *Tracking the American Dream,* Current Housing Reports,
Series H121/94-1 (Washington, DC: US Government Printing Office,
1994), 29.

137. *Civil Rights Cases,* 109 U.S. 3, 8 (1883). See also Blair L. M. Kelley, *Right to
Ride: Streetcar Boycotts and African American Citizenship in the Era of
Plessy v. Ferguson* (Chapel Hill: University of North Carolina Press, 2010).

138. *Civil Rights Cases,* 109 U.S. at 24, 25.

139. Rutherglen, "Badges and Incidents of Slavery," 173.

140. *Civil Rights Cases,* 109 U.S. at 24–25 (emphasis added).

141. *Plessy v. Ferguson,* 163 U.S. 537, 540 (1896).
142. Keith Weldon Medley, *We as Freemen: Plessy v. Ferguson* (New Orleans: Pelican, 2003), Kindle ed., loc. 164–65.
143. *Plessy v. Ferguson,* 163 U.S. at 542.
144. *Plessy v. Ferguson,* 163 U.S. at 543.
145. *Plessy v. Ferguson,* 163 U.S. at 551.
146. *Plessy v. Ferguson,* 163 U.S. at 551.
147. *Plessy v. Ferguson,* 163 U.S. at 552.
148. Memsy Price, "To Buy the World a Coke," *IndyWeek,* February 15, 2012, https://indyweek.com/news/archives-news/buy-world-coke.
149. *Plessy v. Ferguson,* 163 U.S. at 556 (Justice Harlan dissenting).
150. *Plessy v. Ferguson,* 163 U.S. at 557 (Justice Harlan dissenting).
151. *Plessy v. Ferguson,* 163 U.S. at 560 (Justice Harlan dissenting).
152. *Plessy v. Ferguson,* 163 U.S. at 560–61 (Justice Harlan dissenting).
153. *Plessy v. Ferguson,* 163 U.S. at 562 (Justice Harlan dissenting).
154. He was just as racist as his brethren when it came to Asian immigrants, of whom he wrote: "There is a race so different from our own that we do not permit those belonging to it to become citizens of the United States. Persons belonging to it are, with few exceptions, absolutely excluded from our country. I allude to the Chinese race." *Plessy v. Ferguson,* 163 U.S. at 561 (Justice Harlan dissenting).
155. Linda Przybyszewski, *The Republic According to John Marshall Harlan* (Chapel Hill: University of North Carolina Press, 1999), 23.
156. Peter S. Canellos, *The Great Dissenter: The Story of John Marshall Harlan, America's Judicial Hero* (New York: Simon & Schuster, 2021), 42–43.
157. Canellos, *Great Dissenter,* 43.
158. Canellos, *Great Dissenter,* 42.
159. Canellos, *Great Dissenter,* 47.
160. Przybyszewski, *Republic According to Harlan,* 23.
161. Canellos, *Great Dissenter,* 47.
162. Canellos, *Great Dissenter,* 47–48.
163. Canellos, *Great Dissenter,* 49.
164. Canellos, *Great Dissenter,* 49.
165. Canellos, *Great Dissenter,* 56.
166. Canellos, *Great Dissenter,* 60–62.
167. Canellos, *Great Dissenter,* 65–68.
168. *Hodges v. United States,* 203 U.S. 1 (1906).
169. *Hodges v. United States,* 203 U.S. at 17–18.
170. He was joined in his dissent by Justice William R. Day.
171. Peter S. Canellos, "Separate but Equal, the Court Said. One Voice Dissented," *New York Times,* May 19, 2021.
172. Sanford Levinson et al., *Processes of Constitutional Decisionmaking: Cases and Materials* (Lowell, MA: Aspen Publishing, 2022), 1120.
173. *Holmes v. City of Atlanta,* 350 U.S. 879 (1955), cited in Levinson et al., *Processes of Constitutional Decisionmaking,* 1120.

174. *Browder v. Gayle*, 352 U.S. 903 (1956), cited in Levinson et al., *Processes of Constitutional Decisionmaking*, 1120.

175. *New Orleans City Park Improvement Association v. Detiege*, 358 U.S. 54 (1958), cited in Levinson et al., *Processes of Constitutional Decisionmaking*, 1120.

176. Holloway, "In California, a Case of Black Land Loss."

177. Francis et al., "Black Land Loss," 38.

178. "Historically Denied 'Pivotal' Loans, Black Farmers Still Struggle to Get Support," *PBS NewsHour*, December 7, 2021.

179. Thomas W. Mitchell, "From Reconstruction to Deconstruction: Undermining Black Landownership, Political Independence, and Community Through Partition Sales of Tenancies in Common," *Northwestern Law Review* 95, no. 2 (2001): 505–80.

180. "Industrialization, economic shifts, and political pressure ended widespread convict leasing by World War II." Equal Justice Initiative, "Convict Leasing," November 1, 2013, https://eji.org/news/history-racial -injustice-convict-leasing.

181. Tom LoBianco, "Report: Aide Says Nixon's War on Drugs Targeted Blacks, Hippies," CNN, March 24, 2016.

182. Sentencing Project, "Crack Cocaine Sentencing Policy: Unjustified and Unreasonable," n.d., https://www.prisonpolicy.org/scans/sp/1003.pdf.

183. US Sentencing Commission, *Special Report to Congress: Cocaine and Federal Sentencing Policy*, February 1995, 162.

184. US Sentencing Commission, *Special Report to Congress*, xi.

185. Dan Weikel, "War on Crack Targets Minorities over Whites: Cocaine: Records Show Federal Officials Almost Solely Prosecute Nonwhites. U.S. Attorney Denies Race Is a Factor," *Los Angeles Times*, May 21, 1995.

186. Weikel, "War on Crack Targets Minorities."

187. Weikel, "War on Crack Targets Minorities."

188. Weikel, "War on Crack Targets Minorities."

189. *Whren v. United States*, 517 U.S. 806 (1996).

190. "Blacks were almost twice as likely to be searched as whites, even though the searches of blacks were less likely than whites to result in contraband being found (21% vs. 34%)." Dorothy A. Brown, "Ferguson's Perfect Storm of Racism," CNN, March 5, 2015. See also Tracey Maclin, "Race and the Fourth Amendment," *Vanderbilt Law Review* 51 (1998): 350–54.

191. Fair Sentencing Act of 2010, Pub. L. 111-220, 124 Stat. 2372-2375 (August 3, 2010), https://www.congress.gov/111/plaws/publ220/PLAW-111publ220.pdf.

192. Kelly Welch, "Black Criminal Stereotypes and Racial Profiling," *Journal of Contemporary Criminal Justice* 23, no. 3 (2007): 276–88; Addis Adeno, "'Hell Man They Did Invent Us': The Mass Media, Law, and African Americans," *Buffalo Law Review* 41, no. 2 (1993): 523–626.

193. Tera Eva Agyepong, *The Criminalization of Black Children: Race, Gender, and Delinquency in Chicago's Juvenile Justice System, 1899–1945* (Chapel Hill: University of North Carolina Press, 2018).

194. Kristin Henning, *The Rage of Innocence: How America Criminalizes Black Youth* (New York: Vintage Books, 2021), 135.
195. Henning, *Rage of Innocence,* 136.
196. Henning, *Rage of Innocence,* 136.
197. Henning, *Rage of Innocence,* xv.
198. Henning, *Rage of Innocence,* 276, 295–96.
199. Henning, *Rage of Innocence,* 296.
200. Federal Bureau of Prisons, "Inmate Race," October 26, 2024, https://www.bop.gov/about/statistics/statistics_inmate_race.jsp.
201. Terry-Ann Craigie, Ames Grawert, and Cameron Kimble, "Conviction, Imprisonment, and Lost Earnings: How Involvement with the Criminal Justice System Deepens Inequality," Brennan Center for Justice, September 15, 2020, 6.
202. "In an experiment where applicants' ethnicity and criminal history (none vs. drug-related felony) were manipulated, 34% of White applicants without criminal records received call-backs followed by White applicants with criminal records (17%), Black applicants without criminal records (14%), and Black applicants with criminal records (4%)." Christopher R. Beasley and Y. Jenny Xiao, "Incarceration History and Ethnic Bias in Hiring Perceptions: An Experimental Test of Intersectional Bias & Psychological Mechanisms," *PLOS ONE* 18, no. 1 (2023): 2.
203. "White men and women with a conviction earn about $49,000 a year on average, eclipsing the $39,000 a year that Black people with *no* conviction earn over the same period." Craigie, Grawert, and Kimble, "Conviction, Imprisonment, and Lost Earnings," 20.
204. Jhacova A. Williams, Trevon D. Logan, and Bradley L. Hardy, "The Persistence of Historical Racial Violence and Political Suppression: Implications for Contemporary Regional Inequality," *Annals* 694 (2021): 93.
205. Williams, Logan, and Hardy, "Persistence of Historical Racial Violence," 93.
206. Emily A. Shrider, *Poverty in the United States, 2023*, Current Population Reports no. P60-283, September 2024, https://www2.census.gov/library/publications/2024/demo/p60-283.pdf.
207. "Poverty Status in the Past 12 Months" (table), in US Census Bureau, *2023 American Community Survey,* subject table S1701. I want to thank Danilo Trisi, an affiliate scholar with the Georgetown Center for Poverty and Inequality, and Lelaine Bigelow, the executive director, for assistance with this data.
208. Equal Justice Initiative, *Lynching in America: Confronting the Legacy of Racial Terror,* 3rd ed., https://lynchinginamerica.eji.org/report.
209. "*Mississippi Today*'s Anna Wolfe Explains Sprawling Welfare Fraud Case," *Mississippi Today,* December 23, 2021, https://mississippitoday.org/2021/12/23/anna-wolfe-mississippi-welfare-fraud-case.
210. Ana Hernández Kent and Lowell R. Ricketts, "Racial and Ethnic Household Wealth Trends and Wealth Inequality," Federal Reserve Bank

of St. Louis, November 29, 2022, https://www.stlouisfed.org/institute-for
-economic-equity/the-real-state-of-family-wealth/racial-and-ethnic
-household-wealth#:~:text=This%20bar%20chart%20shows%20
the,on%20average%2C%20than%20white%20families.

211. Richard Fausset and Rick Rojas, "Where Ahmaud Arbery Ran, Neighbors
Cast Wary Eyes," *New York Times,* May 22, 2020.

212. Jeremy Townsley and Unai Miguel Andres, "The Lasting Impacts of
Segregation and Redlining," *Savi,* June 24, 2021, https://www.savi.org/
lasting-impacts-of-segregation/#:~:text=Redlining%20and%20
segregation%20lowered%20earnings,born%20to%20low%2Dincome%20
families.

213. Brown, *Whiteness of Wealth,* 92.

214. Keeanga-Yamahtta Taylor, *Race for Profit: How Banks and the Real Estate
Industry Undermined Black Homeownership* (Chapel Hill: University of
North Carolina Press, 2019), Kindle ed., loc. 5.

215. Merritt, *Masterless Men,* 38.

216. Shanks, "Homestead Act," 32.

217. Merritt, *Masterless Men,* 331.

218. Katherine Franke, *Repair: Redeeming the Promise of Abolition* (Chicago:
Haymarket Books, 2019), 136.

219. Lewan and Barclay, "Torn from the Land."

220. Francis et al., "Black Land Loss," 38.

221. O'Connell, "Historical Shadows," 322.

222. O'Connell, "Historical Shadows," 323.

223. Dick M. Carpenter II and John K. Ross, *Victimizing the Vulnerable: The
Demographics of Eminent Domain Abuse,* Institute for Justice, June 2007,
https://ij.org/wp-content/uploads/2015/03/Victimizing_the_Vulnerable.pdf.

224. "The condemnation went through despite the fact that the firm that
conducted the 'blight' study that justified the condemnation had been on
Columbia's payroll, and much of the blight used to justify the takings was
actually on land that Columbia already owned, thereby making it likely
that Columbia itself had created the 'blight' that justified the use of
eminent domain." Statement of Ilya Somin, in US Commission on Civil
Rights, *The Civil Rights Implications of Eminent Domain Abuse,* June 2014,
46, https://www.usccr.gov/files/pubs/docs/FINAL_FY14_Eminent
-Domain-Report.pdf.

225. Davarian L. Baldwin, *In the Shadow of the Ivory Tower: How Universities
Are Plundering Our Cities* (New York: Bold Type Books, 2021), 12–13,
17–18.

226. "FACT SHEET: Delivering on Tulsa Commitments to Build Black Wealth,"
White House, June 1, 2022, https://www.whitehouse.gov/briefing-room/
statements-releases/2022/06/01/fact-sheet-delivering-on-tulsa
-commitments-to-build-black-wealth.

227. Joe R. Feagin, "Documenting the Costs of Slavery, Segregation and

Contemporary Racism: Why Reparations Are in Order for African Americans," *Harvard Blackletter Law Journal* 20 (2004): 53.

228. Thomas Craemer et al., "Wealth Implications of Slavery and Racial Discrimination for African American Descendants of the Enslaved," *Review of Black Political Economy* 47, no. 3 (2020): 228; William A. Darity, Jr., and Kristen Mullen, *From Here to Equality: Reparations for Black Americans in the Twenty-First Century* (Chapel Hill: University of North Carolina Press, 2020), 261. Their estimates, with interest calculated at a 2018 present value, range between $8.6 trillion and $17.1 trillion depending upon the interest rate used.

229. Craemer et al., "Wealth Implications of Slavery and Racial Discrimination," 236.

230. Matthew Desmond, "Capitalism," in *The 1619 Project*, ed. Nikole Hannah-Jones et al. (New York: One World, 2021), 175.

231. Desmond, "Capitalism," 176.

232. Julian Kunnie, "Justice Never Too Late: The Historical Background to Current Reparations Movements Among Africans and African Americans," *Journal of African American History* 103, no. 12 (2018): 52.

233. Craig Steven Wilder, *Ebony & Ivy: Race, Slavery, and the Troubled History of America's Universities* (New York: Bloomsbury, 2014), Kindle ed., loc 17.

234. Kunnie, "Justice Never Too Late," 53.

235. Georgetown provides the 272 descendants who apply to Georgetown with a plus factor in the admissions process, but they charge those admitted regular tuition. Rachel Swarns, *The 272: The Families Who Were Enslaved and Sold to Build the American Catholic Church* (New York: Random House, 2023), 226–27.

236. Kyla Matthews, a Georgetown Law student, describes how lots of people think she gets a scholarship as a 272 descendant, but she does not. Kyla Matthews, interview by Trymaine Lee, in "The 272," bonus episode of *Uncounted Millions: The Power of Reparations* (podcast), April 12, 2024, https://www.msnbc.com/msnbc-podcast/uncounted-millions-bonus -gu272-rcna147610.

237. Adeel Hassan, "Georgetown Students Agree to Create Reparations Fund," *New York Times*, April 12, 2019.

238. "Reconciliation Fund," Georgetown University, https://www.georgetown .edu/slavery/reconciliation-fund.

239. "Update on Actions Emory Is Taking for Racial Justice," Emory University, https://president.emory.edu/communications/2020/10/racial-justice -update.html#:~:text=Establishing%20the%20Descendants%20 Endowment,whose%20land%20Emory%20was%20built.

240. Numerous emails that I sent to the office of the president did not result in any substantive response.

241. Fisher, "Chevy Chase, 1916."

242. President Joe Biden, "Remarks at Signing of the Juneteenth National Independence Day Act," White House, June 17, 2021, https://www.whitehouse.gov/briefing-room/speeches-remarks/2021/06/17/remarks-by-president-biden-at-signing-of-the-juneteenth-national-independence-day-act.

243. *Jones v. Alfred Mayer*, 392 U.S. at 445 (Justice Douglas concurring).

Part III: Righting Wrongs

1. Clint Smith, *How the Word Is Passed: A Reckoning with the History of Slavery Across America* (New York: Little, Brown, 2021), 192.

2. Smith, *How Word Is Passed*, 175; Ron Tyler and Lawrence R. Murphy, eds., *The Slave Narratives of Texas* (Austin, TX: State House Press, 1997), 132. Haywood self-identifies as age ninety-two.

3. Smith, *How Word Is Passed*, 192.

4. "To date, slavery reparations have been the subject of little survey research, and only one poll conducted by ABC News in 1997 has been scientifically administered." Shelly Campo, Teresa Mastin, and M. Somjen Frazer, "Predicting and Explaining Public Opinion Regarding U.S. Slavery Reparations," *Howard Journal of Communications* 15 (2004): 117.

5. Peter Baker, "Clinton Sounds Call for Dialogue on Race," *Washington Post*, June 14, 1997.

6. Campo et al., "Predicting and Explaining Public Opinion Regarding Reparations," 117; Melissa R. Michelson, "The Black Reparations Movement," *Journal of Black Studies* 32, no. 5 (2002): 578.

7. Michelson, "Black Reparations Movement," 578.

8. Jesse H. Rhodes et al., "Why Reparations? Race and Public Opinion Toward Reparations," *Journal of the Social Sciences* 10, no. 3 (2024): 32.

9. Kiana Cox and Khadijah Edwards, *Black Americans Have a Clear Vision for Reducing Racism but Little Hope It Will Happen*, Pew Research Center, August 30, 2022.

10. Carrie Blazina and Kiana Cox, *Black and White Americans Are Far Apart in Their Views of Reparations for Slavery*, Pew Research Center, November 28, 2022.

11. "Estimates for Asian adults are representative of English speakers only. Note: Black adults include those who say their race is Black Alone and non-Hispanic; multiracial, non-Hispanic Black; or Black and Hispanic. White and Asian respondents include those who report being only one race and are not Hispanic. Hispanics are of any race. 'Some college' includes adults who have an associate degree and those who attended college but did not obtain a degree." Blazina and Cox, *Black and White Americans Are Far Apart*. But Tatishe M. Nteta points out, "the results of a 2023 UMass Poll, which found that about 30% of the white population in the U.S. now support reparations for Black Americans." See "Reparations Now," episode 5 of Trymaine Lee, *Uncounted Millions:*

The Power of Reparations (podcast), March 14, 2024, https://www
.msnbc.com/msnbc-podcast/uncounted-millions-reparations-now
-rcna142865.

12. Blazina and Cox, *Black and White Americans Are Far Apart.*
13. Blazina and Cox, *Black and White Americans Are Far Apart.*
14. Blazina and Cox, *Black and White Americans Are Far Apart.*
15. Blazina and Cox, *Black and White Americans Are Far Apart.*
16. Cox and Edwards, *Black Americans Have a Clear Vision.*
17. Some preliminary research suggests that when Asian Americans are
    reminded that Japanese Americans received reparations, they are more
    likely to support reparations for black Americans. Michael W. Kraus and
    A. Chyei Vinluan, "Reminders of Japanese Redress Increase Asian
    American Support for Black Reparations," *Communications Psychology*
    (2023): 1–33. I am not aware of any polling of Tribal members on the issue
    of reparations for black Americans.
18. Dorothy A. Brown, *The Whiteness of Wealth: How the Tax System
    Impoverishes Black Americans—And How We Can Fix It* (New York:
    Crown, 2021).
19. "We [Georgetown Law] are a faculty of 120, and, to my knowledge, the
    number of professors who are openly conservative, or libertarian, or
    Republican or, in any sense, to the right of the American center, is three—
    three out of 120. There are more conservatives on the nine-member U.S.
    Supreme Court than there are on this 120-member faculty. Moreover, the
    ideological median of the other 117 seems to lie not just left of center, but
    closer to the left edge of the Democratic Party. Many are further left than
    that." Nicholas Quinn Rosenkranz, "Intellectual Diversity in the Legal
    Academy," *Harvard Journal of Law and Public Policy* 37, no. 1 (2014): 137
    (citations omitted).
20. Drew Westen, *The Political Brain: The Role of Emotion in Deciding the Fate
    of the Nation* (New York: PublicAffairs, 2008).
21. Caitlin O'Kane, "Over 1600 Books Were Banned in U.S. School Districts
    in One Year—And the Number Is Increasing," CBS News, September 20,
    2022; Anemona Hartocollis and Eliza Fawcett, "The College Board Strips
    Down Its A.P. Curriculum for African American Studies," *New York Times,*
    February 2, 2023.
22. Executive Order 13950, "Combating Race and Sex Stereotyping," *Federal
    Register* 85, no. 188 (September 28, 2020), 60,683, https://www.govinfo
    .gov/content/pkg/FR-2020-09-28/pdf/2020-21534.pdf.
23. Janel George, "Deny, Defund, and Divert: The Law and American
    Miseducation," *Georgetown Law Journal* 112, no. 3 (2024): 547.
24. George, "Deny, Defund, and Divert," 548.
25. See James Fishkin et al., "Can Deliberation Have Lasting Effects?"
    American Political Science Review (2024): 1–21. See also John Gastil, "The
    Lessons and Limitations of Experiments in Democratic Deliberation,"
    Annual Review of Law and Social Science 14 (2018): 271–91; and Selen

Ercan et al., eds., *Research Methods in Deliberative Democracy* (Oxford: Oxford University Press, 2023).

26. I would like to thank the Robert Wood Johnson Foundation for their financial support for this expanded messaging research project.

27. Quoted in Sonya Singh, "California Faces Backlash As It Weighs Historic Reparations for Black Residents," *Guardian,* July 11, 2023.

28. Ta-Nehisi Coates, " 'Better Is Good': Obama on Reparations, Civil Rights, and the Art of the Possible," *Atlantic,* December 21, 2016.

29. "In 1989, Representative John Conyers Jr., who retired in 2017, introduced legislation to create a commission to develop proposals for reparations. He introduced it every year for nearly 30 years. It went nowhere. Even President Barack Obama opposed reparations, calling the idea impractical." Sheryl Gay Stolberg, "At Historic Hearing, House Panel Explores Reparations," *New York Times,* June 19, 2019.

30. Stolberg, "At Historic Hearing."

31. "It is that bill, titled the 'Commission to Study and Develop Reparation Proposals for African-Americans Act,' and now sponsored by Representative Sheila Jackson Lee, Democrat of Texas, that the subcommittee has before it. It would authorize $12 million for a 13-member commission to study the effects of slavery and make recommendations to Congress." Stolberg, "At Historic Hearing."

32. "S. 1083 At the request of Mr. BOOKER, the names of the Senator from Massachusetts (Mr. MARKEY), the Senator from New York (Mrs. GILLIBRAND) and the Senator from California (Ms. HARRIS) were added as cosponsors of S. 1083, a bill to address the fundamental injustice, cruelty, brutality, and inhumanity of slavery in the United States and the 13 American colonies between 1619 and 1865 and to establish a commission to study and consider a national apology and proposal for reparations for the institution of slavery, its subsequent de jure and de facto racial and economic discrimination against African-Americans, and the impact of these forces on living African-Americans, to make recommendations to the Congress on appropriate remedies, and for other purposes." *Congressional Record* (May 2, 2019), S2615.

33. "Hearing on Slavery Reparations," C-SPAN, June 19, 2019, https://www.c-span.org/video/?461767-1/hearing-slavery-reparations; and "House Subcommittee Hearing on Slavery Reparations," C-SPAN, February 17, 2021, https://www.c-span.org/video/?509041-1/house-subcommittee-hearing-slavery-reparations.

34. Kevin Freking, "Biden Backs Studying Reparations as Congress Considers Bill," Associated Press, February 17, 2021; "White House Says Biden Supports Study of Slavery Reparations," Reuters, February 18, 2021.

35. Gerren Keith Gaynor, "Would Biden Honor Sheila Jackson Lee with Executive Action on Reparations?," *Grio,* August 2, 2024.

36. Barbara Rodriguez, "Kamala Harris on Reparations for Slavery: 'It Can't Just Be Hey . . . Write Some Checks,' " *Des Moines Register,* August 11, 2019.

37. "We have a long way to go to realize the full promise of America, but we are committed as a party to continuing the work to build a nation where all people are not only created equal, but treated equally throughout their lives. To determine how best to right historical wrongs, Democrats support Congress executing a study of reparations and the continuing impacts of slavery." 2024 Democratic Party Platform, August 19, 2024, https://www.presidency.ucsb.edu/documents/2024-democratic-party -platform.

38. Jordan Fabian and Saagar Enjeti, "Trump on Reparations: 'I Don't See It Happening,'" *Hill*, June 24, 2019, https://thehill.com/homenews/ administration/450126-exclusive-trump-on-reparations-i-dont-see-it -happening.

39. Haris Alic, "Trump Demands China Pay $60T in Reparations for the Coronavirus Pandemic," *Washington Times*, December 19, 2021.

40. This structure with modifications is borrowed from the Treasury Advisory Committee on Racial Equity, of which I was a member from 2022 to September 2024.

41. Executive Order 14023, "Executive Order on the Establishment of the Presidential Commission on the Supreme Court of the United States," White House, April 9, 2021, sec. 4, https://www.whitehouse.gov/briefing -room/presidential-actions/2021/04/09/executive-order-on-the -establishment-of-the-presidential-commission-on-the-supreme-court -of-the-united-states.

42. For example, written testimony included in a 1980 hearing states that "Japanese American organizations conducted several polls nationwide in the mid-1970s. Of the four thousand people who returned their questionnaires, more than 90 percent strongly supported individual compensation as redress." *To Establish the Commission on Wartime Relocation and Internment of Civilians; To Provide for Payments to Certain Individuals of Japanese Ancestry* [sic] *Who Were Interned, Detained, or Forcibly Relocated by the United States During World War II: Hearing on H.R. 5499 Before the Subcomm. on Admin. Law & Governmental Relations of the H. Comm. on the Judiciary,* 96th Cong. 161 (1980) (written testimony of Frank Abe and Karen Seriguchi, National Council for Japanese American Redress). In contrast, a letter to Rep. Les AuCoin (D-OR) and reprinted in a 1986 hearing, stated, also without citation, that "public opinion polls indicate that Americans oppose 'reparations' by a margin of four-to-one." *Hearing on H.R. 442 and H.R. 2415 Before the Subcomm. on Admin. Law and Governmental Relations of the H. Comm. on the Judiciary,* 99th Cong. 1477 (1986) (letter from Henry Kane to Hon. Les AuCoin, June 4, 1983).

43. Executive Order 14023, sec. 3: "The Commission shall produce a report for the President."

44. Linda Greenhouse, "Should We Reform the Court?," *New York Review of Books,* April 7, 2022.

45. Sun Tzu, *The Art of War,* trans. Lionel Giles (India: Fingerprint Classics, 2024), 45.

46. Zach Schonfeld, "Public Opinion Relatively Unchanged After Jan. 6 Hearings: Poll," *Hill,* August 9, 2022; Jennifer Agiesta, "CNN Poll: January 6 Hearings Haven't Changed Opinions Much, But Most Agree Trump Acted Unethically," CNN Politics, July 26, 2022; "National: Jan. 6 Hearings Have No Impact on Opinion," Monmouth University Poll, August 9, 2022, https://www.monmouth.edu/polling-institute/documents/monmouthpoll_us_080922.pdf.

47. Alexandra Hutzler and Jessie DiMartino, "How the Jan. 6 Hearings Changed Public Opinion Ahead of the Midterms," ABC News, October 27, 2022.

48. Brown, *Whiteness of Wealth,* 64–65.

49. Juan F. Perea et al., *Race and Races: Cases and Resources for a Diverse America* (Eagan, MN: West Academic, 2000), 84.

50. Blair L. M. Kelley, *Right to Ride: Streetcar Boycotts and African American Citizenship in the Era of Plessy v. Ferguson* (Chapel Hill: University of North Carolina Press, 2010), 77.

51. Mitchell T. Maki, Harry H. L. Kitano, and S. Megan Berthold, *Achieving the Impossible Dream: How Japanese Americans Obtained Redress* (Urbana: University of Illinois Press, 1999), 225.

52. "African Americans make up 13 percent of the general population, but more than 40 percent of the homeless population." National Alliance to End Homelessness, "Racial Inequalities in Homelessness, by the Numbers," June 1, 2020, https://endhomelessness.org/resource/racial-inequalities-homelessness-numbers/#:~:text=African%20Americans%20make%20up%2013,share%20of%20the%20homeless%20population.

53. Maki, Kitano, and Berthold, *Achieving the Impossible Dream,* 225.

54. Katie Balevic, "Just 11 People Were Responsible for Most 2021–2022 Book Challenges. A Virginia Woman Challenged 71 of the 73 Books She Read," *Business Insider,* October 1, 2023.

55. Karla M. McKanders, "Immigration and Racial Justice: Enforcing the Borders of Blackness," *Georgia State University Law Review* 37, no. 4 (2021): 1139–76.

56. Maki, Kitano, and Berthold, *Achieving the Impossible Dream,* 225.

57. Eleanor Marie Lawrence Brown argues that West Indians are more likely to be homeowners in New York City than African Americans. See Eleanor Brown, "Why Black Homeowners Are More Likely to Be Caribbean American than African American in New York," *American Journal of Legal History* 61 (2021): 3–36. Taking that argument to its logical conclusion could support excluding Caribbean immigrants who outperform African Americans on specific wealth measures. It could also mean giving a lower cash payment to Caribbean immigrants living in the United States. As is obvious, I do not subscribe to the view that all black immigrants receive better treatment than all African Americans.

58. Carol Anderson, *White Rage: The Unspoken Truth of Our Racial Divide* (New York: Bloomsbury, 2016), 1.

59. "White Americans are more likely to favor welfare cuts when they believe that their status is threatened and that minorities are the main beneficiaries of safety net programs." Caitlin Dewey, "White America's Racial Resentment Is the Real Impetus for Welfare Cuts, Study Says," *Washington Post*, May 30, 2018.

60. Dania V. Francis et al., "Black Land Loss: 1920–1997," *AEA Papers and Proceedings* 112 (2022): 38.

61. Alex Albright et al., "After the Burning: The Economic Effects of the 1921 Tulsa Race Massacre," NBER Working Paper no. 28985, July 2021, 1, https://www.nber.org/system/files/working_papers/w28985/w28985.pdf. The lawsuit seeking reparations for Tulsa was recently dismissed by the Oklahoma Supreme Court. Andy Rose and Omar Jimenez, "Oklahoma Supreme Court Dismisses Lawsuit Brought by Survivors of Tulsa Race Massacre," CNN, June 12, 2014.

62. William A. Darity, Jr., and Kristen Mullen, *From Here to Equality: Reparations for Black Americans in the Twenty-First Century* (Chapel Hill: University of North Carolina Press, 2020), 262.

63. Darity and Mullen, *From Here to Equality*, 263.

64. Darity and Mullen, *From Here to Equality*, 260.

65. Brown, *Whiteness of Wealth*.

66. State and local reparations efforts could also include addressing the antiblack bias in our property tax system as skillfully documented in Andrew W. Kahrl, *The Black Tax: 150 Years of Theft, Exploitation, and Dispossession in America* (Chicago: University of Chicago Press, 2024).

67. Kai Ryssdal and Andie Corban, " 'We've Got a Lot More Progress to Go' on Fixing Racial Disparities Caused by the Tax System," *Marketplace*, January 18, 2024; Ali Velshi, " 'It Is a Sin and a Shame': Exposing Racism in the U.S. Tax Code," MSNBC, January 28, 2024.

68. Department of the Treasury, Office of Minority and Women Inclusion, *Annual Report to Congress, FY23*, https://home.treasury.gov/system/files/2016/OMWI-FY23-Annual-Report-to-Congress.pdf.

69. "Treasury Department Announces Inaugural Members of Formal Advisory Committee on Racial Equity" (featured story), October 4, 2022, https://home.treasury.gov/news/featured-stories/treasury-department-announces-inaugural-members-of-formal-advisory-committee-on-racial-equity.

70. For the argument that the Federal Reserve could play a role here, see Matthew Yglesias, "Slavery Reparations Are Workable and Affordable," *Vox*, May 23, 2014. However, even if the Federal Reserve, as an independent agency, were authorized to print money for reparations, it would need to determine that it wanted to spend the money on reparations-type activities. In other words, you would need congressional action through reparations legislation and a progressive Federal Reserve.

71. Ted Barrett, "McConnell Opposes Paying Reparations: 'None of Us Currently Living Are Responsible' for Slavery," CNN, June 19, 2019.

72. Corky Siemaszko, "Sen. Mitch McConnell's Great-Great-Grandfathers Owned 14 Slaves, Bringing Reparations Issue Close to Home," NBC News, July 8, 2019.

73. Philipp Ager, Leah Platt Boustan, and Katherine Eriksson, "The Intergenerational Effects of a Large Wealth Shock: White Southerners After the Civil War," NBER Working Paper no. 25700, September 2019, https://www.nber.org/papers/w25700.

74. Sandy Mazza, "In McConnell's Boyhood Town Where His Family Owned Slaves, the Reparations Debate Thrives," *Courier Journal* (Louisville, KY), July 13, 2019.

75. Mazza, "In McConnell's Boyhood Town Where His Family Owned Slaves"; Siemaszko, "McConnell's Great-Great-Grandfathers Owned 14 Slaves."

76. Sara Francis Fujimura, "U.S. at War: Mystery Virus Leaps Around the Globe Killing Scores in Its Path. Scientists Race to Find a Cure," Pan American Health Organization, c. 2003, https://www.paho.org/en/who -we-are/history-paho/purple-death-great-flu-1918.

77. Amber Phillips, "Meet Jenean Hampton, the first black statewide officeholder in Kentucky. And, she's a Republican," *Washington Post,* November 4, 2015.

78. Mazza, "In McConnell's Boyhood Town Where His Family Owned Slaves."

79. Antonin Scalia, "The Disease as Cure: In Order to Get Beyond Racism, We Must First Take Account of Race," *Washington University Law Quarterly* (1979): 152.

80. *California v. Bakke,* 438 U.S. 265, 314 (1978).

81. *Students for Fair Admissions, Inc. v. Harvard,* 600 U.S. 181 (2023).

82. Sally Kohn, "Affirmative Action Has Helped White Women More Than Anyone," *Time,* June 17, 2013.

83. Marin Scotten, "After Years of Discrimination, U.S. Makes a Historic $2.2 Billion Payout to Black Farmers," *Salon,* August 22, 2024.

84. See also Akhil Amar, "Forty Acres and a Mule," *Harvard Journal of Law and Public Policy* 13 (1990): 39–43.

85. *Jones v. Alfred Mayer,* 392 U.S. at 440.

86. *Jones v. Alfred Mayer,* 392 U.S. at 412–13.

87. *Jones v. Alfred Mayer,* 392 U.S. at 443.

88. *Jones v. Alfred Mayer,* 392 U.S. at 445 (Justice Douglas concurring).

89. Stolberg, "At Historic Hearing."

90. Wesley Lowery, "Aren't More White People than Black People Killed by Police? Yes, But No," *Washington Post,* July 11, 2016.

91. Brown, *Whiteness of Wealth,* 66–71.

92. *Brown v. Board of Education,* 347 U.S. 483 (1954).

93. In 2012 the Department of Justice settled with Wells Fargo. "The Department of Justice today filed the second largest fair lending

settlement in the department's history to resolve allegations that Wells Fargo Bank, the largest residential home mortgage originator in the United States, engaged in a pattern or practice of discrimination against qualified African-American and Hispanic borrowers in its mortgage lending from 2004 through 2009. The settlement provides $184.3 million in compensation for wholesale borrowers who were steered into subprime mortgages or who paid higher fees and rates than white borrowers because of their race or national origin." "Justice Department Reaches Settlement with Wells Fargo Resulting in More than $175 Million in Relief for Homeowners to Resolve Fair Lending Claims" (press release), July 12, 2012, https://www.justice.gov/opa/pr/justice-department-reaches -settlement-wells-fargo-resulting-more-175-million-relief. The prevalence of subprime mortgages could help explain why high-income black Americans have a larger mortgage interest deduction than their white peers. According to a recent Treasury analysis, "Average benefits for higher income Black and Hispanic families are slightly higher than for higher income White families (8th and 9th deciles)." See Julie-Anne Cronin, Portia DeFilippes, and Robin Fisher, "Tax Expenditures by Race and Hispanic Ethnicity: An Application of the U.S. Treasury Department's Race and Hispanic Ethnicity Imputation," Office of Tax Analysis Working Paper no. 122, January 2023, 39, https://home.treasury.gov/system/ files/131/WP-122.pdf.

94. See Debra Kamin, "Home Appraised with a Black Owner: $472,000. With a White Owner: $750,000," *New York Times,* August 12, 2022.

95. Khalil Gibran Muhammad, *The Condemnation of Blackness* (Cambridge, MA: Harvard University Press, 2011).

96. Jeffrey M. Jones, "Supreme Court Trust, Job Approval at Historical Lows," Gallup, September 29, 2022, https://news.gallup.com/poll/402044/ supreme-court-trust-job-approval-historical-lows.aspx?version=print.

97. Devan Cole, "Supreme Court Approval Rating Declines Amid Controversy over Ethics and Transparency: Marquette Poll," CNN, May 24, 2023.

98. Jacquelyne Germain, "The Fight for Reparations Has Stalled in Congress. Here's What They Look Like in State and Local Government," CNN, July 13, 2022.

99. *Jones v. Alfred Mayer,* 392 U.S. at 445 (Justice Douglas concurring).

100. *Tee-Hit-Ton Indians v. United States,* 348 U.S. 272 (1955) (Court took away indigenous land rights in Alaska); *City of Sherrill v. Oneida Indian Nation of New York,* 544 U.S. 197 (2005) (Court used laches to diminish the rights of the Oneida over land within their reservation).

101. Carey L. Biron, "U.S. Cities Start Racism Reparations as National Efforts Languish," *Context,* January 12, 2024, https://www.context.news/money -power-people/us-cities-start-racism-reparations-as-national-efforts -languish.

102. California Task Force to Study and Develop Reparation Proposals for

African Americans, *Final Report,* June 29, 2023, https://oag.ca.gov/ab3121/report.

103. Germain, "Fight for Reparations Has Stalled in Congress."
104. Germain, "Fight for Reparations Has Stalled in Congress"; Michael Casey, "Slavery Reparations in Amherst Massachusetts Could Include Funding for Youth Programs and Housing," Associated Press, October 16, 2023.
105. Nordea Lewis, "Hearing on Bill to Create Reparations Commission in Maryland," WMAR, March 1, 2023.
106. Michelle Watson, "New York Governor Signs Law Establishing Reparations and Racial Justice Commission," CNN, December 19, 2023.
107. Oregon Legislative Assembly, 2021 Regular Sess., Senate Bill 619, https://olis.oregonlegislature.gov/liz/2021R1/Downloads/MeasureDocument/SB0619/Introduced; Robin Quirke, "Efforts to Provide Reparations Take Root in Oregon," *Portland Tribune,* November 21, 2022.
108. Ethan Bakuli, "BTV City Council Votes to Create Task Force to Study Reparations for Slavery," *Burlington Free Press* (Vermont), August 11, 2020.
109. *Flinn et al. v. City of Evanston,* Complaint 04269, filed May 23, 2024.
110. Brown, *Whiteness of Wealth,* 20–21.
111. Tatjana Meschede et al., "'Family Achievements?': How a College Degree Accumulates Wealth for Whites and Not for Blacks," *Federal Reserve Bank of St. Louis Review* 99, no. 1 (2017): 121–37.
112. "This disparity is driven by the preferential rates for capital gains, 92 percent of the benefits of which accrue to White families." Cronin et al., "Tax Expenditures by Race and Hispanic Ethnicity," 43.
113. Brown, *Whiteness of Wealth,* 189.
114. Franklin, "Civil Rights Act Revisited," 1135.
115. Toni Morrison, "A Humanist View," speech at Portland State University, 1975, in "12 of Toni Morrison's Most Memorable Quotes," *New York Times,* August 6, 2019.
116. Westen Strategies, LLC, on file with author.
117. "Racism is a national security issue," writes Sherrilyn Ifill, in "It's Time to Face the Facts: Racism Is a National Security Issue," *Washington Post,* December 18, 2018.
118. James Weldon Johnson, "Lift Every Voice and Sing," https://www.poetryfoundation.org/poems/46549/lift-every-voice-and-sing.

Appendix

1. Much of this language is taken verbatim from the Commission on the Supreme Court established by Executive Order 14023.
2. This section was modeled after California Assembly Bill 3121, which established the California Reparations Task Force, file:///C:/Users/14042/Downloads/20190AB3121_95.pdf.

ABOUT THE AUTHOR

Dorothy A. Brown is a professor of law and holder of the Martin D. Ginsburg Chair in Taxation at Georgetown University Law Center. She is the author of *The Whiteness of Wealth*. A graduate of Fordham University and Georgetown Law, she received her LLM in taxation from New York University. A nationally recognized scholar in the areas of race, class, and tax policy, she has published dozens of articles, essays, and book chapters on the topic. She has appeared on ABC's *The View,* CNN, MSNBC, PBS, NPR, *The Armchair Expert, New Yorker Radio Hour,* and *Code Switch,* and her opinion pieces have been published in *The Atlantic, The New York Times,* and *The Washington Post.* Born and raised in the South Bronx in New York City, Dorothy Brown currently resides in Washington, DC.